Sente Diagramming

Level 2

Sentence Diagramming products available in print or eBook form.

Beginning • Level 1 • Level 2

Written by
Angela Carter

Edited by
Patricia Gray

Graphic Design by
Scott Slyter

THE CRITICAL THINKING CO.™
www.CriticalThinking.com
Phone: 800-458-4849 • Fax: 541-756-1758
1991 Sherman Ave., Suite 200 • North Bend • OR 97459
ISBN 978-1-60144-855-2

Printed in the United States of America by McNaughton & Gunn, Inc., Saline, MI (Jan. 2021)

Table of Contents

About This Book

I began writing this series while teaching elementary children how to diagram sentences. I just couldn't find quality resources out there that laid out diagramming as a logical process, building on itself from simple subject-verb sentences up through complex sentences with dependent clauses—at least not for the younger crowd. I found myself making up sentences and planning quick lessons on my own, so I decided to write them down and share!

I first fell in love with sentence diagramming in college. Through elementary and middle school our grammar lessons had us "circle the adjective and draw a line from the adjective to the noun it modifies." I found this task to be messy and disorganized, lines crossing over each other squeezed between the words on the page. It was confusing to look at and made me grumpy. I was thrilled when, in "English Grammar 101," I learned to sort and organize all the words of a sentence onto lines, showing their relationships and the structure of the sentence! For me—and many other visual learners—this visual representation of the English language was very helpful!

During my career as an elementary and middle school teacher and private tutor, I have seen many students labor over grammar exercises similar to the ones in my old grammar books. Students' handwriting is sloppy; their lines go all over the place; they can't find the direct object to save their lives. They are told to write a paragraph which includes at least two complex sentences with dependent clauses, yet they don't truly understand what a dependent clause or a subordinating conjunction is. I started thinking about how very visually-oriented students of the 21st century are and decided to bring back diagramming. My students were amazed at how fun diagramming can actually be. They found sense in the structure of a sentence and a clear and true sense of satisfaction with each completed diagram. Even the kids who were traditionally more "math minded" began to enjoy English lessons. One even called diagramming "the math of English class." They started asking how to diagram more and more complex sentences, looking for examples in the books they were reading, trying to stump me by composing the most complex sentences they could imagine. The grammar lessons were actually spilling over into the writing lessons!

I find the benefits of sentence diagramming to be multi-faceted. Students learn critical thinking skills in a way never presented to them before. They learn information organization skills, and how to make a visual representation of language. They begin to truly understand the finer points of English grammar. Their writing becomes more complex and mature. For many students, boring old grammar lessons become fun.

I hope you will find much success with *Sentence Diagramming: Level 2*. Please feel free to extend the lessons beyond what is written in this book. Find sentences to diagram from literature, magazines, your own conversations, and the students' own writings! Draw diagrams large, on marker boards, butcher paper, and poster boards. Embrace the "visual organization" of language—and most of all—have fun!

Review of Diagramming Concepts

Sentence Diagramming: Beginning taught the basics of sentence diagramming starting with simple subjects and main verbs. Adjectives, adverbs, prepositional phrases, direct objects, and predicate nouns/adjectives were added as the book progressed.

Sentence Diagramming: Level 1 taught more advanced diagramming structures, such as compound subject, predicates, and sentences; interrogative and imperative sentences (questions and commands); indirect objects, intensifiers, and appositives.

Declarative Sentence with Modifiers

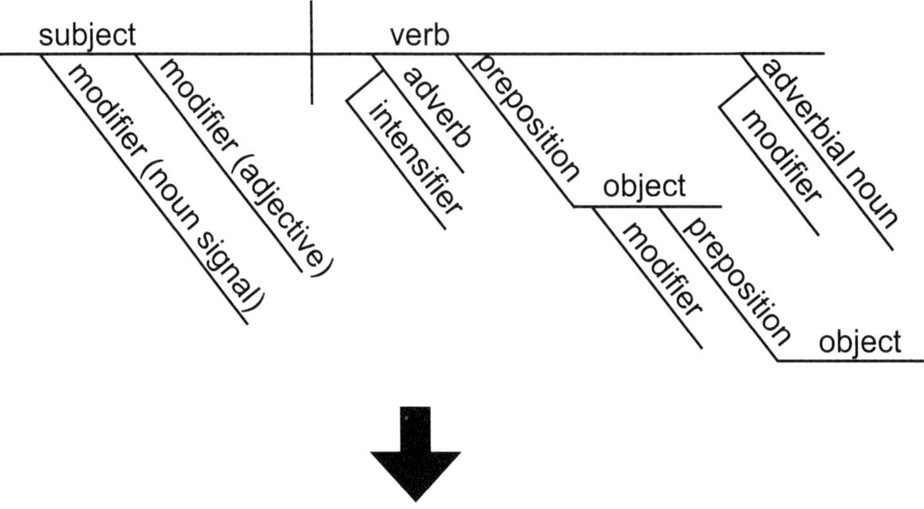

The playful penguins slide quite happily on the ice hills in Antarctica every day.

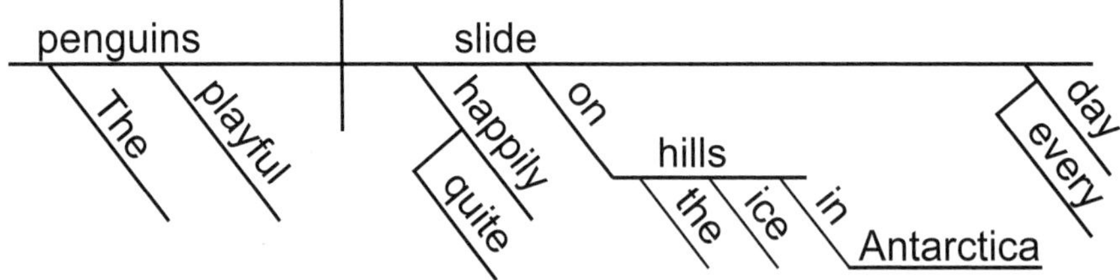

Imperative Sentences (Commands)

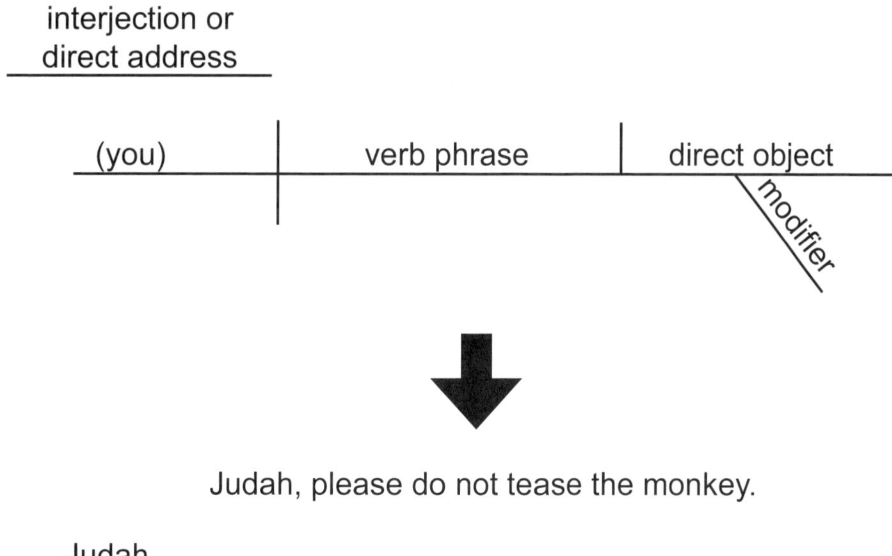

Judah, please do not tease the monkey.

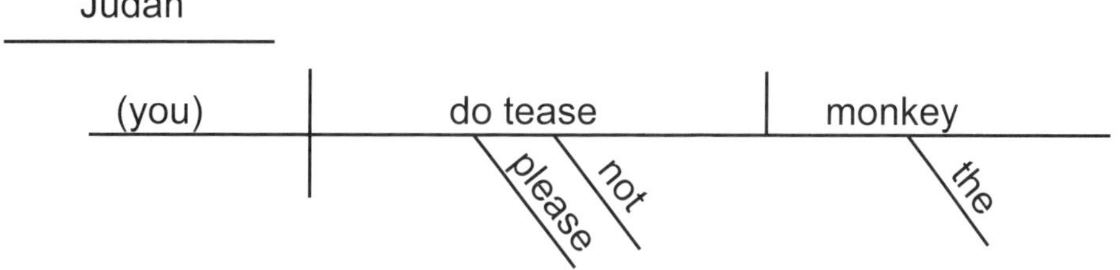

Interrogative Sentences (Questions)

Rearrange the words into a declarative sentence, then diagram.

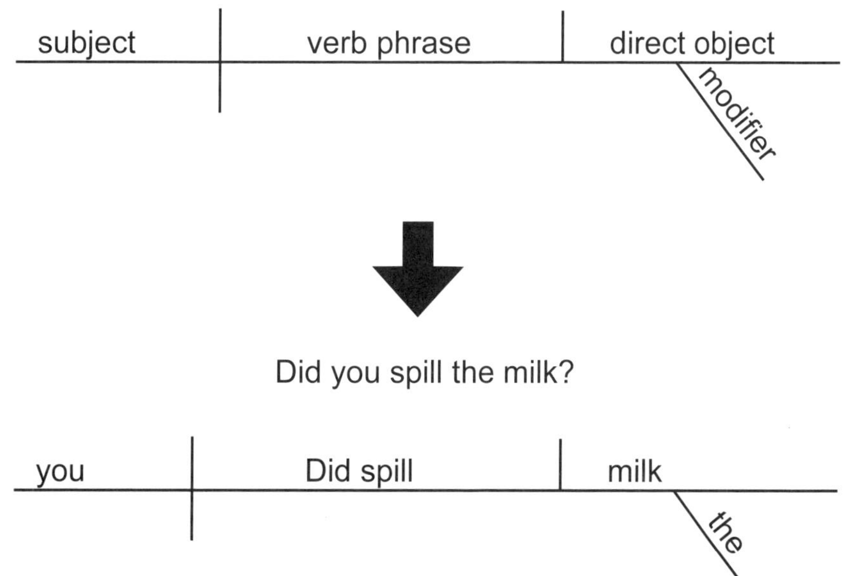

Did you spill the milk?

Appositive

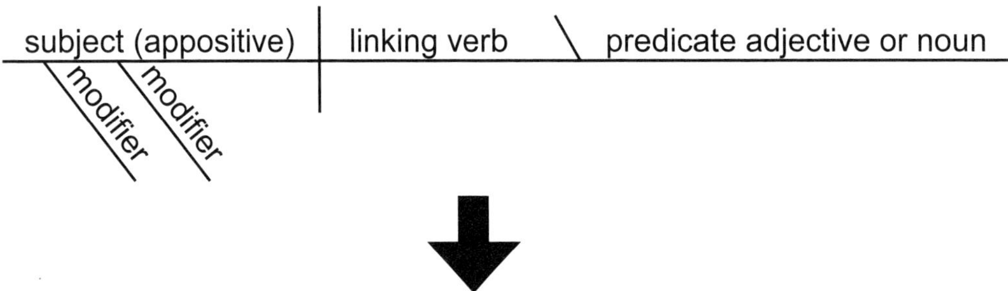

Her favorite cookies, snickerdoodles, are delicious.

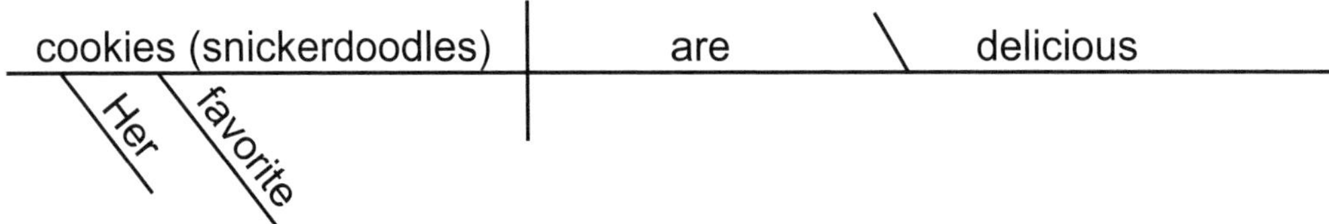

Indirect Object

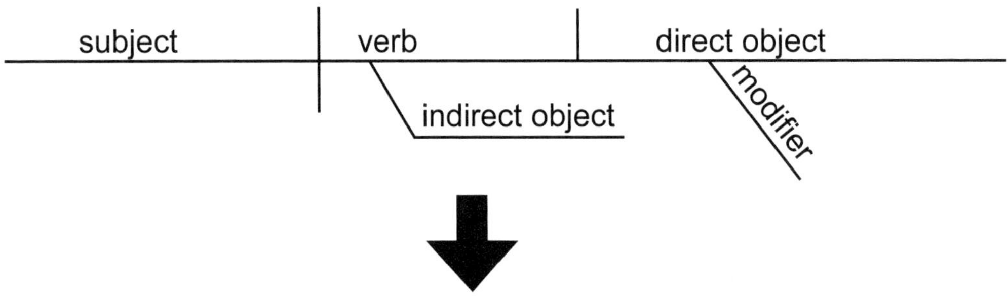

Emmie bought Dad some saltwater taffy.

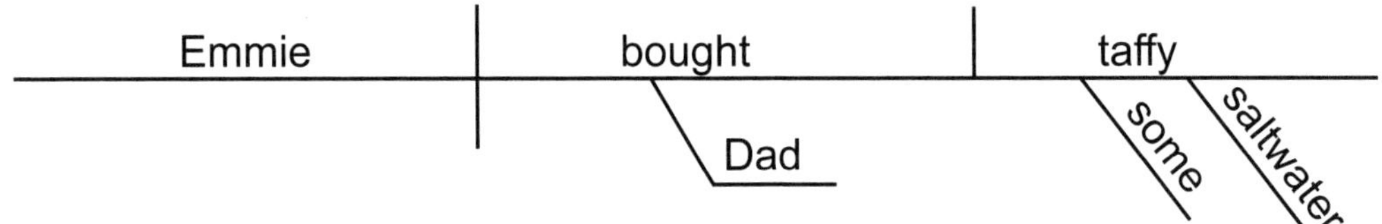

Compound Subject and Predicate

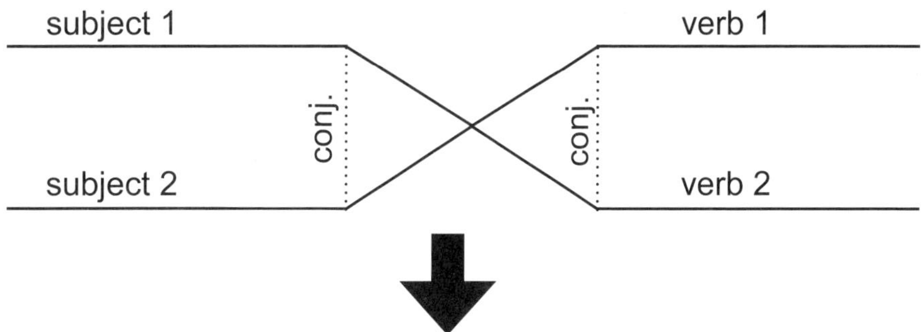

Dick and Jane laughed and played.

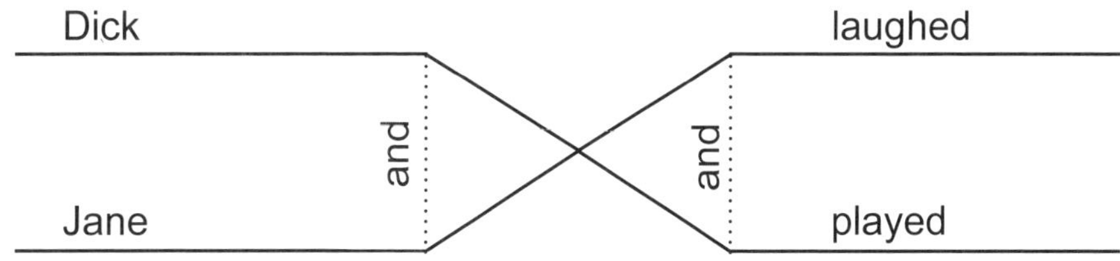

Compound Sentences

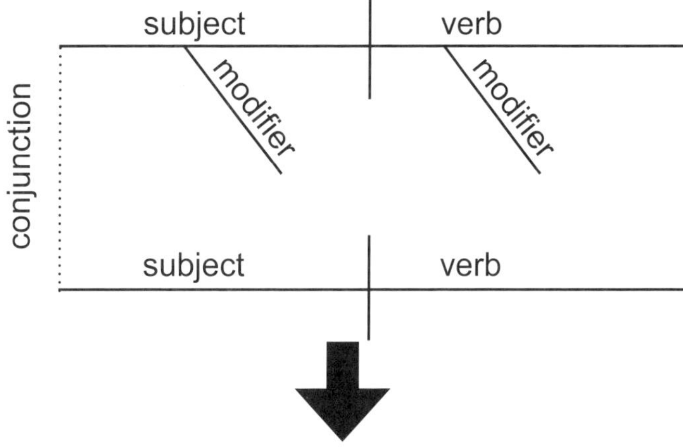

The ambulance arrived quickly, but nobody was injured.

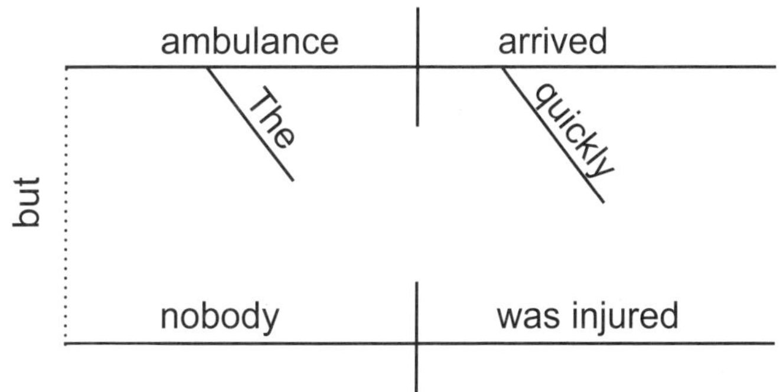

Lesson 1: Appositives and Appositive Phrases

An **appositive** is a noun or pronoun that renames or identifies another *noun* or pronoun right beside it. It gives extra information not essential to the meaning of the sentence. Comma(s) are used to set it off from the rest of the sentence. The appositive is diagrammed in parentheses on the main line directly after the noun that is renamed.

The very tall man in the corner is my *teacher*, **Mr. Dalton**.

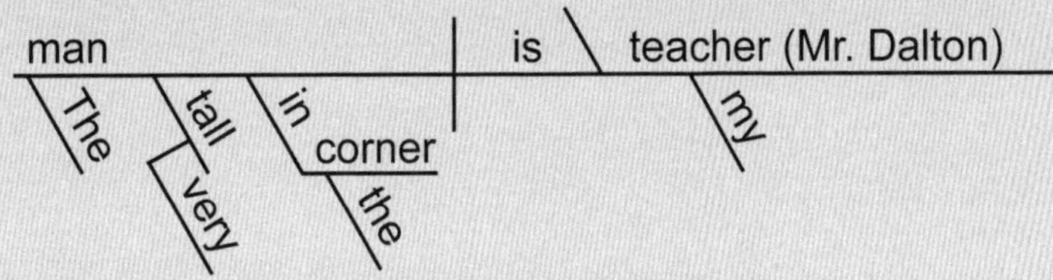

An **appositive phrase** consists of an appositive and its modifiers.

My teacher is **Mr. Dalton**, the very tall man in the corner.

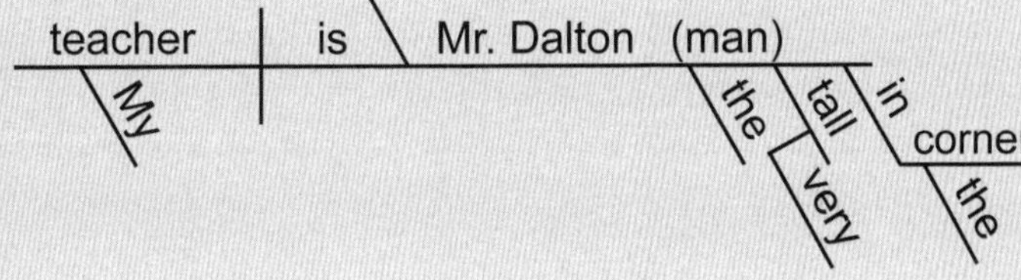

1. Each sentence diagram below has an error. Diagram each sentence correctly.

a. Bugs Bunny, my favorite cartoon character, is seventy-six years old!

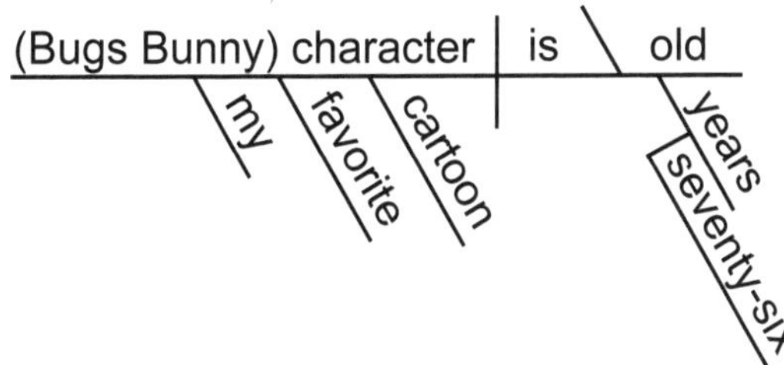

b. I visited Charleston, the most amazing city!

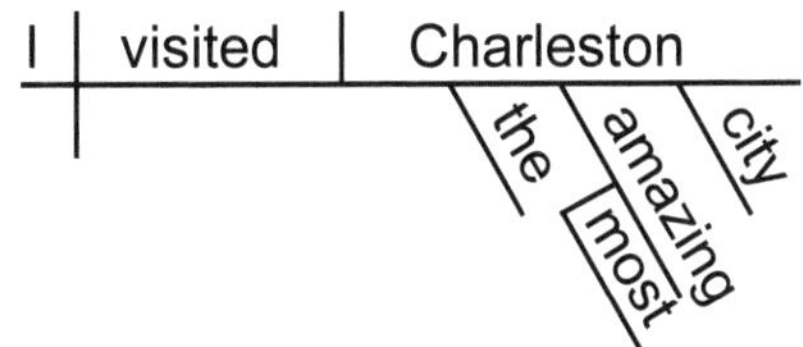

c. You baked macaroons, my favorite cookie!

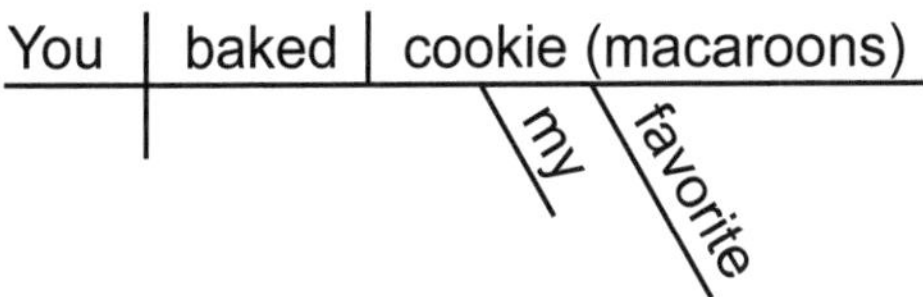

2. Fill in the diagram for each sentence.

   a. Auntie Lola will bring sushi, my favorite food!

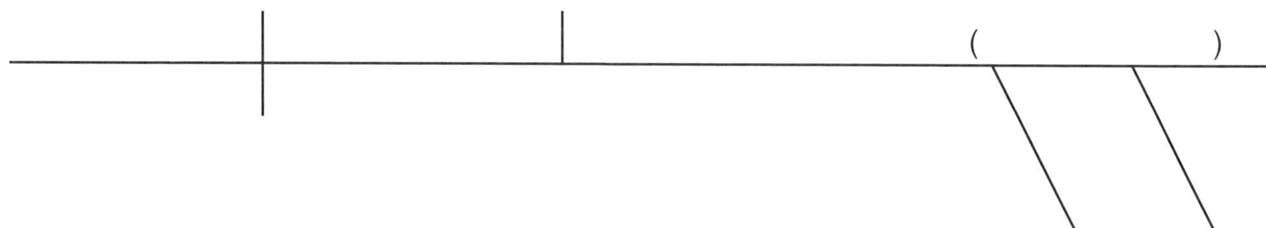

   b. Bobby was drinking chocolate milk, a healthy and delicious drink!

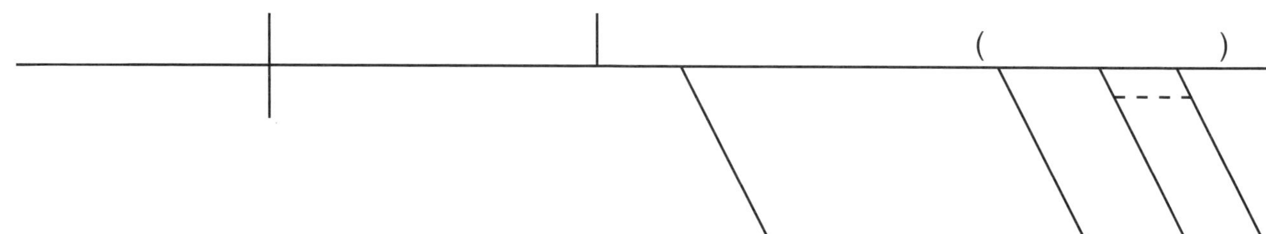

   c. Mom's gift, a hand-knit sweater, and Cheryl's present, a box of stationery, are my favorite gifts.

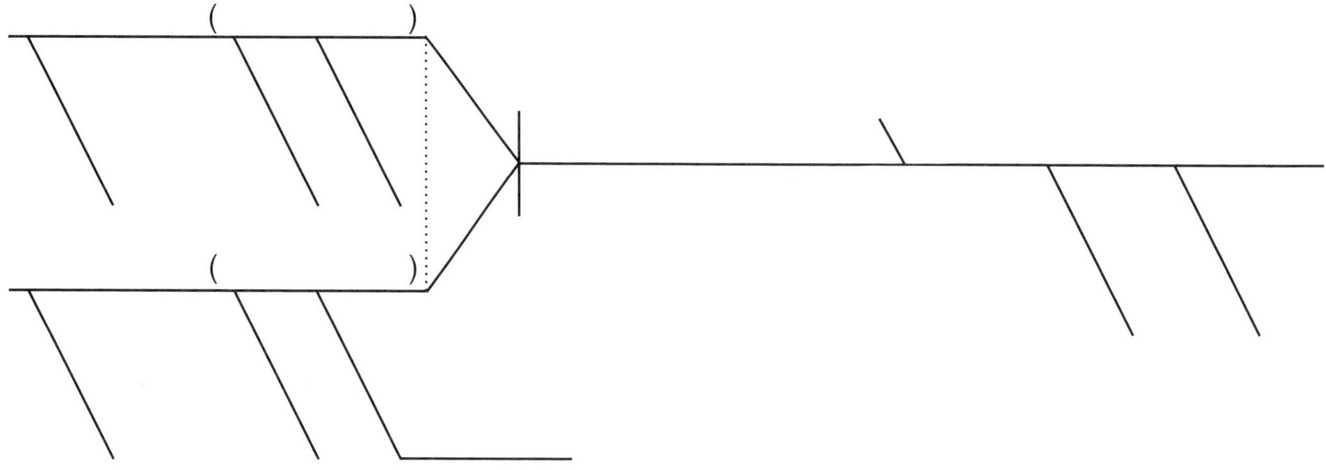

d. My crazy Aunt Kathy, the blond lady in roller skates, is celebrating her 70th birthday.

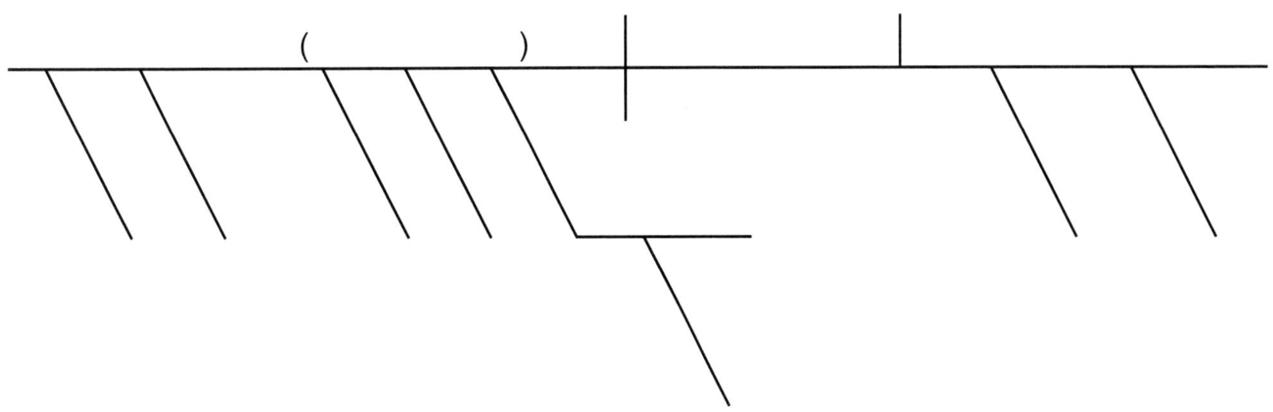

e. She will probably buy the cheaper car, the red one with cloth seats.

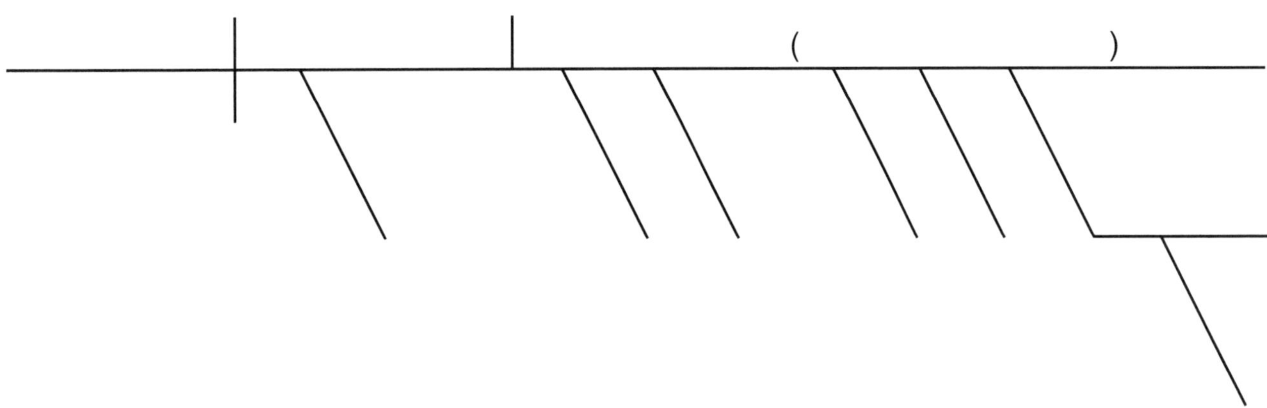

f. Plant the daylilies near Shannon's flowers, the red and yellow tulips.

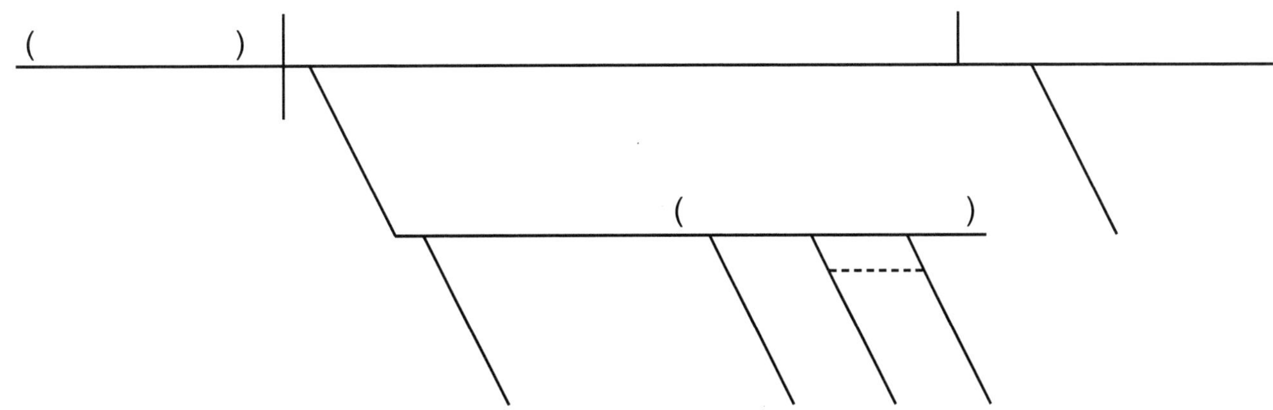

3. Write a sentence to match each diagram. Then complete the diagram.

a. ....

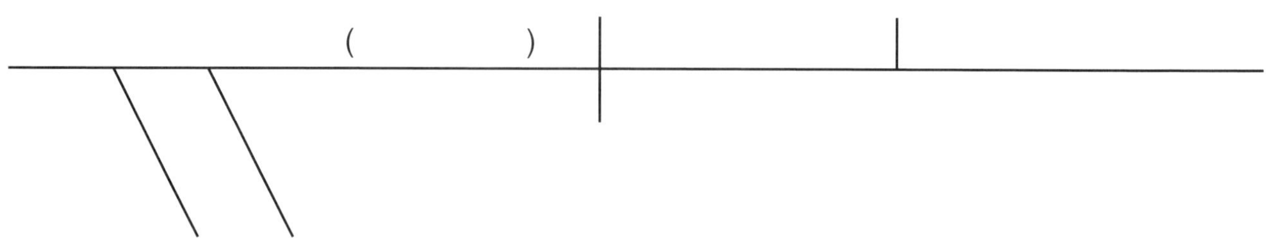

b. ....

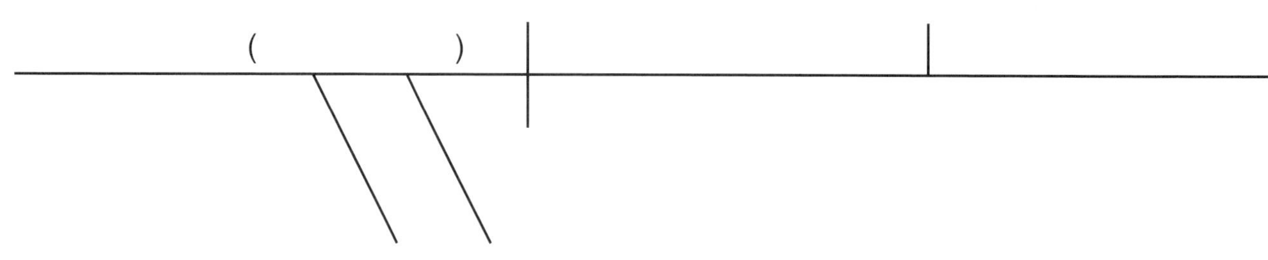

c. ....

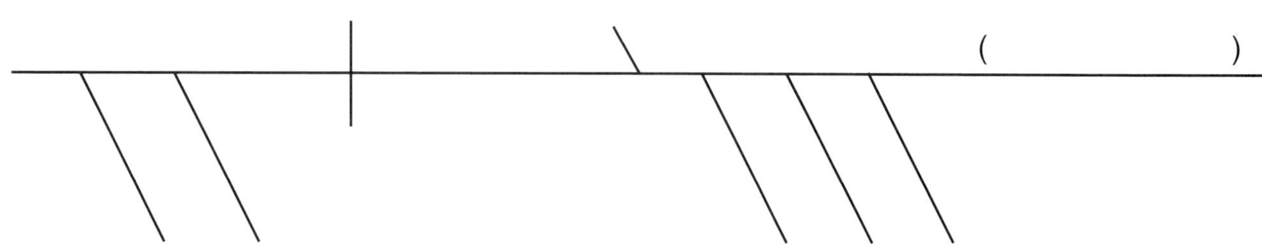

d. ....

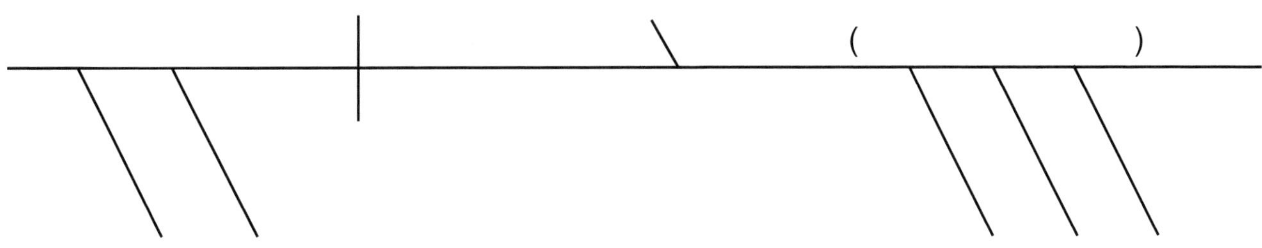

e. ....

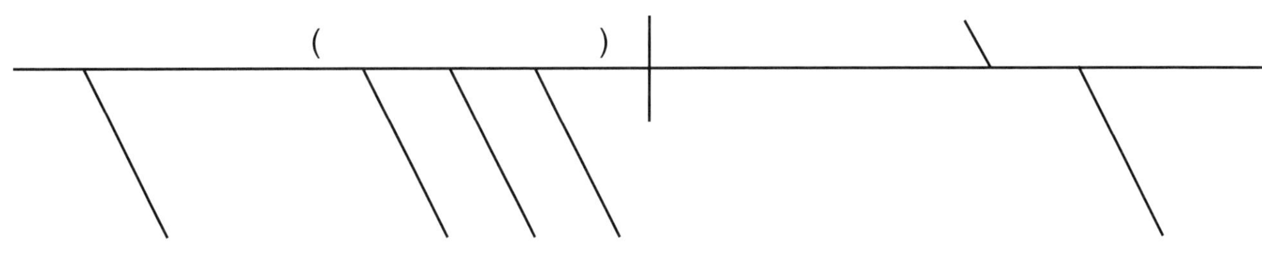

f. ....

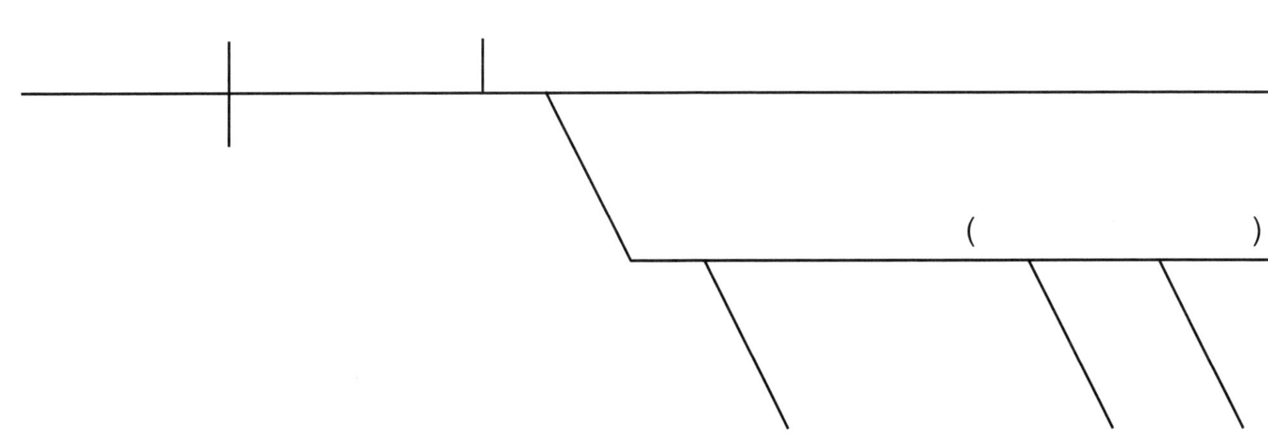

4. Diagram each sentence.

   a. My much older sister, Darla, is leaving for college next week.

   b. Nathan, my oldest brother, visited the Big Apple, New York City!

   c. Charlie, the big black Newfoundland, and Max, the noisy little beagle, are my favorite dogs.

d. My brother, Abel, was hiding in the cellar, our favorite hiding place.

e. The Library of Congress, the largest library in the world, houses 16 million books and 838 miles of bookshelves.

f. The movie, *Victoria and Albert*, is about Queen Victoria and her husband, Prince Albert.

Lesson 2: Objective Complements

An **objective complement** is a word following a *direct object* that further describes or renames the direct object. It sounds and looks like an appositive, but is essential to the meaning of the sentence.

Appositive: I held their new *baby*, Charles.

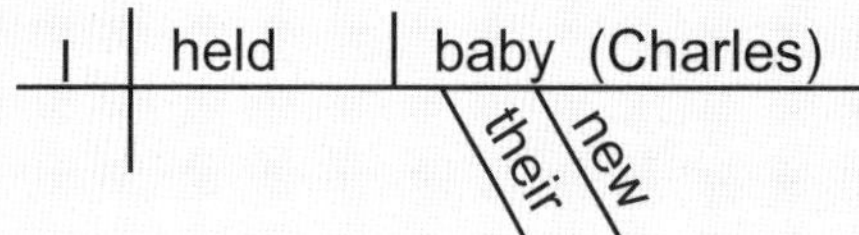

Objective Complement: The couple named their new *baby*, ***Charles***.

The fact that the baby's name is Charles is the main point of the sentence. If the word "Charles" is taken out, the sentence wouldn't make sense. The reader would be wondering, "What? What did they name the baby?"

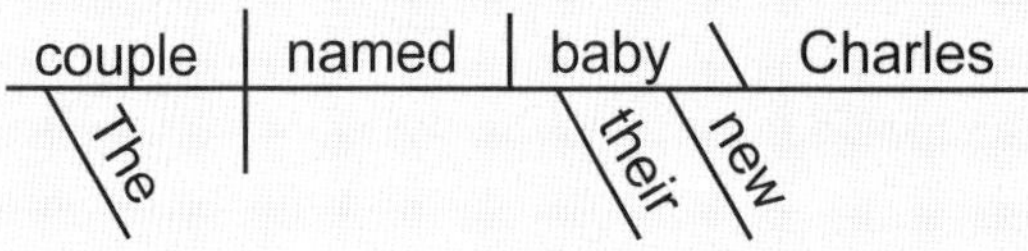

1. Each sentence diagram below has an error. Diagram each sentence correctly.

   a. The king dubbed him Sir Galahad.

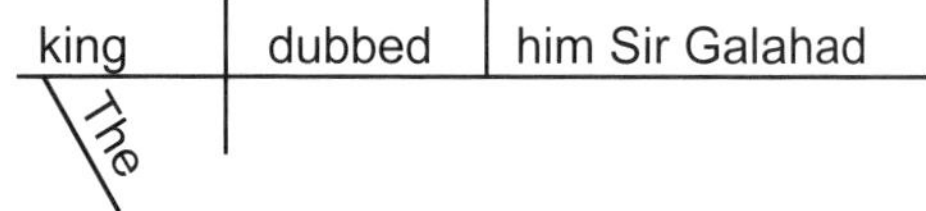

   b. We elected Victor president.

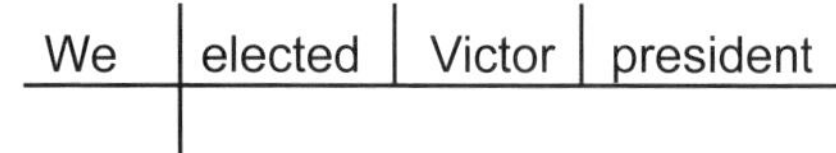

   c. Everyone considers firemen heroes.

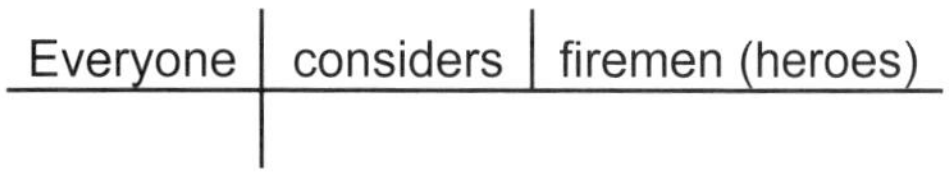

Everyone | considers | firemen (heroes)

Objective complements can also be adjectives.

The tomb raiders found the grave empty.

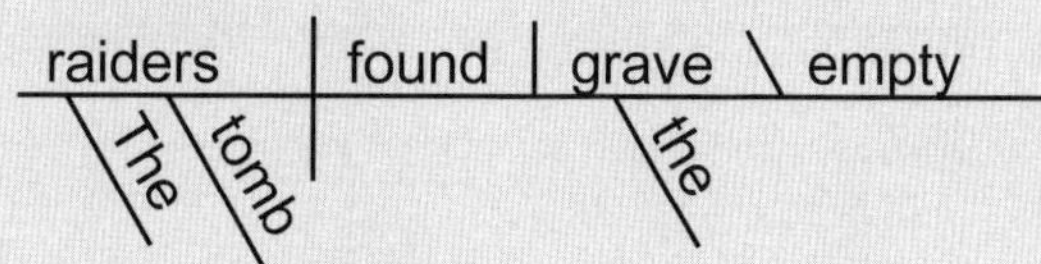

Objective complements can also have modifiers.

We painted our garage *door* dark **brown**.

The adjective "dark" describes "brown" and is diagrammed directly under the word "brown."

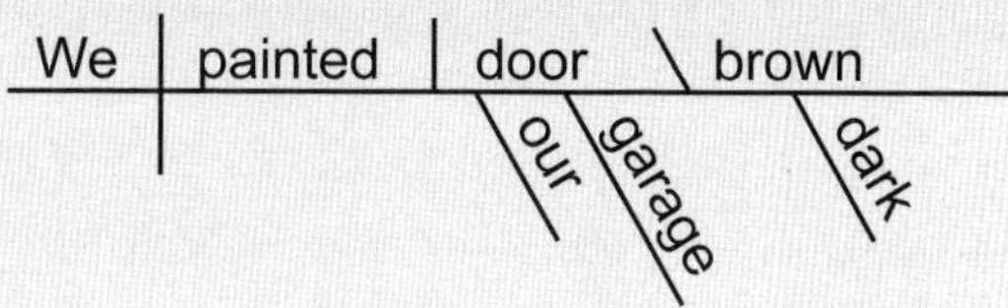

2. Fill in the diagram for each sentence.

a. Math homework keeps me very busy.

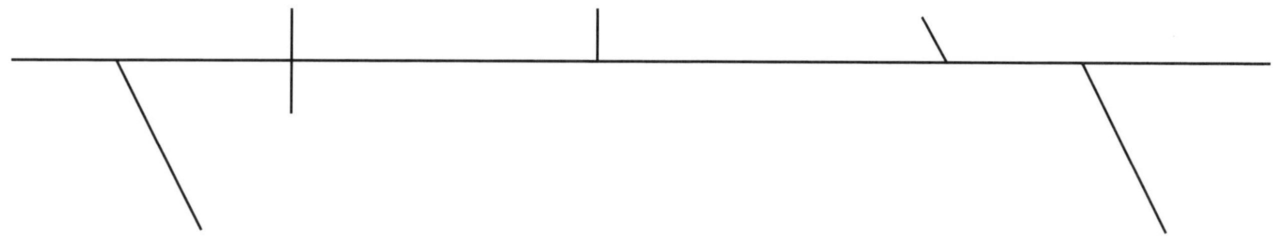

b. Last month's electric bill made my dad very angry.

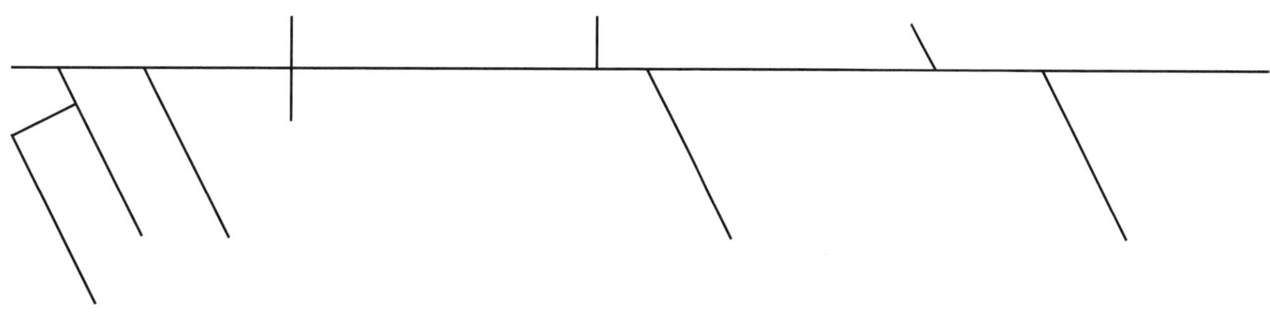

c. Surprisingly, the king named his youngest son his successor.

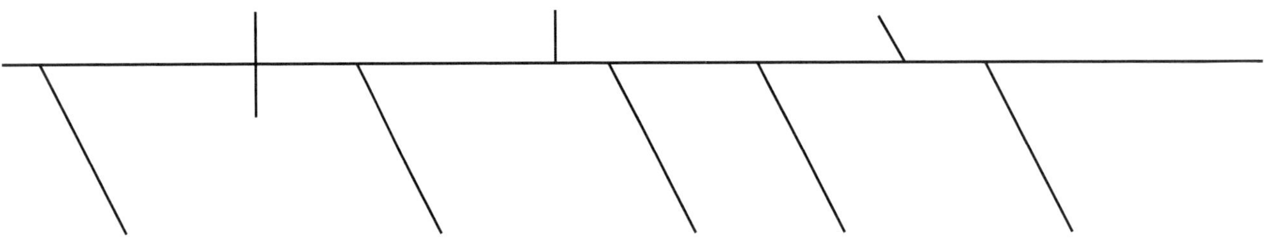

d. The director awarded Sarai most improved actor.

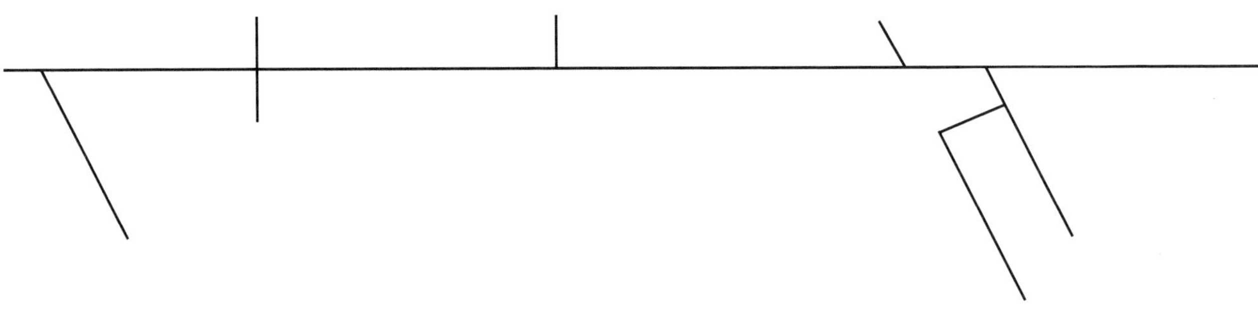

e. My son keeps his car very clean.

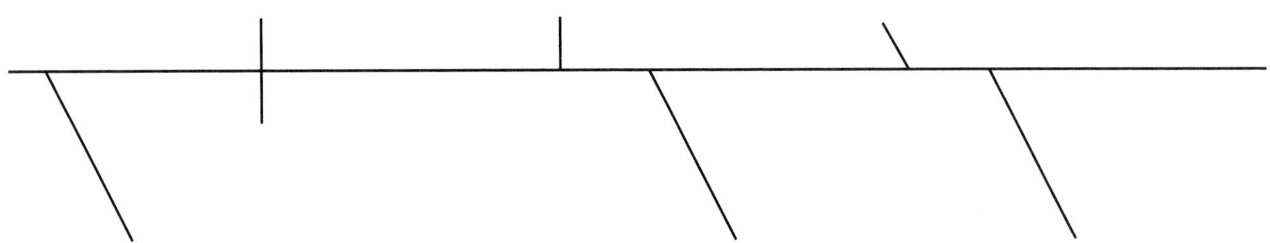

Objective complements can also be modified by *prepositional phrases.*

We painted the garage **door** dark brown *with tan stripes.*

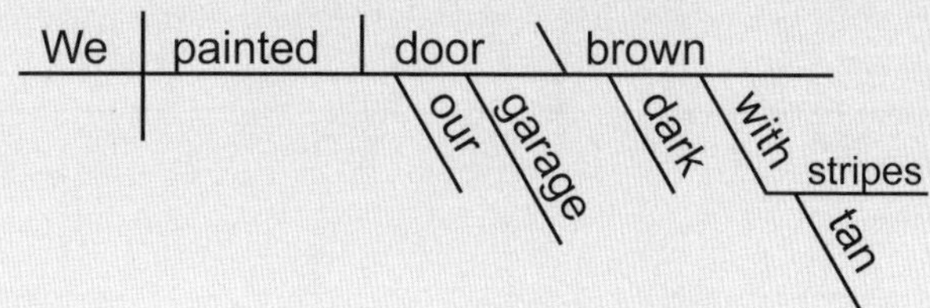

3. Write a sentence to match each diagram. Then complete the diagram.
   (Hint: Choose from the following verbs: named, called, elected, appointed, awarded)

   a. ....

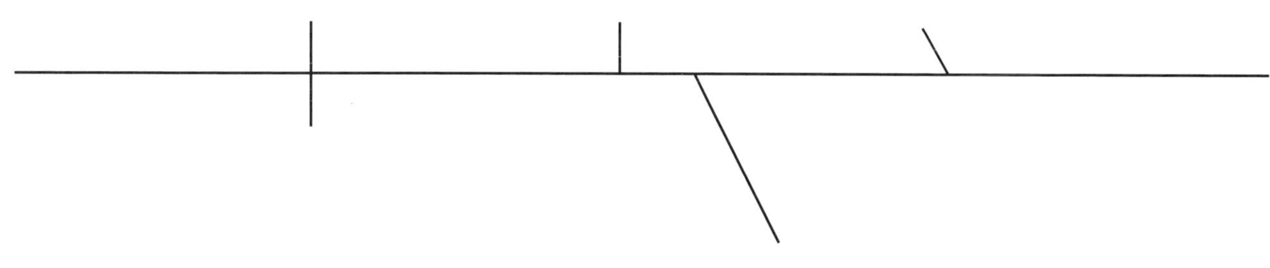

   b. ....

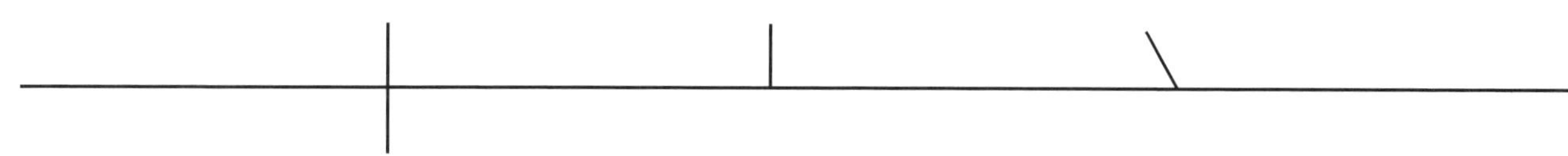

   c. ....

d. ....

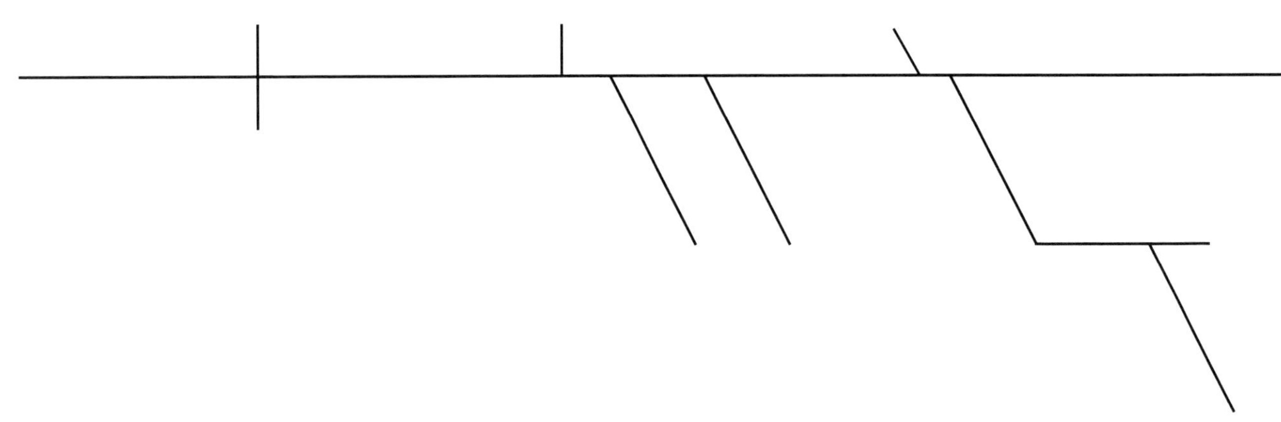

e. ....

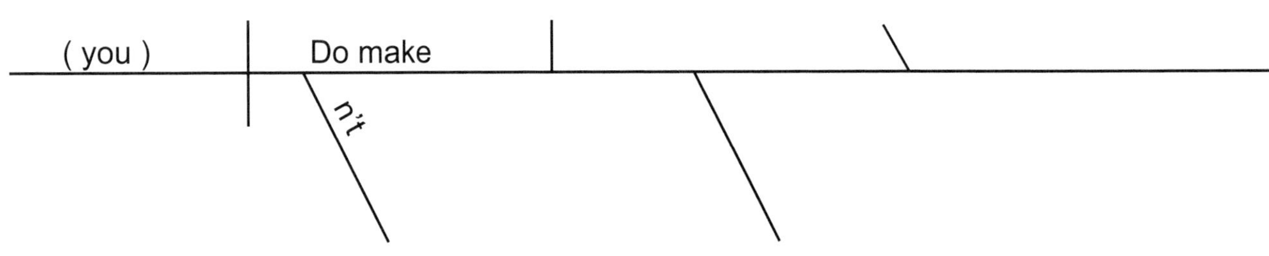

f. ....

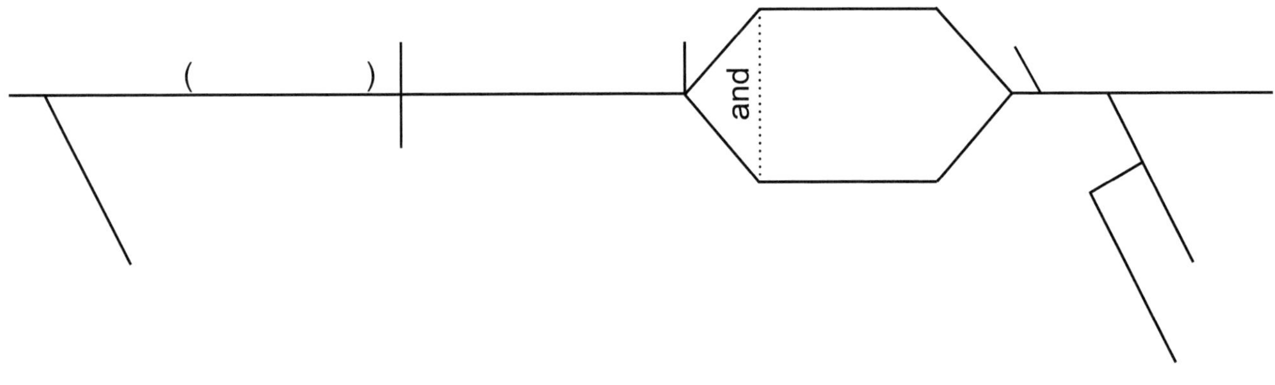

Compound objective complements are diagrammed on a split main line, joined by a dotted line with the conjunction.

The chef made the *soup* **spicy** and **delicious**.

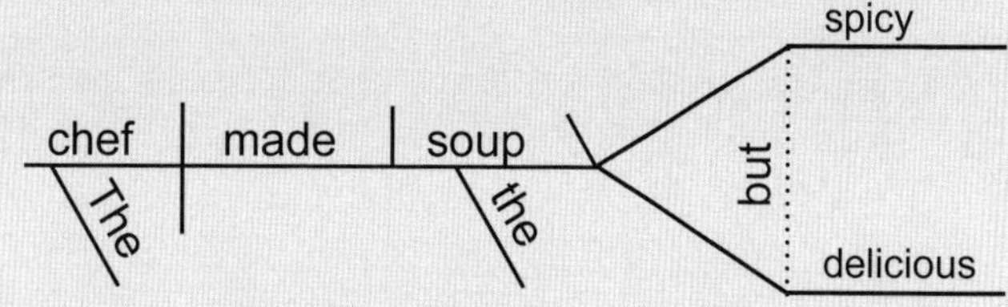

4. Diagram each sentence.

   a. They call me Bob.

   b. We appointed Lisa Fleming chairman of the board.

c. Can you make Grandma's pound cake more buttery?

d. Please make your posters neat and colorful.

e. My silly, little sister painted her walls pink and purple!

Lesson 3: Gerunds and Gerund Phrases

A **gerund** is a verb behaving like a noun. It always ends with the suffix "-ing." A verb can end with "-ing" when it is not a gerund. If the "-ing" word tells what someone is doing, it's a *verb*. If it is a thing, and it acts like a noun, it is a gerund. Gerunds are diagrammed on a stepped line connected by a forked line to the rest of the diagram.

Verb: I am *running*. ("Running" is what the person is doing.)

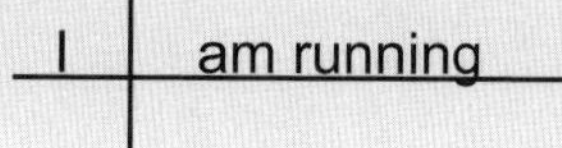

Gerund: **Running** is fun. ("Running" is the thing the person finds fun.)

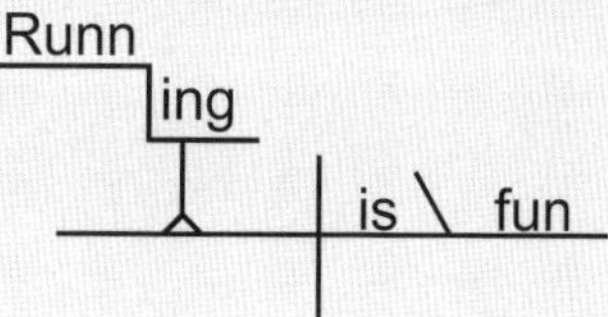

Gerund: I like **running**. ("Running" is the thing the person likes.)

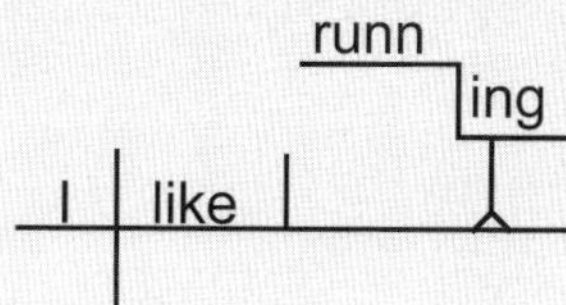

1. Each sentence contains an "-ing" word that may or may not be a gerund. Each diagram below has an error. Diagram each sentence correctly.

   a. Reading is my favorite hobby.

Reading | is \ hobby
my
favorite

   b. She will be baking later today.

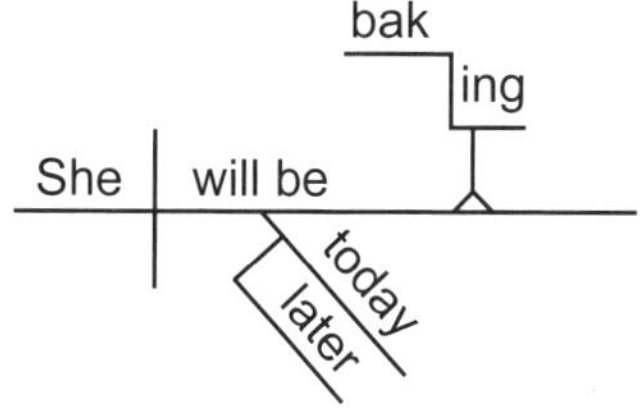

   c. I really enjoy dancing.

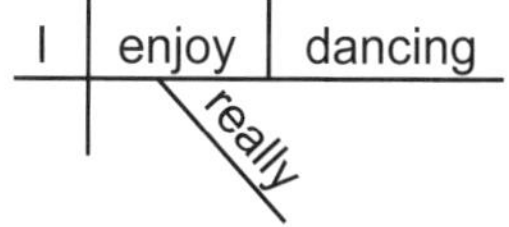

A **gerund** can be modified by an adverb or a *prepositional phrase*. It is diagrammed below the gerund's step line.

Chewing loudly is rude.

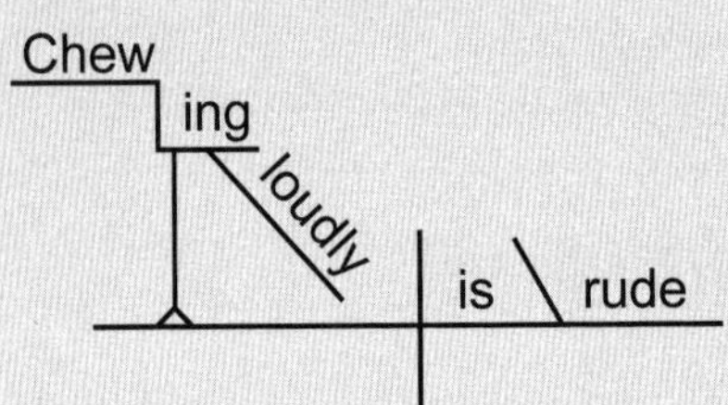

I enjoy **dancing** *with my dad*.

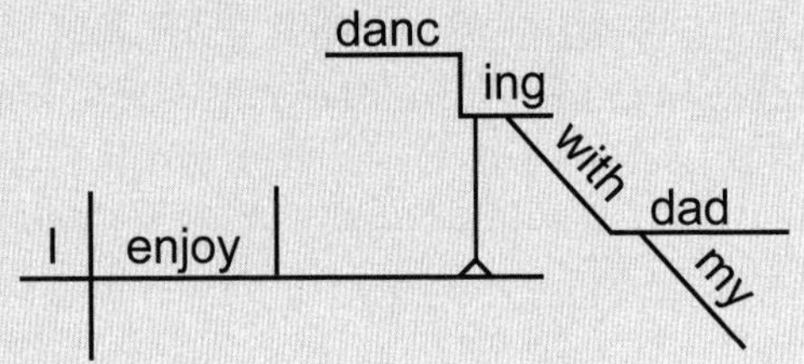

2. Fill in the diagram for each sentence.

   a. Prim and Polly enjoyed sledding.

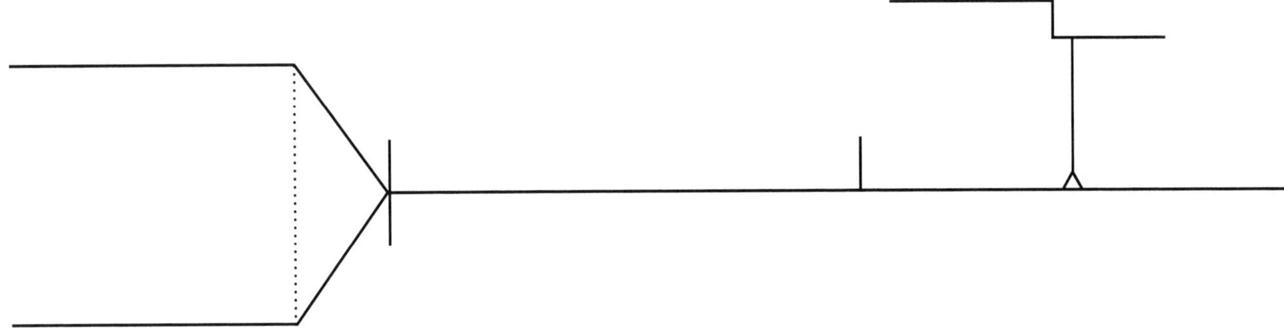

   b. Eating quickly is not good for you.

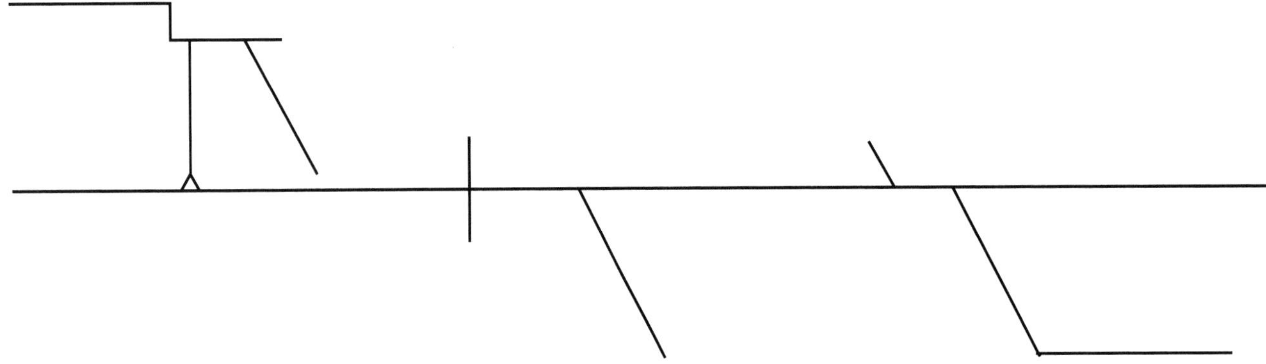

c. Napping after Thanksgiving dinner is a family tradition.

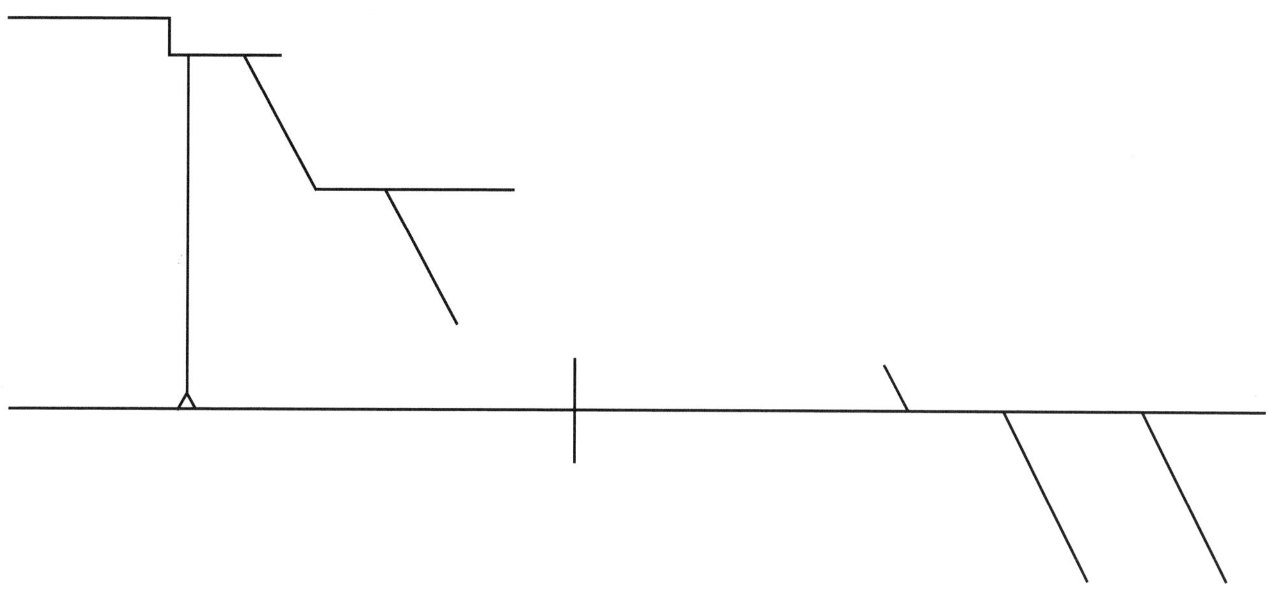

d. On May Day, Ms. Sheryl's students enjoyed dancing around the Maypole with ribbons.

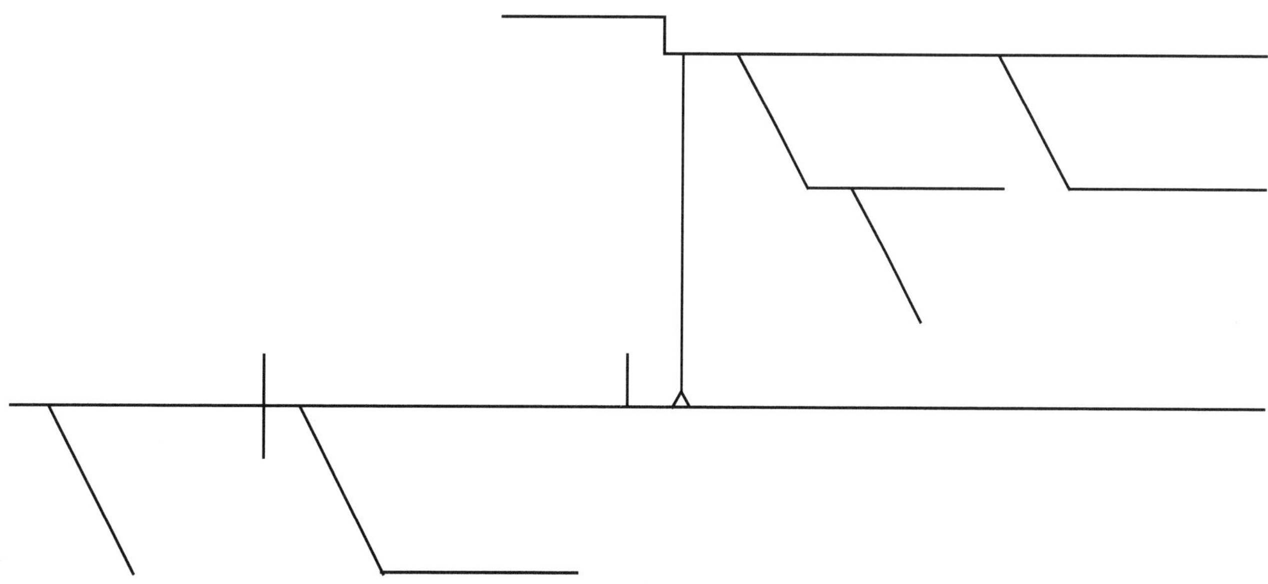

A **gerund phrase** is a gerund with a direct object. It includes objective complements and appositives.

The queen's guards do not enjoy painting the roses red.

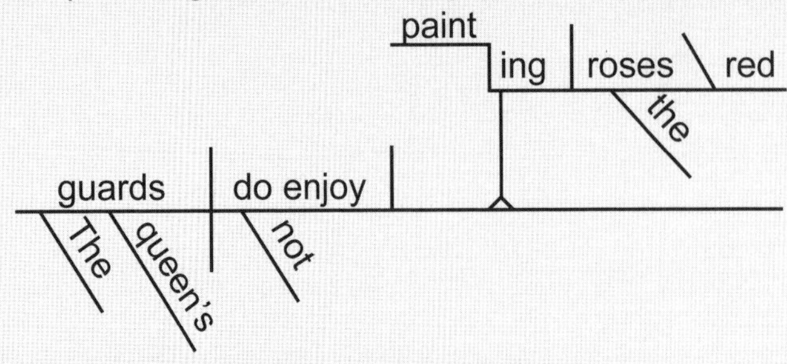

I like **tickling my little brother**, Jackson.

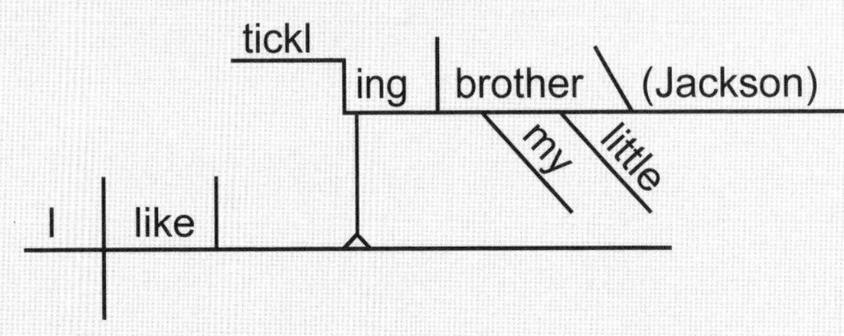

3. Write a sentence to match each diagram. Then complete the diagram.

a. ....

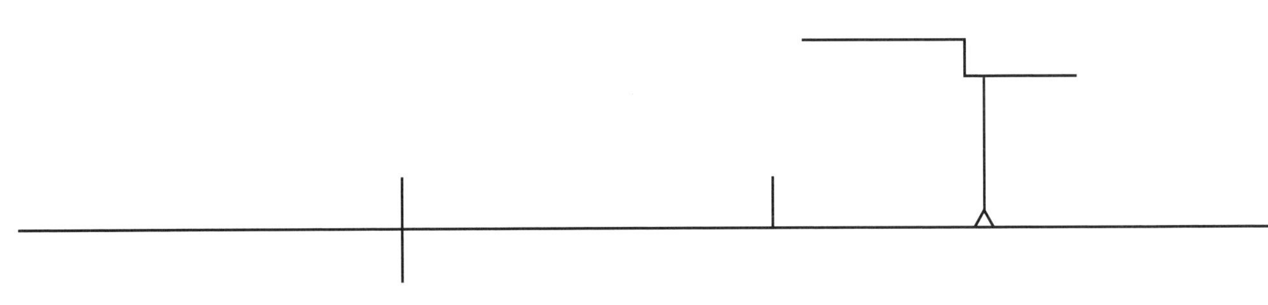

b. ....

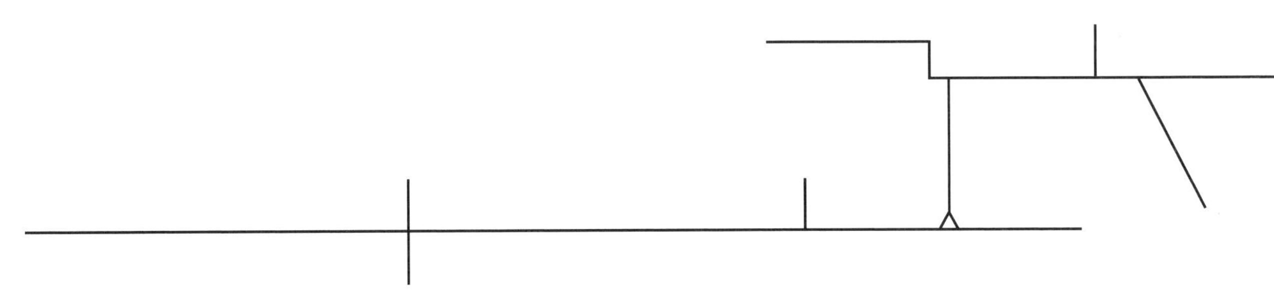

c. ....

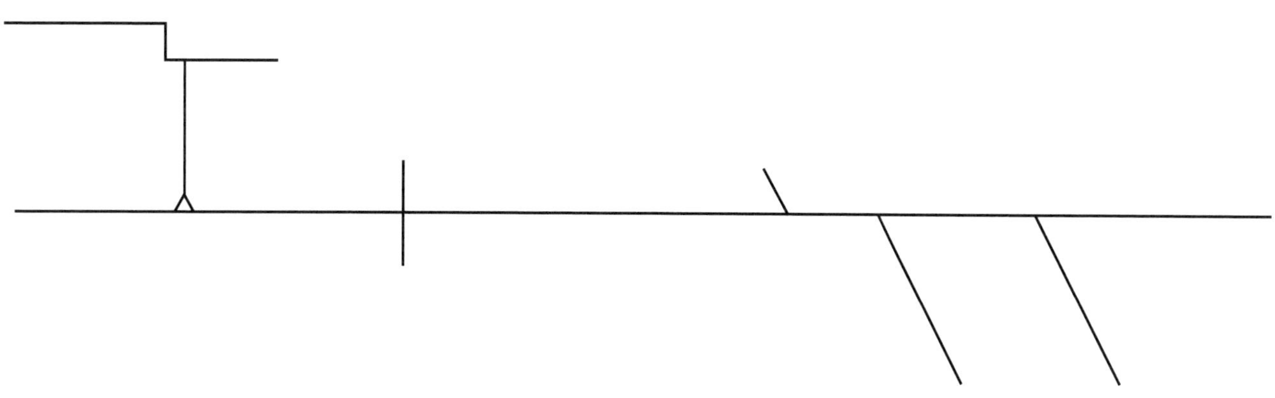

d. ....

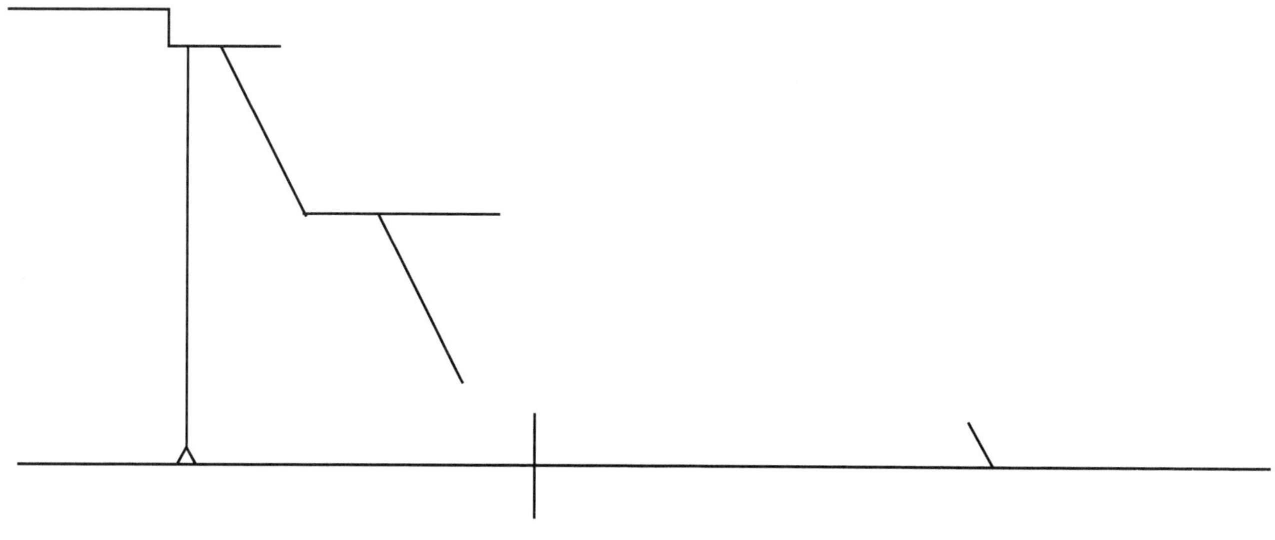

A **gerund** acting like a noun can also be the object of a preposition.

Nick annoys Uncle Hermann by **screeching**.

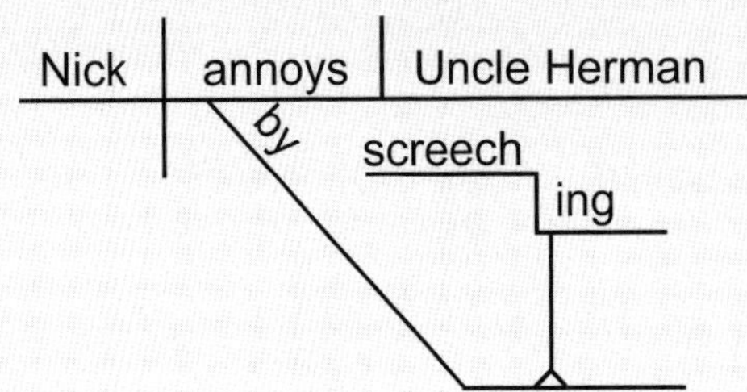

4. Diagram each of these sentences.

   a. Skiing professionally looks very hard.

   b. Exercising in the morning is so refreshing!

c. I don't mind doing homework on Saturday.

d. I helped Aunt Patty by vacuuming the whole house.

e. Diagramming sentences makes me happy!

Lesson 4: Participles Modifying Nouns

A participle is a verb behaving like an adjective or a noun. A **present participle**, like a gerund, ends with the suffix "-ing." If the "-ing" word tells what someone is doing, it's a verb. If it is a thing, it's a gerund. If it is describing something, it's a participle. Participles are diagrammed on a curved line.

Verb: The baby is **crying**. ("Crying" is what the baby is doing.)

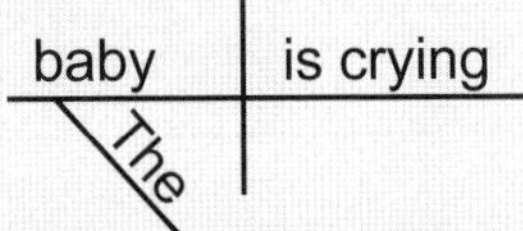

Gerund: **Crying** is not fun. ("Crying" is the thing the person finds no fun.)

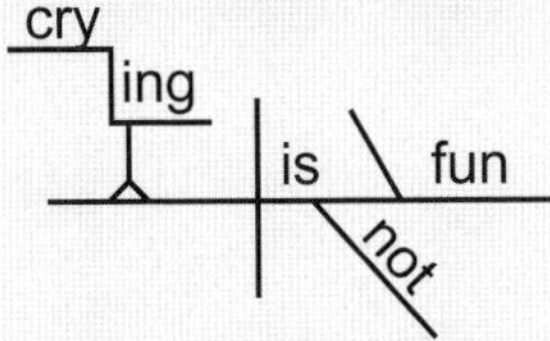

Present Participle: The **crying** baby was hungry. ("Crying" is describing the baby. It is acting like an adjective.)

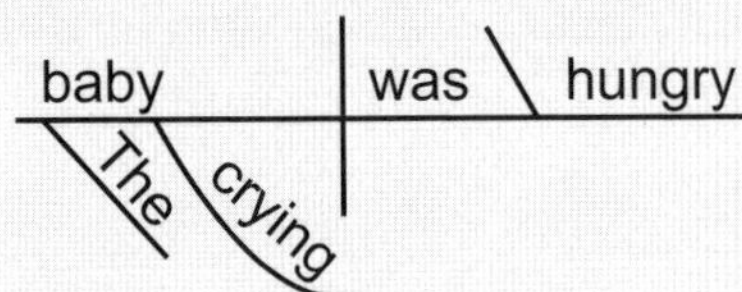

1. Each sentence contains an "-ing" word that may or may not be a participle. Each diagram contains an error. Diagram each sentence correctly.

   a. The bunny was hopping across the yard.

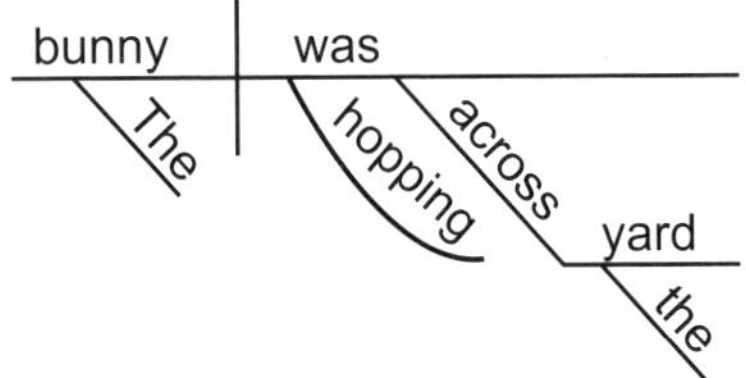

   b. The hopping bunny took a rest under the bush.

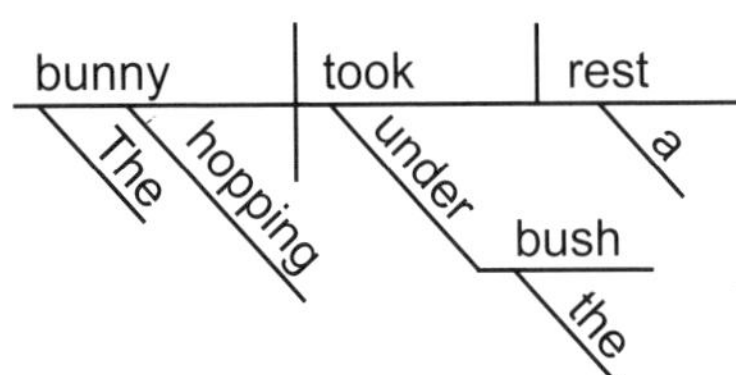

A **past participle** ends with "-ed."

The **frightened** child ran to her mother.

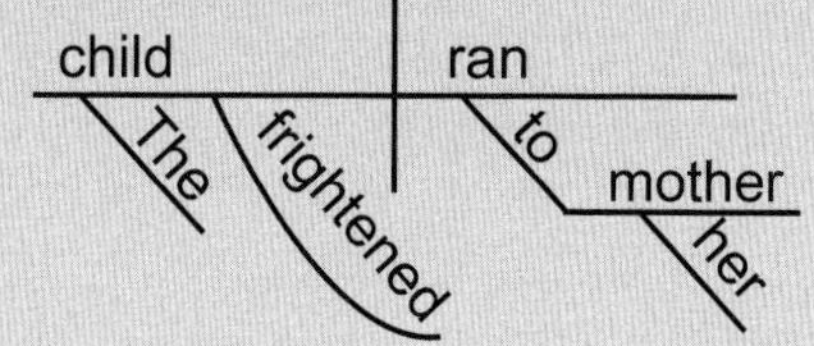

The tow truck took away the **wrecked** car.

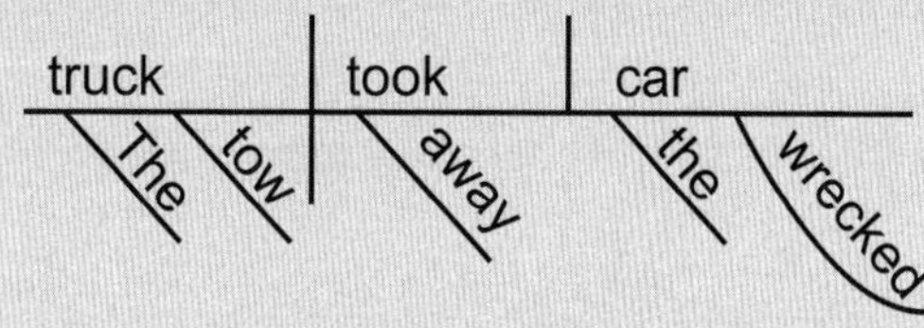

2. Fill in the diagram for each sentence.

a. The cracked windows are dangerous.

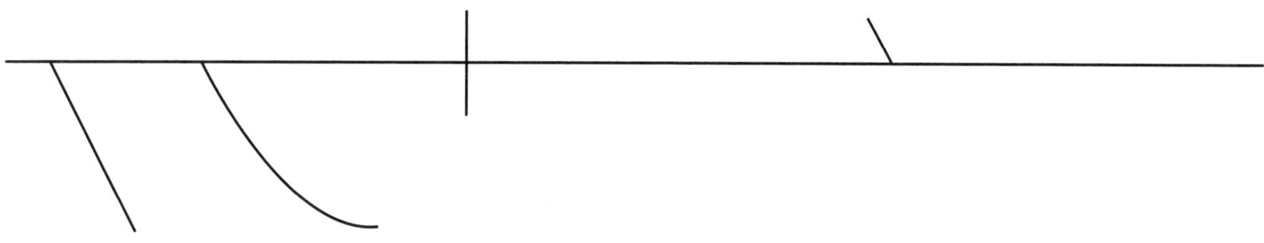

b. Who is making that buzzing noise?

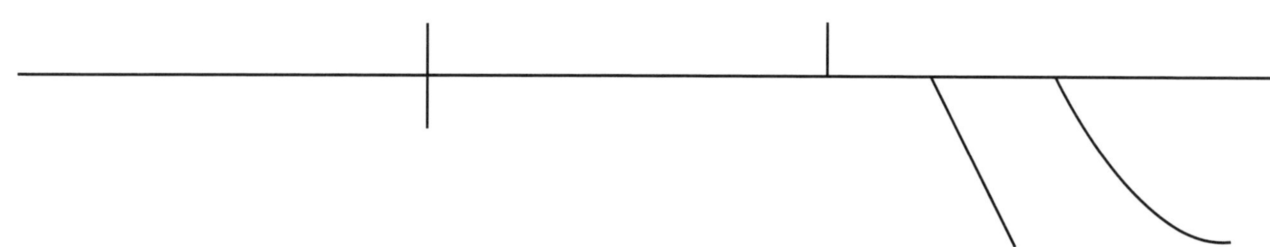

c. Boiling water is very hot!

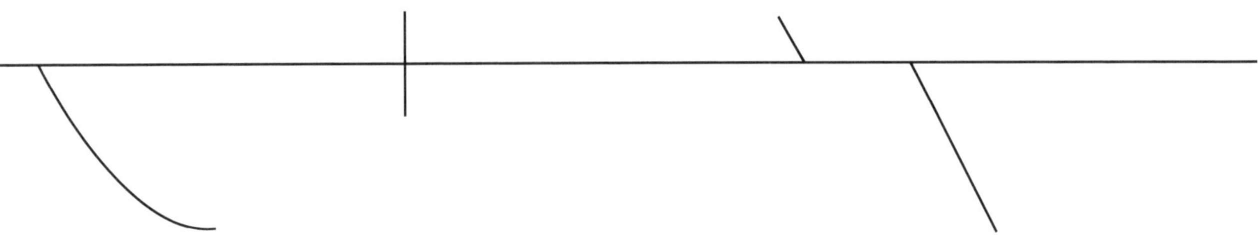

d. Can you repair the creaking floorboards in the kitchen?

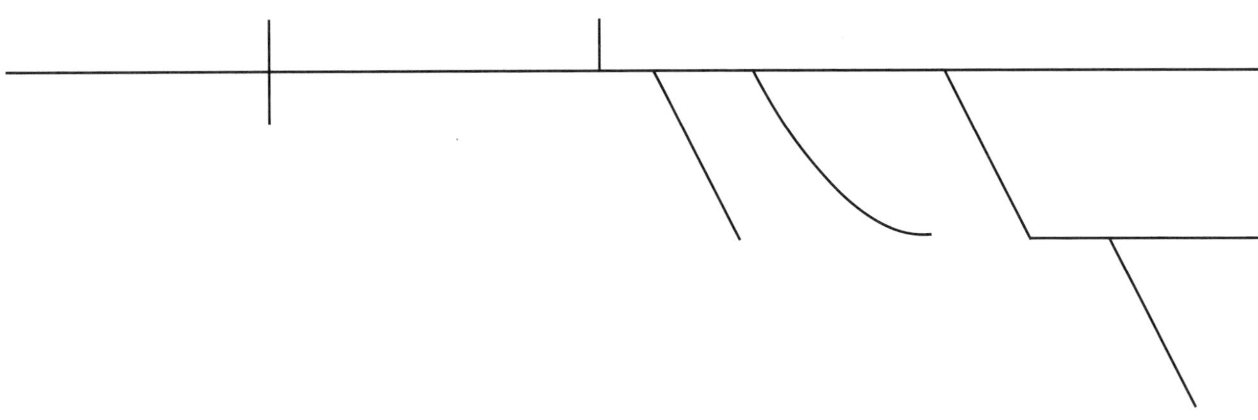

e. The enchanted children listened to every word of the fairy tale!

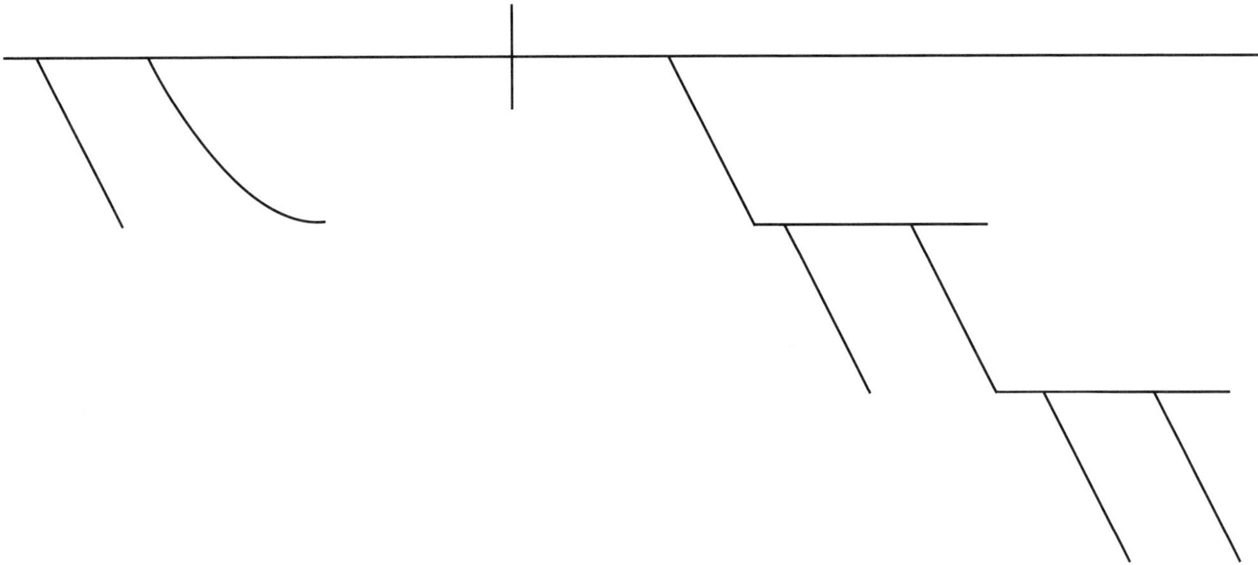

A **participle** is often used as a sentence opener, giving us a brief description of the subject. It is separated from the subject by a comma.

Frightened, the small child ran to her mother.

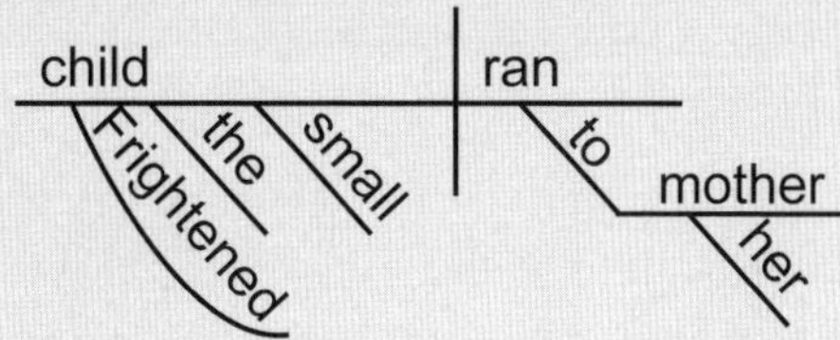

Smirking, the mischievous child poured his milk on the floor.

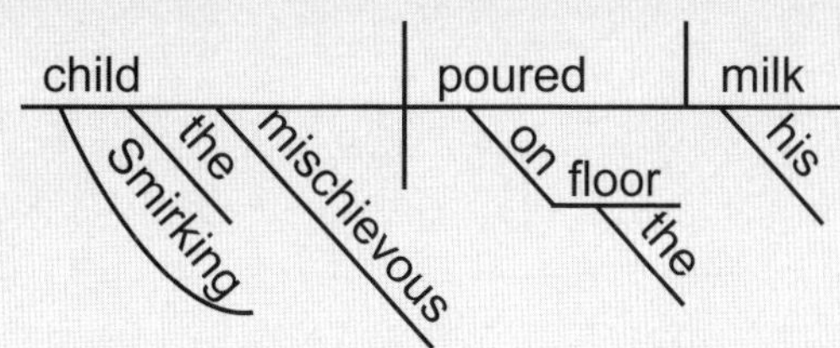

3. Write a sentence, using the prompt, to match each diagram. Then complete the diagram.

a. ....
(Present Participle)

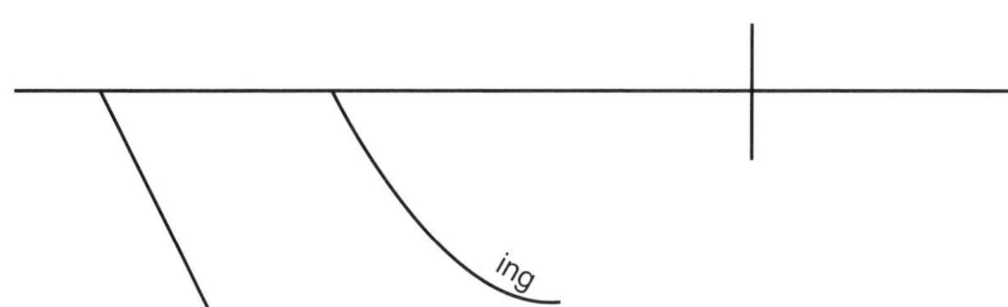

b. ....
(Present Participle)

c. ....
(1st Word Present Participle)

d. ....
(1st Word Past Participle)

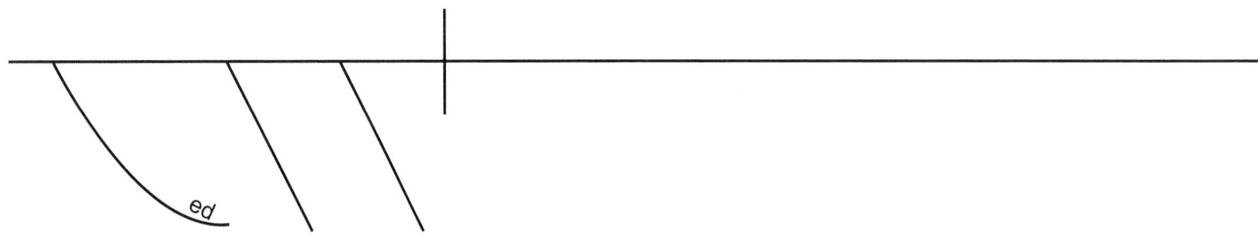

e. ....
(1st 2 Words Past Participles)

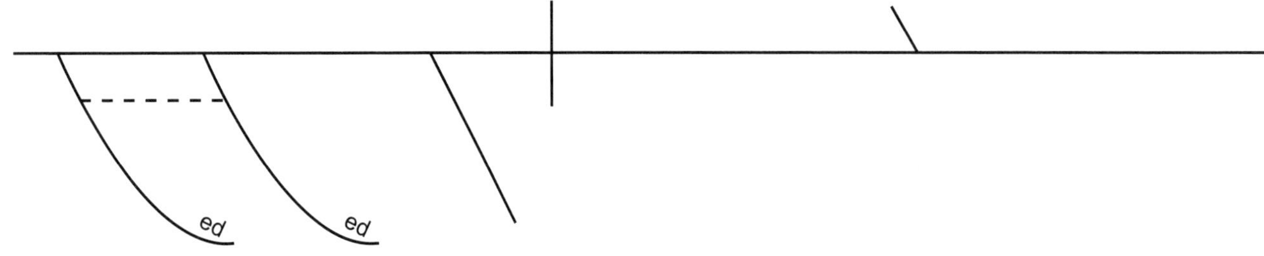

An **irregular past participle** does NOT end with "-ed." It ends with "-en," "–d," "-n,"or "-t" or has a different spelling.

tore/tor**n** broke/brok**en** bend/ben**t** fine/foun**d** beat/beat**en** become/**became**

4. Diagram each sentence.

   a. Forgotten, the toy doll sat on the swing set for a week.

   b. The injured runner bravely jumped back into the race.

c. Mr. Bell repaired Alice's mangled teddy bear.

d. The mewing and hissing kitten did not like the rain.

e. Bent and broken, Ronnie's finger looked painful.

Lesson 5: Participial Phrases

A **participial** phrase begins with a *present* or *past* participle. It includes objects and/or modifiers. The whole phrase functions as an adjective to describe the noun. The modifiers are diagrammed below the participle.

Smiling brightly *at her new students*, Miss Day welcomed them to kindergarten.

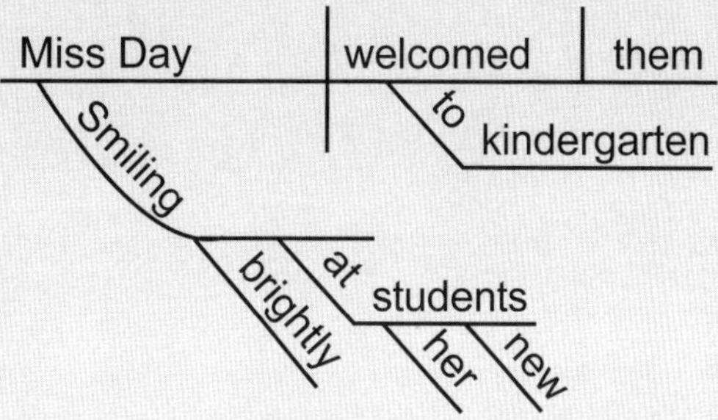

Excited *about her party*, Charley cleaned house all day!

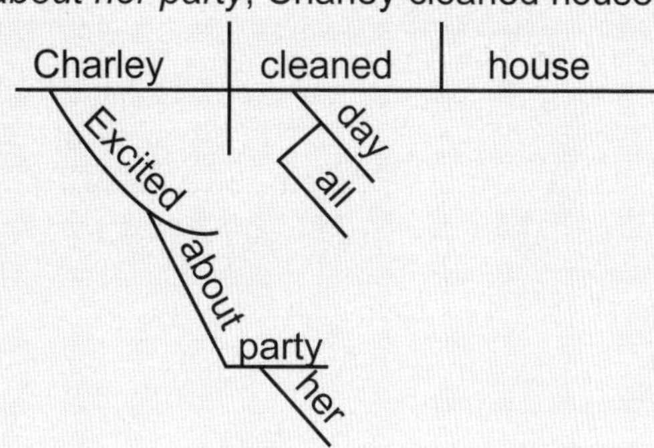

1. Each sentence diagram below has an error. Diagram each sentence correctly.

   a. Frozen in the early snowstorm, Mom's roses died.

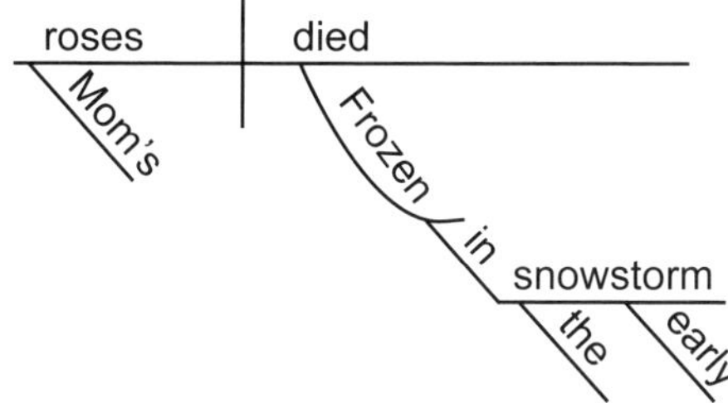

   b. Charmed by the seven dwarves, Snow White felt safe in their home.

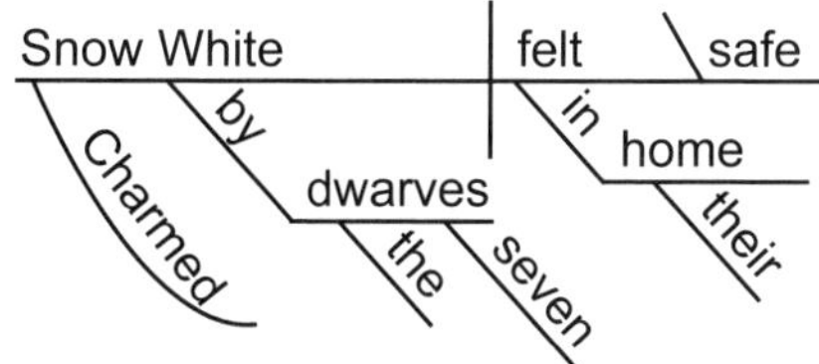

A **participle** can take on a direct object. It is diagrammed after a short vertical line following the participle.

Carefully **checking** his answers, Matthew felt confident about his test score.

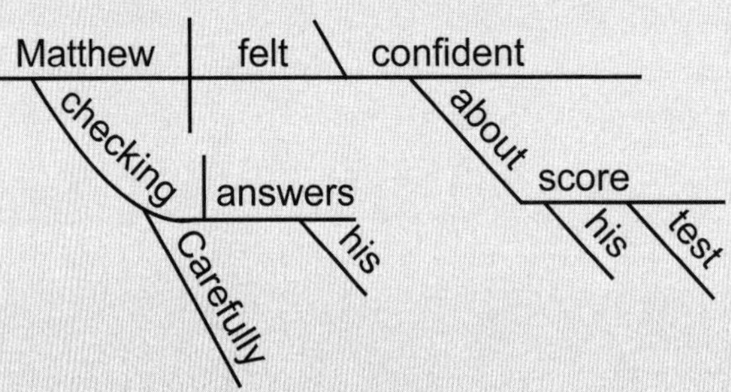

2. Fill in the diagram for each sentence.

   a. Skipping steps, Charlie raced up the stairs.

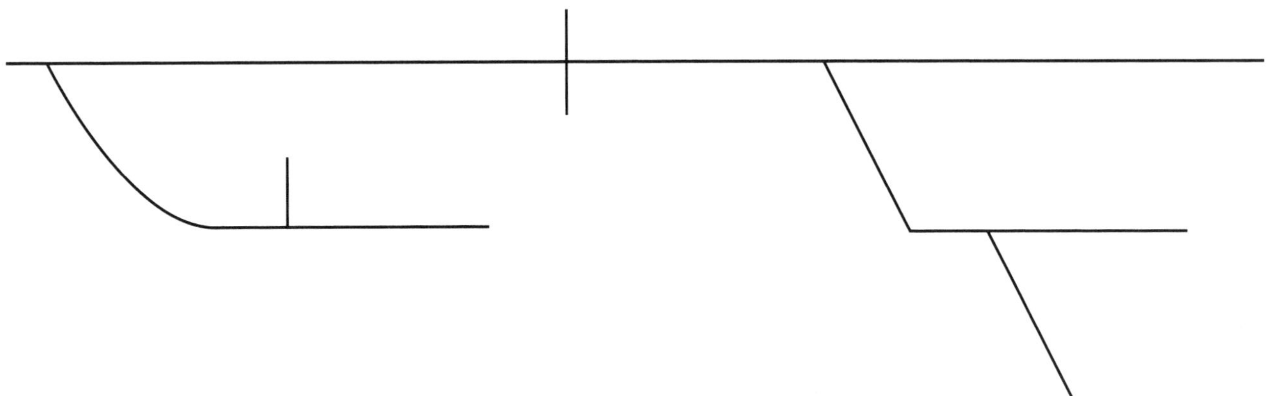

   b. Bothered by the heat, Angelina jumped into the pool.

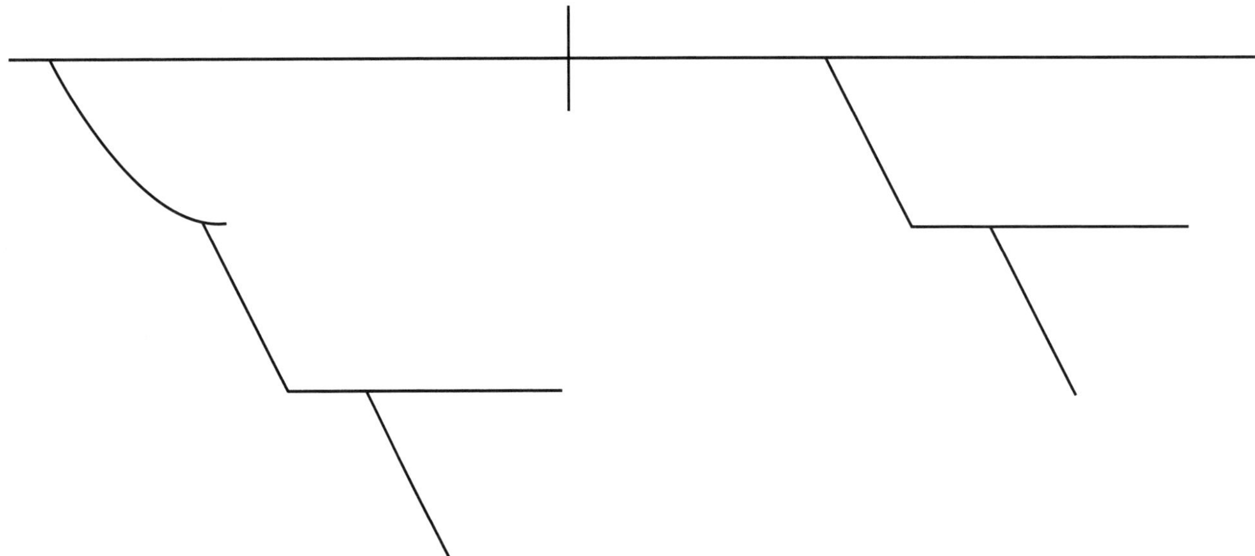

c. Munching popcorn happily, Marcus enjoyed the movie.

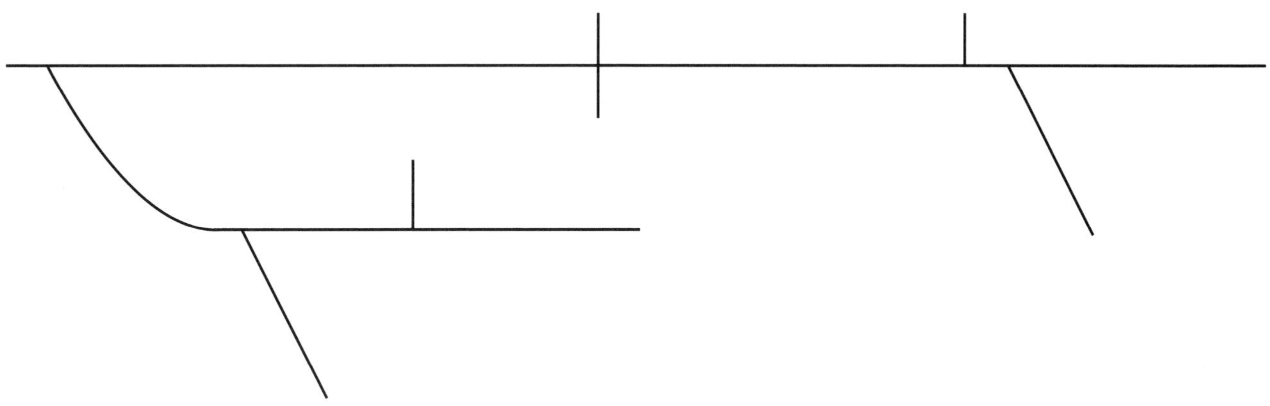

d. Quietly humming Christmas carols, Mom baked our favorite cookies.

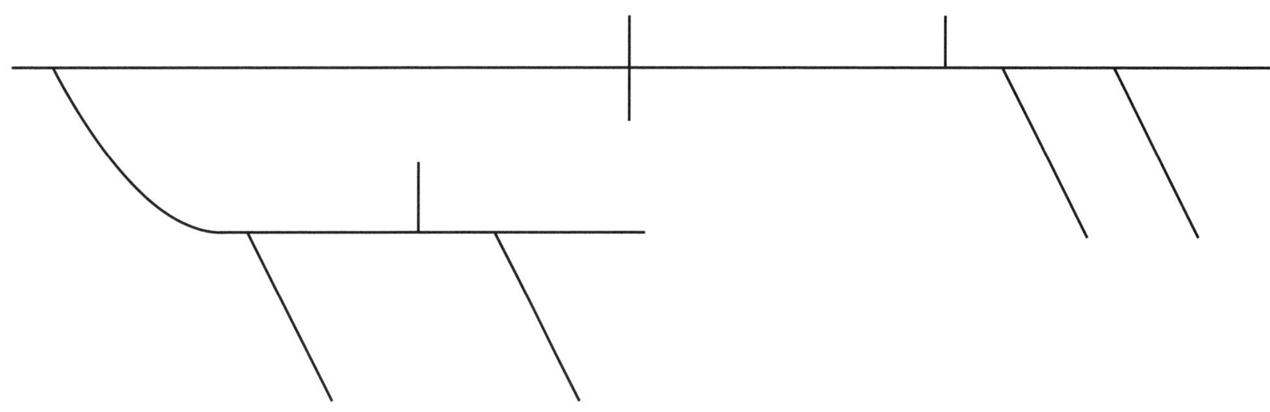

e. Gently rubbing his back, the nanny soothed the crying child.

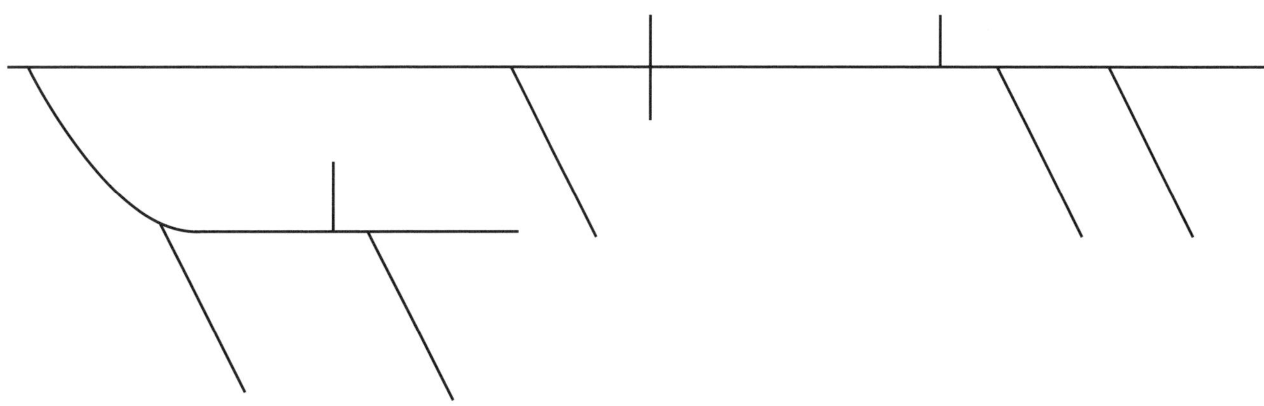

A **participial phrase** is not always at the beginning of a sentence. It can come after the subject.

The old dog, **frightened by fireworks**, was hiding under a bed.

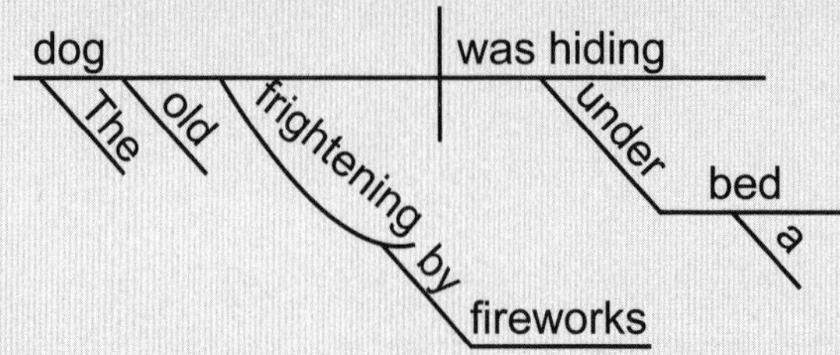

A **participial phrase** can modify any noun in the sentence, not just the subject.

I saw a YouTube video of lemmings **jumping off a cliff**.

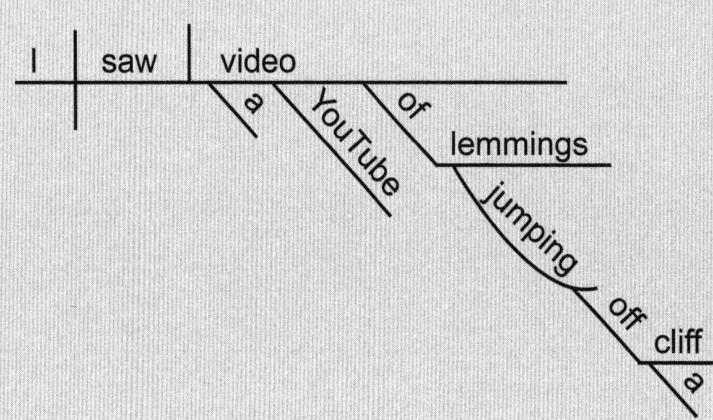

3. Write a sentence to match each diagram. Then complete the diagram.

a. ....

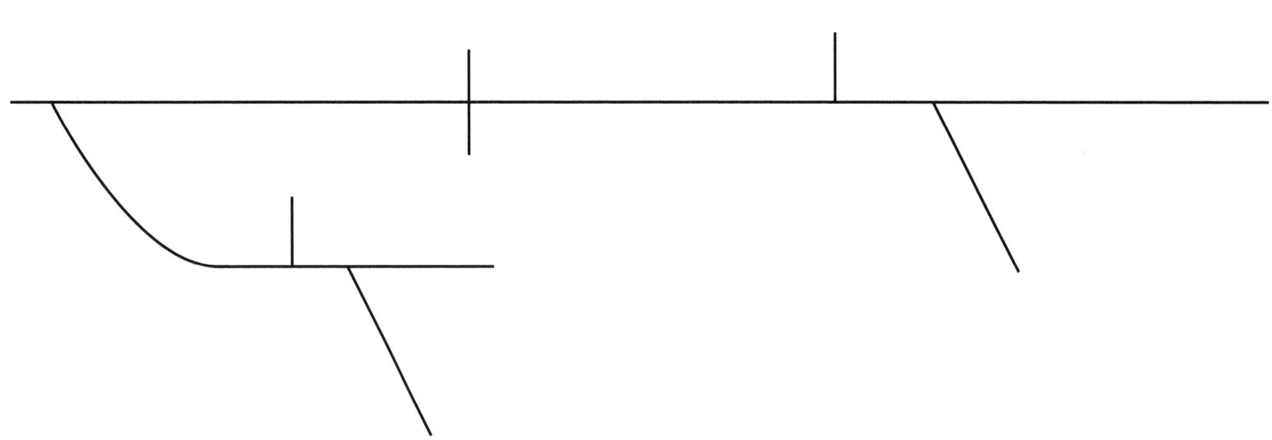

b. ....

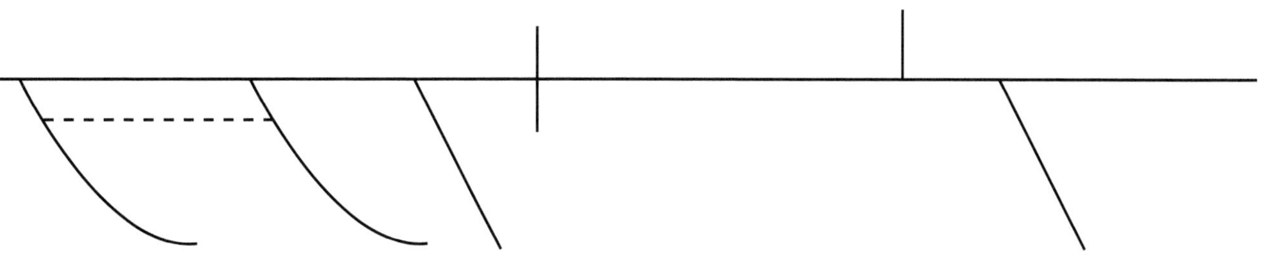

c. ....

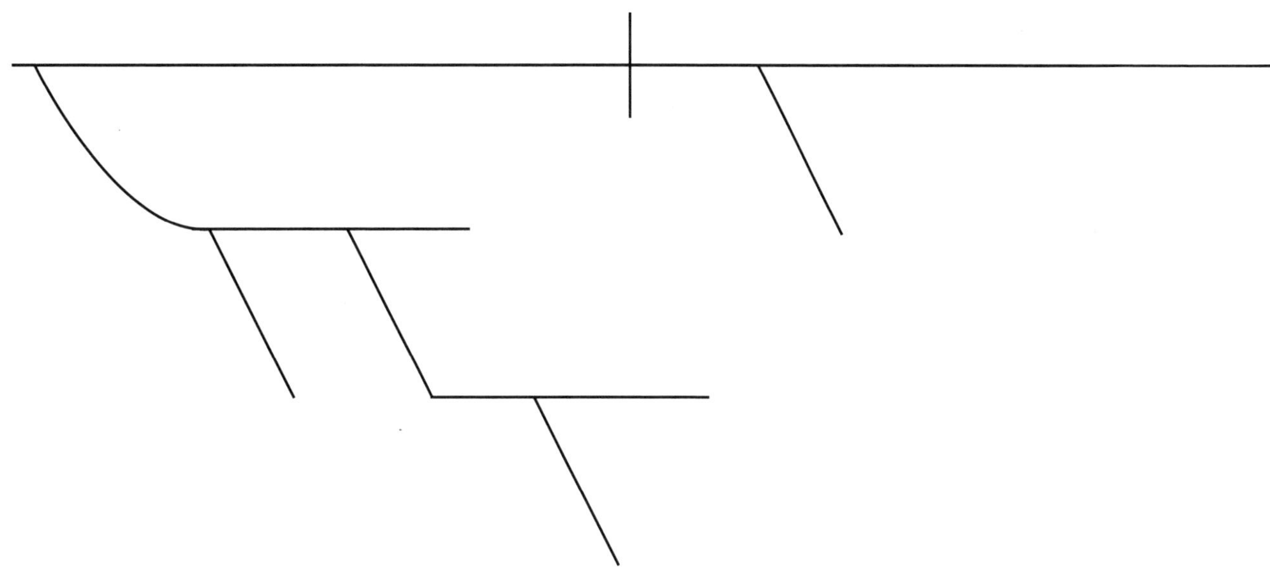

d. ....

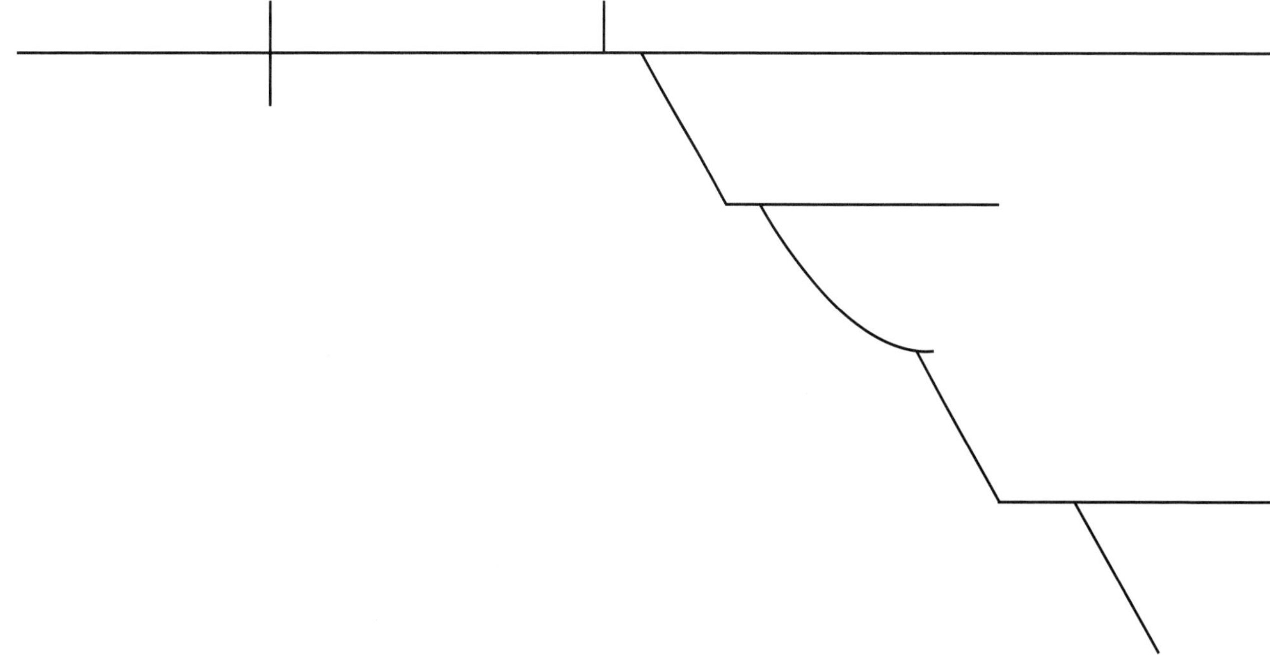

Gerund phrases and **participial phrases** are easily confused because they both begin with a verb ending with "-ing."

Gerund Phrase: Skiing on smooth water at sunset is an thrilling. (The "thing" that is enjoyed.)

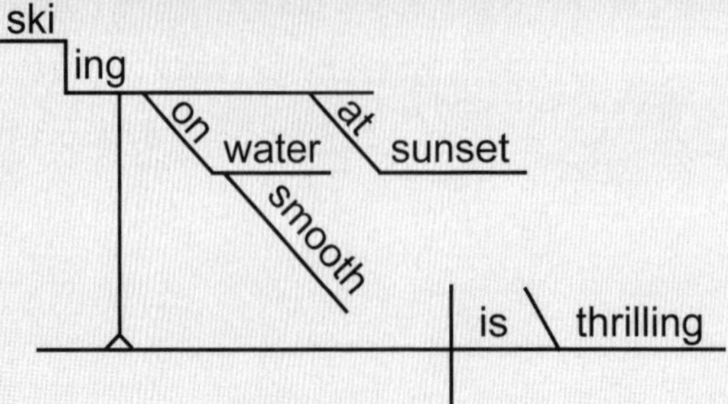

Participial Phrase: **Skiing on smooth water at sunset**, *Mike felt relaxed but also re-energized.* ("Skiing on smooth water at sunset" is describing the subject of the sentence, Mike. The comma sets the participial phrase apart from the main clause of the sentence.)

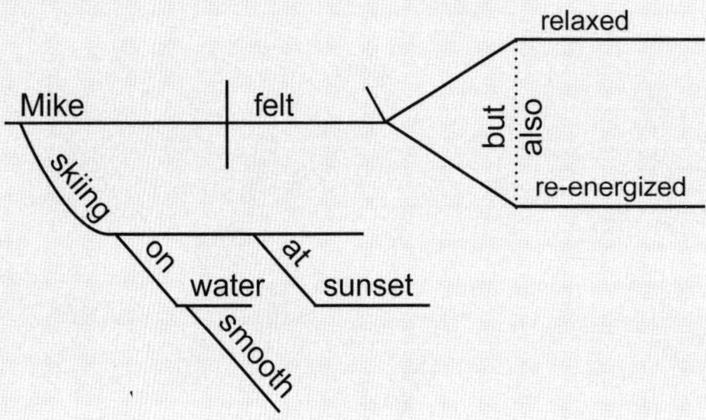

4. Diagram each sentence.

   a. Clenching her teeth nervously, Anabelle stepped up to the microphone.

b. The lifeguard, mindlessly twirling her whistle, carefully watched the swimmers.

c. The children were amazed by the busker juggling swords.

d. Licking the spatula, Uncle Matt was enjoying cleaning the brownie bowl.

Lesson 6: Infinitives

An **infinitive** is another way that a verb can behave like another part of speech. An infinitive is made with the word "to" plus the simplest form of any verb.

An **infinitive** can be a direct object. It is diagrammed in a prepositional-phrase type formation on top of a forked line.

Megan likes **to sing**.

1. Each sentence diagram below has an error. Diagram each sentence correctly.

   a. Ashton hates to type.

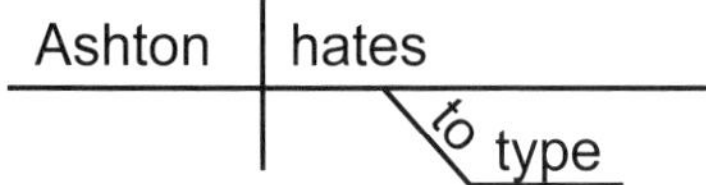

   b. Mrs. Jones prefers to email.

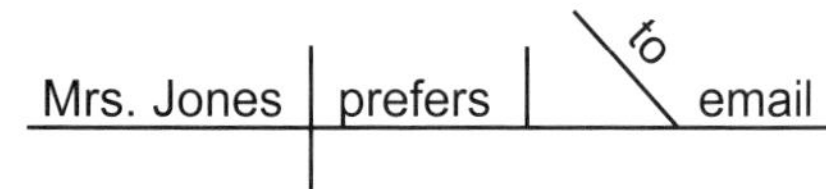

   c. My old piano teacher really liked to laugh.

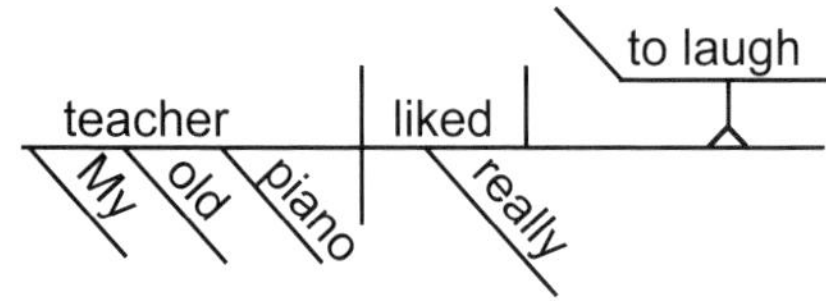

   d. During recess the kindergarteners like to scream and shout.

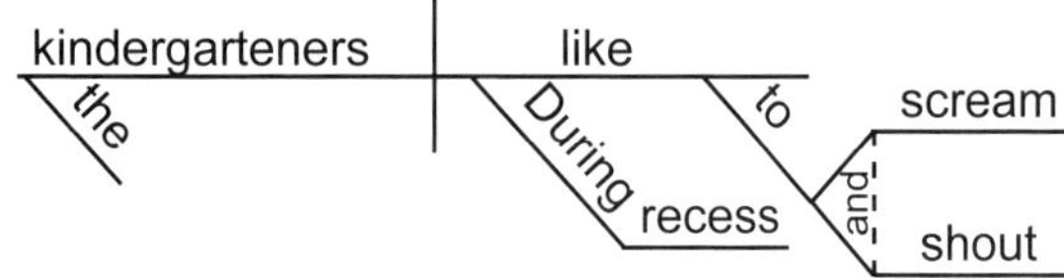

An **infinitive** can also be used as the <u>subject</u> of a sentence.

<u>To procrastinate</u> is foolish.

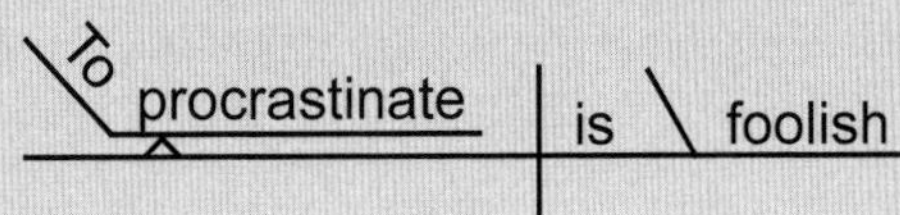

2. Fill in the diagram for each sentence.

   a. To act is my greatest desire.

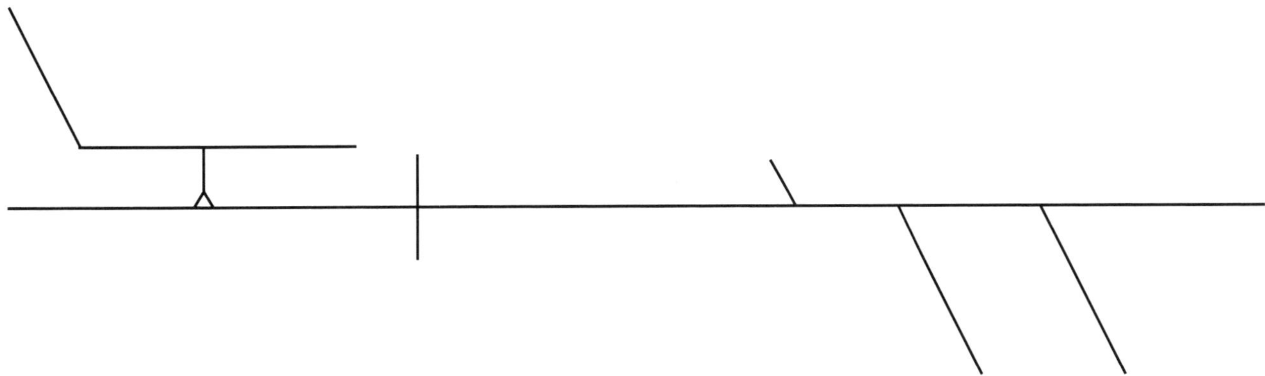

   b. I want to leave.

c. To fail is to learn.

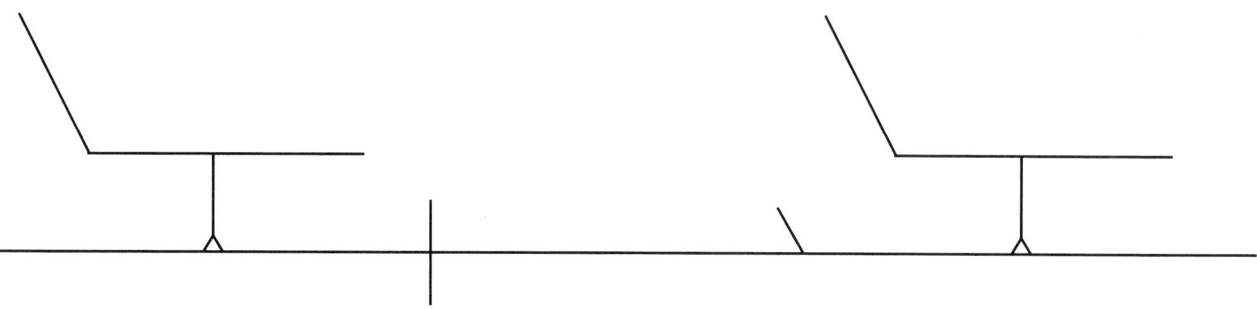

d. My sister finally learned to whistle!

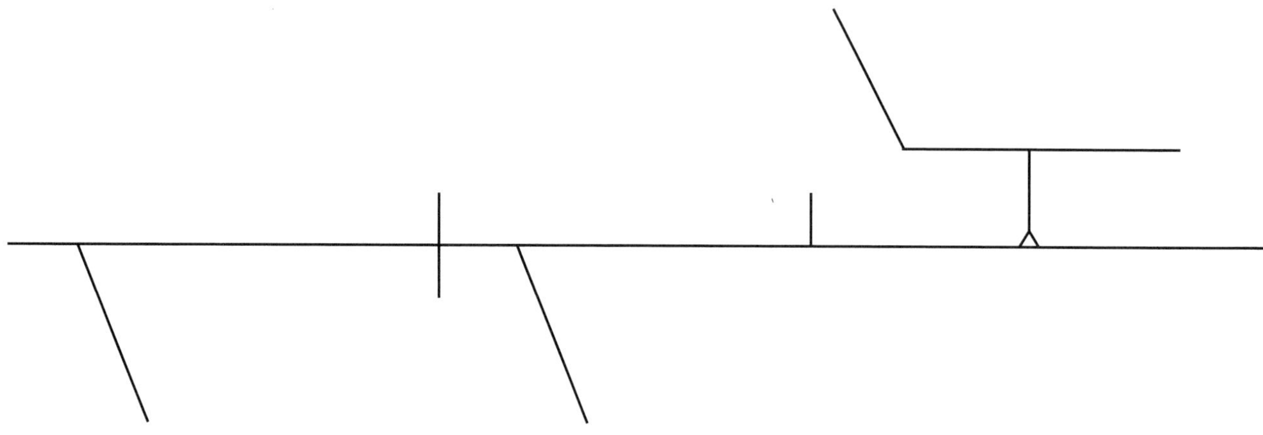

e. To win will take a lot of hard work and dedication.

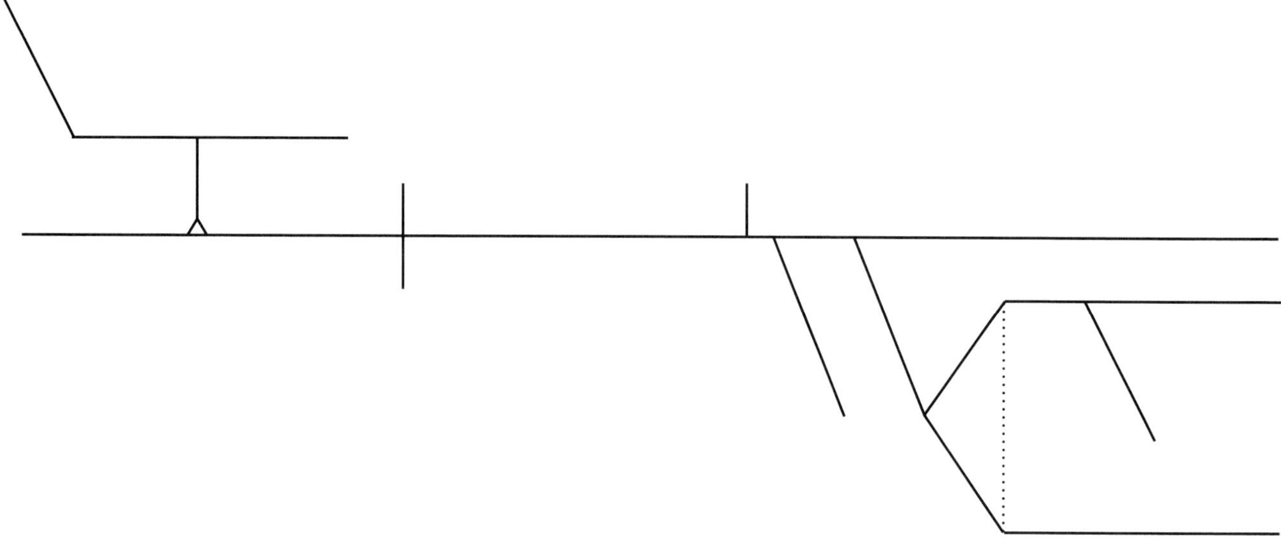

An **infinitive** always begins with the word "to," but the word "to" can also be the first word in a *prepositional phrase*. If a verb comes right after the word "to," then it is an infinitive. If "to" is followed by an article (a, an, the) and a noun, then it is a prepositional phrase.

Infinitive: Grandma likes ***to knit***. ("To" is followed by the verb "knit.")

Prepositional Phrase: We must go *to the store*. ("To" is followed by the article "the" and the noun "store.")

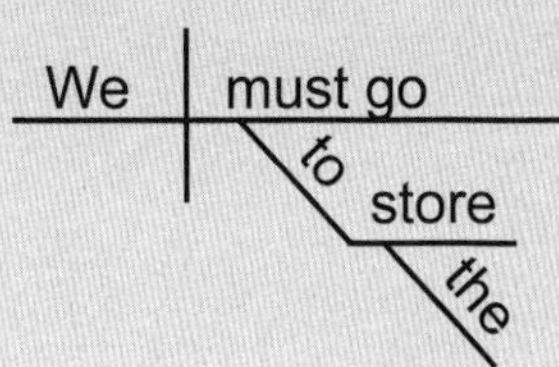

3. Write a sentence to match each diagram. Then complete the diagram.

a. ....

b. ....

c. ....

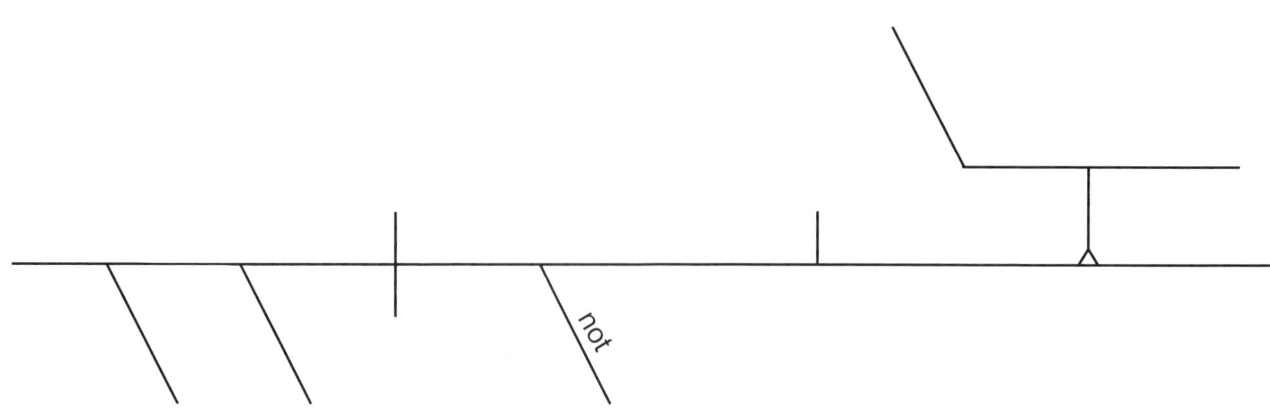

d. ....

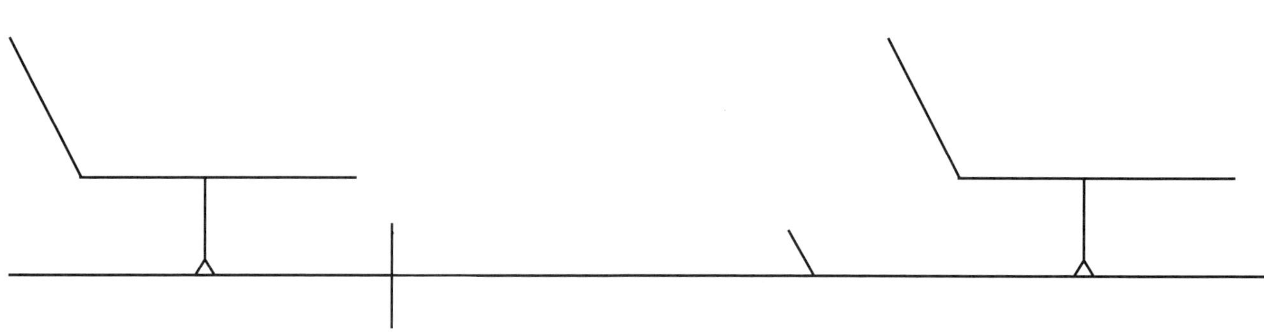

e. ....

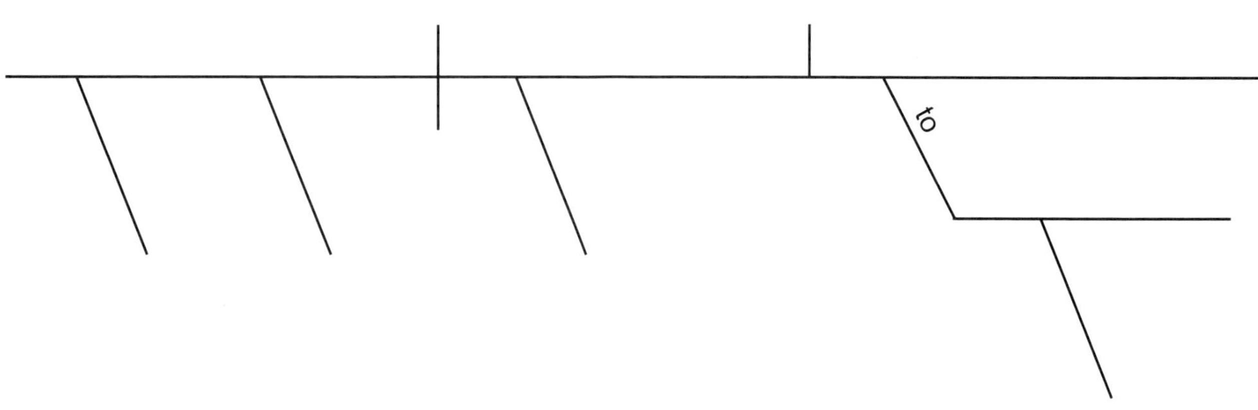

4. Diagram each sentence.

   a. Tired children often like to whine.

   b. Would you like to listen?

   c. Tell Lucy to hurry!

d. To be or not to be is the question.

e. Please teach me to ski.

f. At summer camp, Ellie learned to sing.

Lesson 7: Infinitive Phrases

Like other verbals (gerunds and participles), an infinitive can take on modifiers, creating an **infinitive phrase**. The modifiers can be adverbs or adverbial nouns and come right after the infinitive. They are diagrammed below the infinitive.

I try **to read daily**.

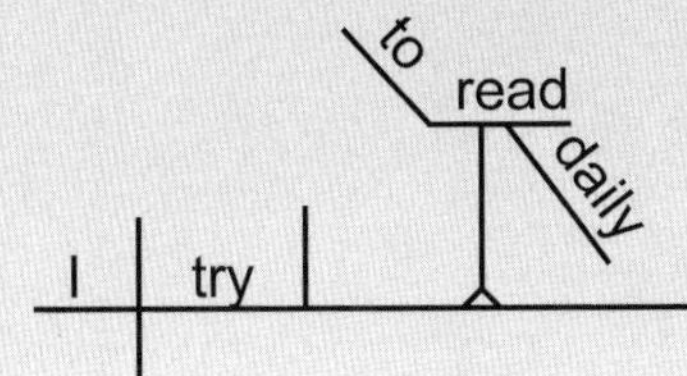

I try **to read every day**.

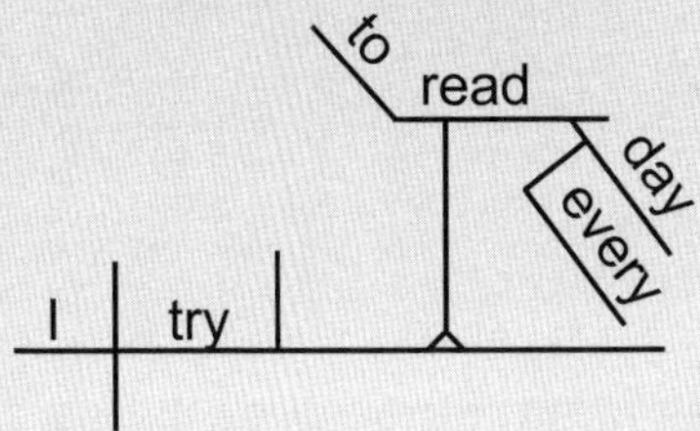

1. Each sentence diagram below has an error. Diagram each sentence correctly.

   a. You ought to exercise daily.

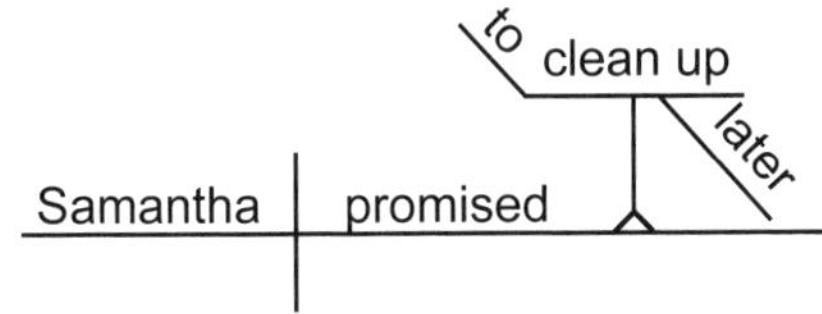

   b. Samantha promised to clean up later.

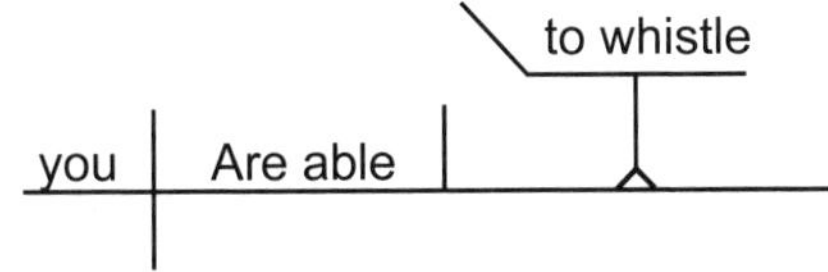

   c. Are you able to whistle?

to whistle

you | Are able

An **infinitive phrase** can have its own direct object. It is diagrammed after a short vertical line following the verb part of the infinitive.

I try **to read poetry every day**.

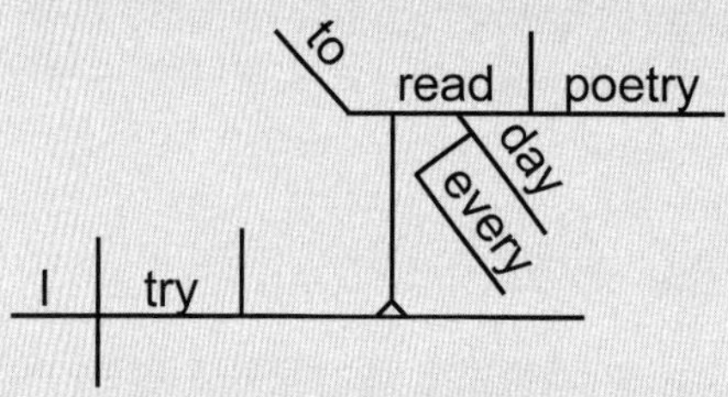

2. Fill in the diagram for each sentence.

a. I want to inspire people.

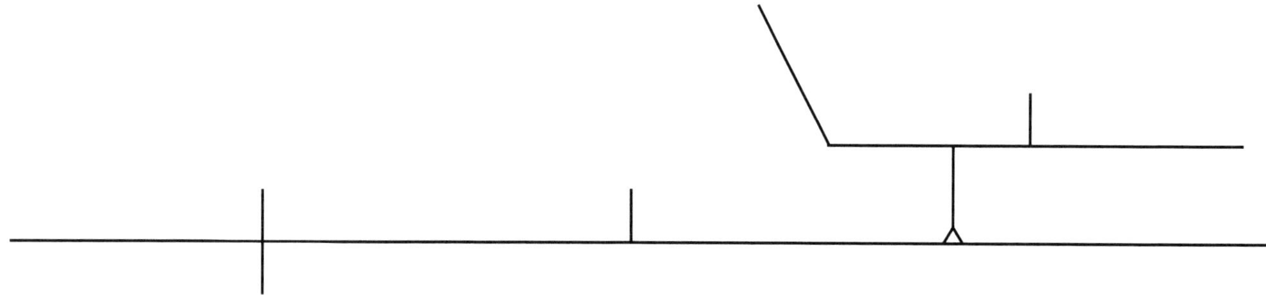

b. Sebastian agreed to watch *Romeo and Juliet* tonight.

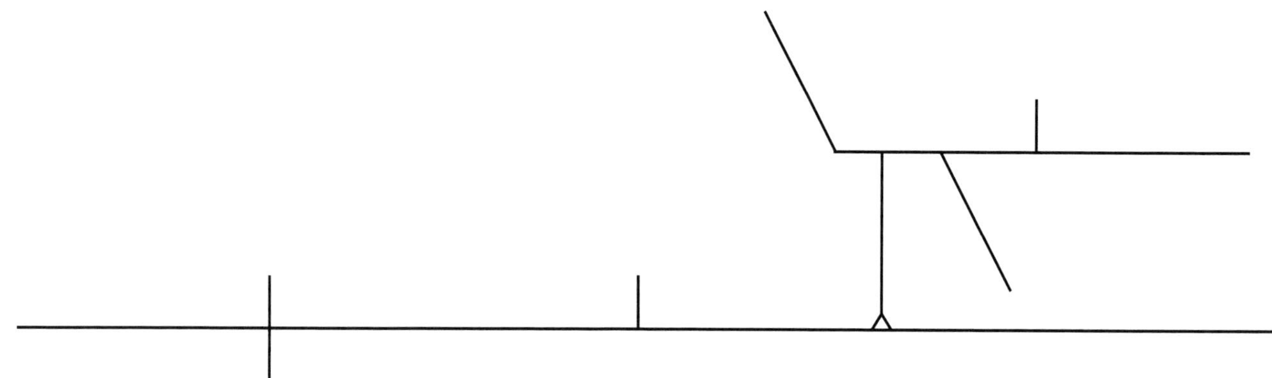

c. Jaya, you are required to write one paragraph every afternoon.

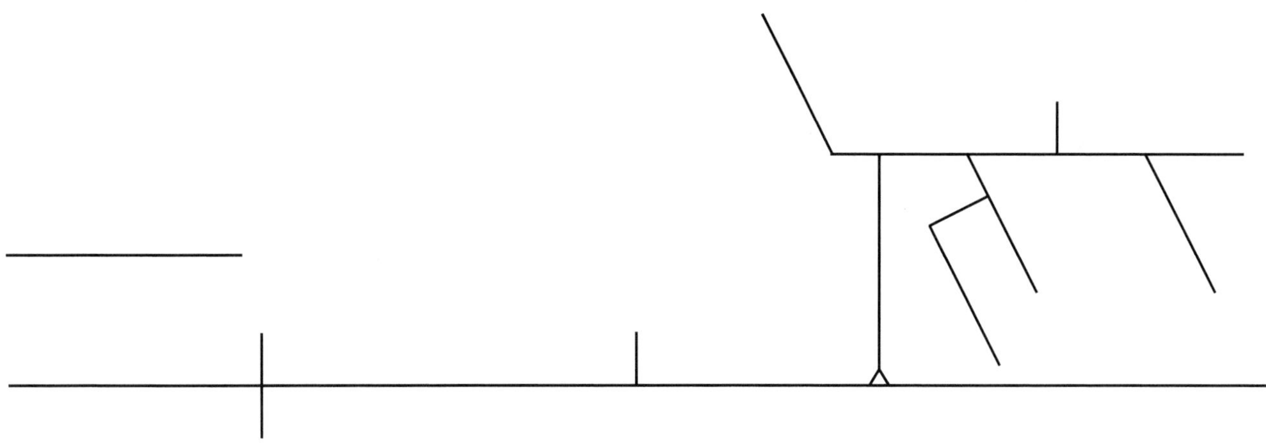

d. Jackson needs to buy a new laptop soon!

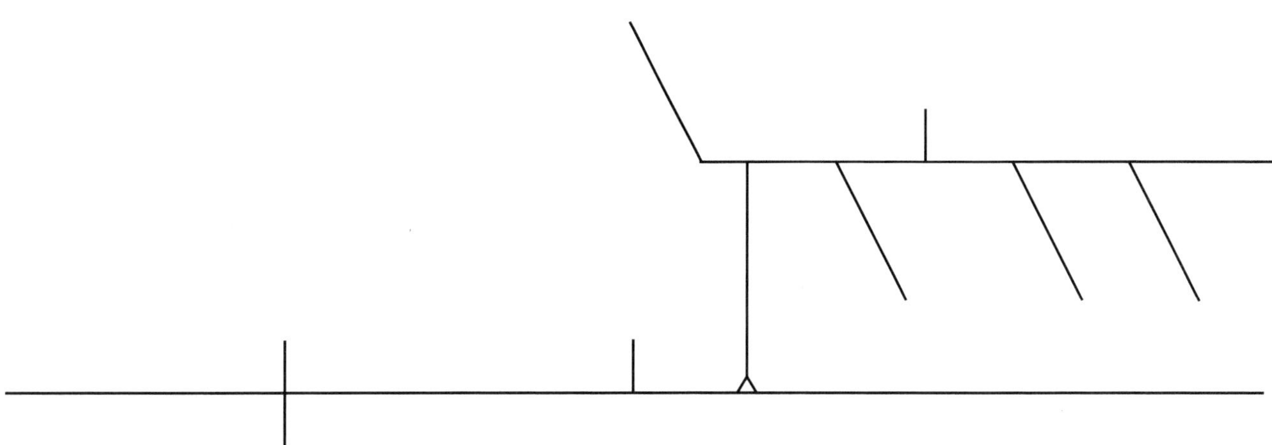

e. To win the Boston Marathon is a great achievement!

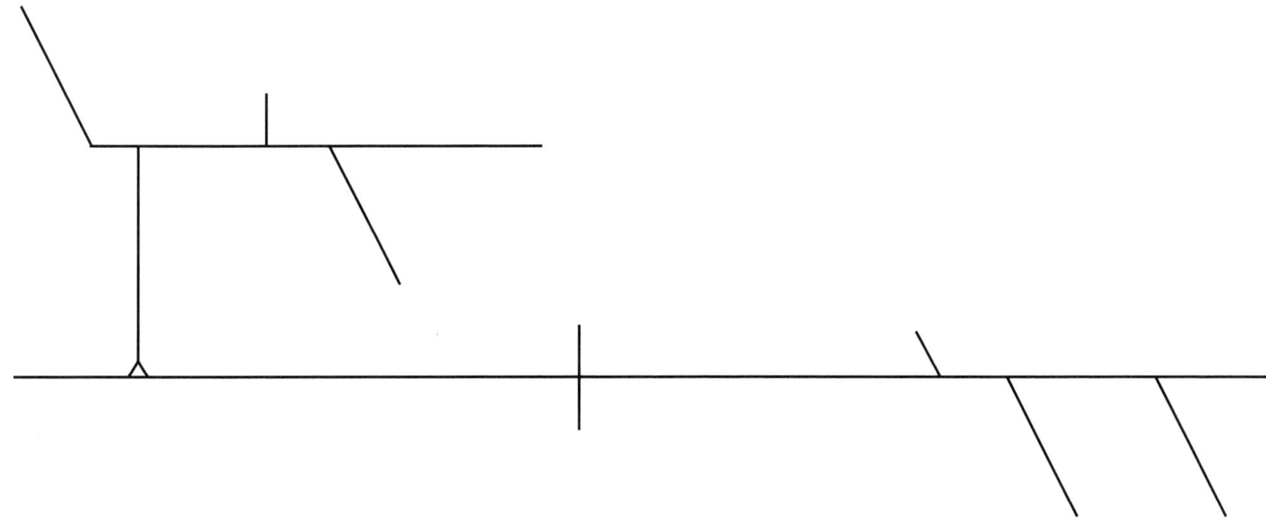

An **infinitive** can be followed by a *prepositional phrase* telling where, when, or how the action happens.

I try **to read** *before breakfast*.

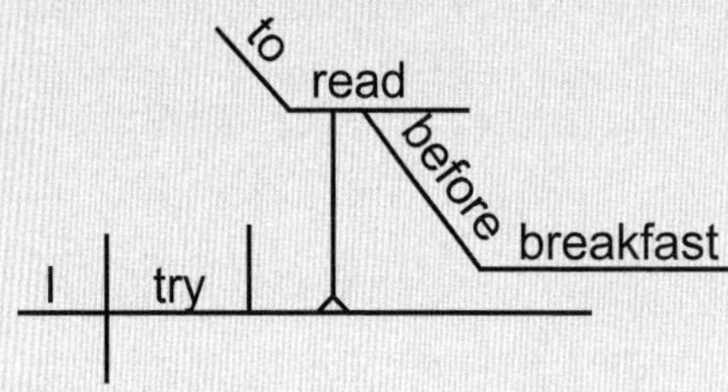

3. Write a sentence to match each diagram. Then complete the diagram.

a. ....

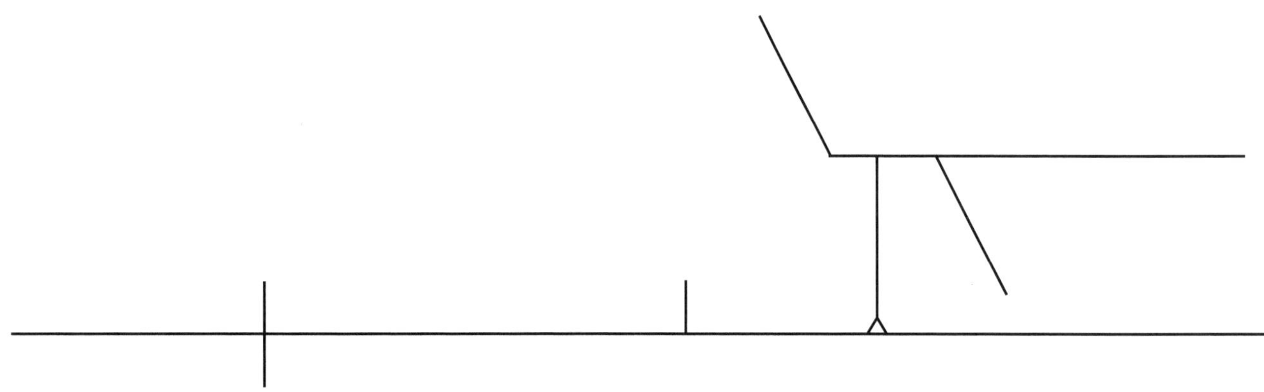

b. ....

c. ....

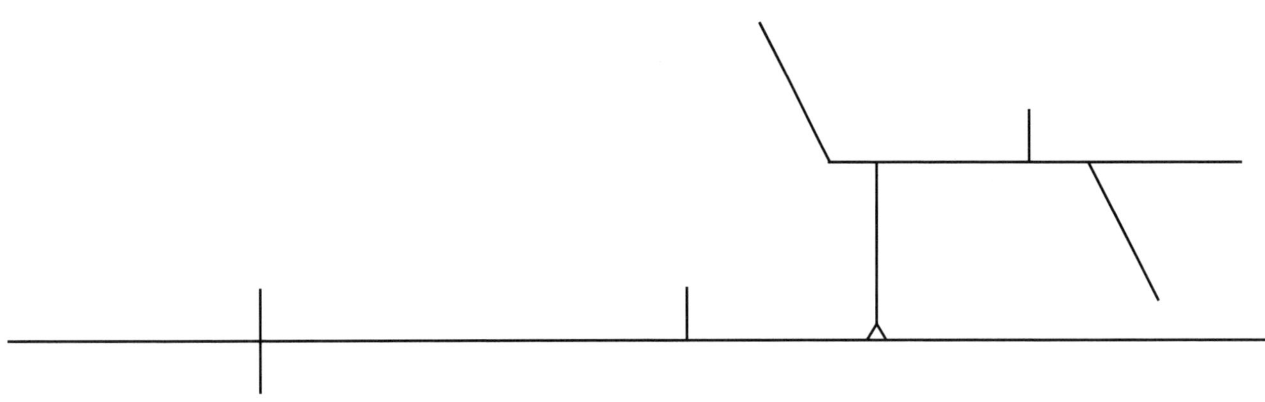

d. ....

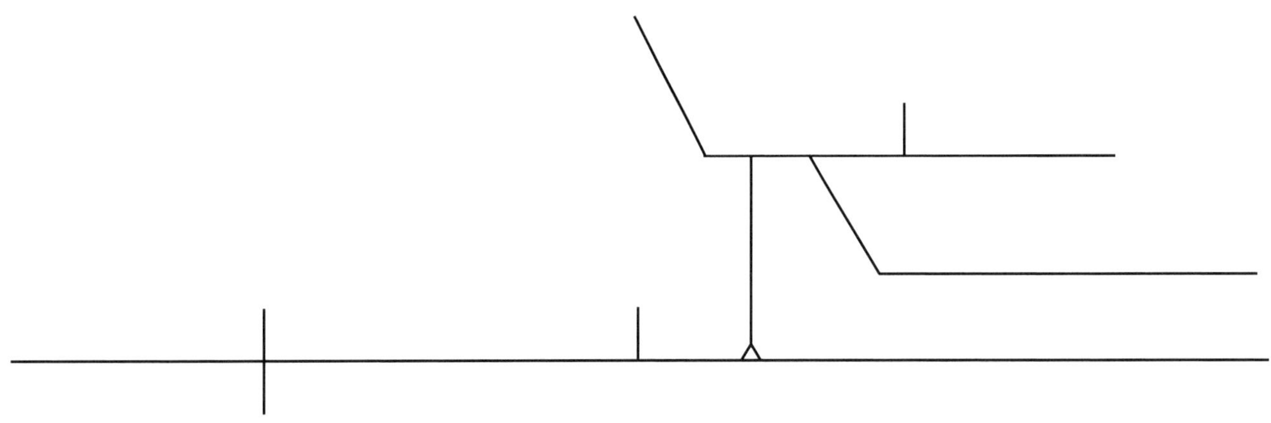

e. ....

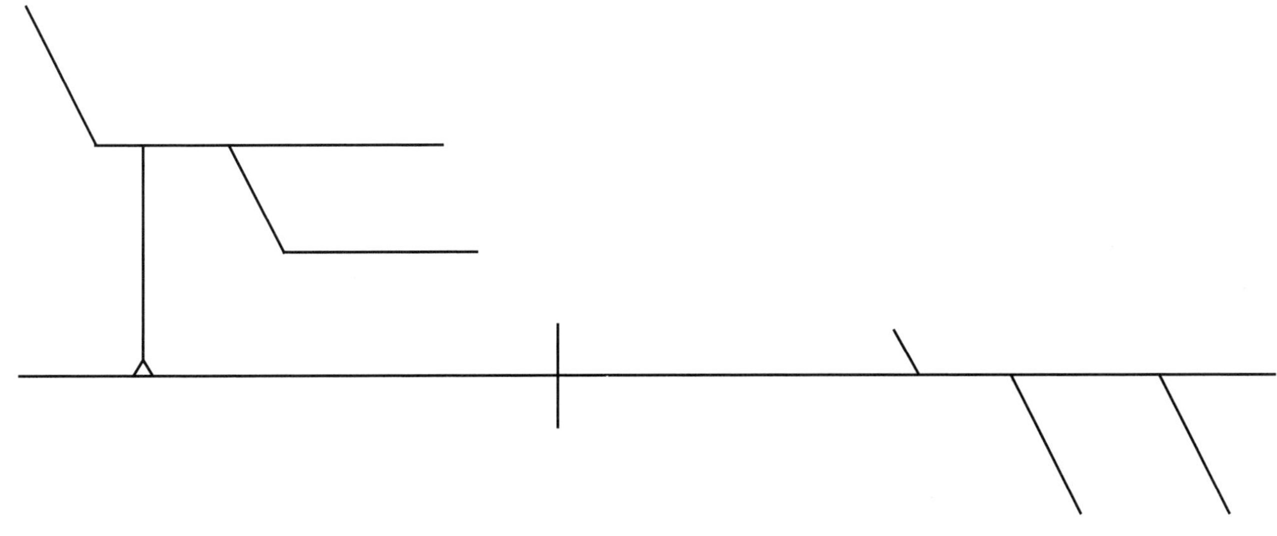

4. Diagram each sentence.

   a. To graduate with honors is a noble goal.

   b. Peter doesn't want to jump off the diving board.

   c. Does Maggie want to hang the new ornaments on the tree?

d. I try to read poetry every day before breakfast.

e. To become an Eagle Scout takes hard work and dedication!

f. Tony needs to go to the store tonight.

Lesson 8: Noun Clauses

A **noun clause** is a dependent clause, complete with a subject and a verb, which is acting like a noun. It can be found anywhere in a sentence that a noun would be, such as the subject, direct object, object of a preposition, etc. A noun clause often starts with the signal word "that." It is diagrammed on its own main line resting on a forked line. The word "that" floats above on a dotted line.

I think **that it tastes good**.

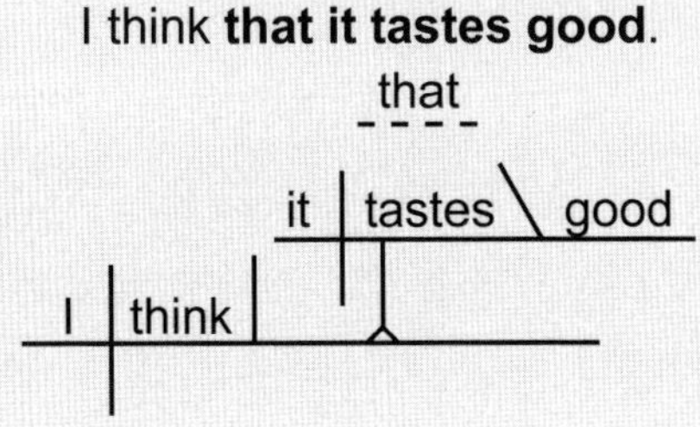

1. Each sentence diagram below has an error. Diagram each sentence correctly.

   a. Johanna thinks that the movie was great!

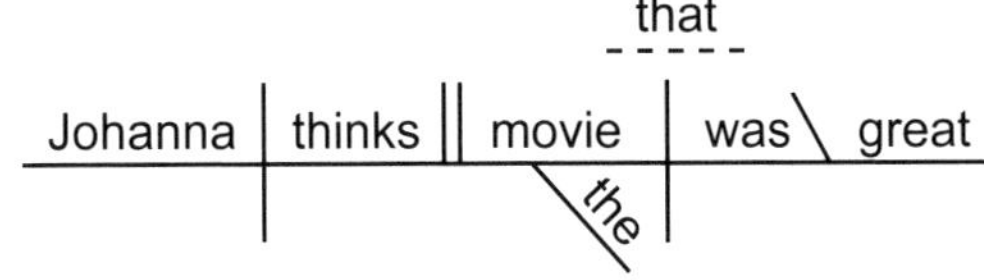

   b. Mrs. Criswell likes that you printed so neatly!

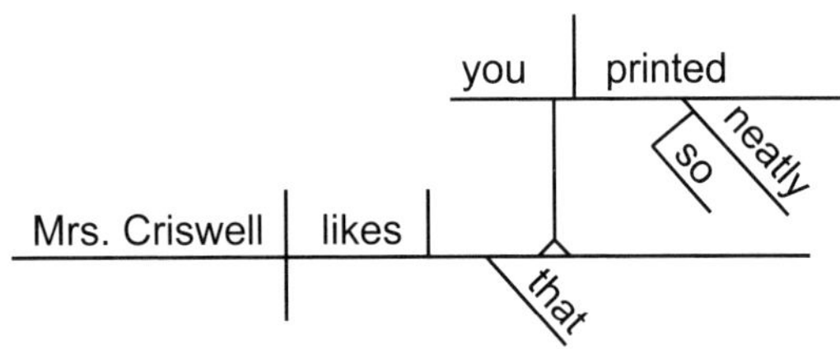

   c. I heard that a snowstorm is coming!

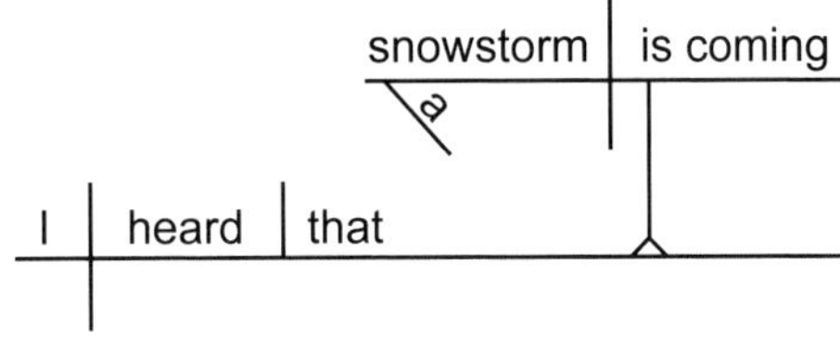

A **noun clause** appearing as a direct object can begin with signal words other than "that." It will often begin with a word that asks a question.

Question Words

what where who when why how

To diagram, put the whole clause on its own main line above a forked line.

I don't know **how you do it**!

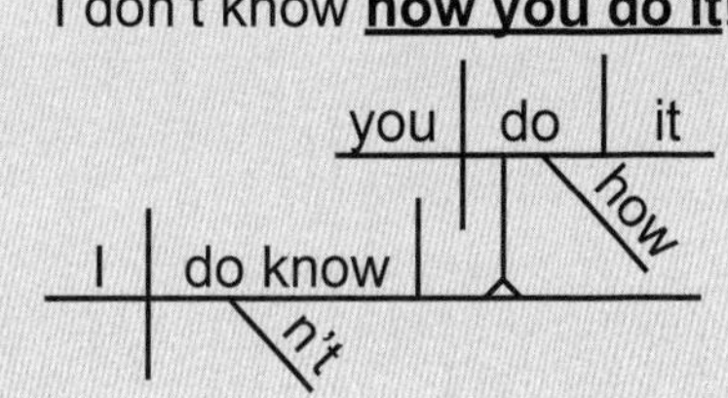

2. Fill in the diagram for each sentence.

a. Devon said that she feels ill.

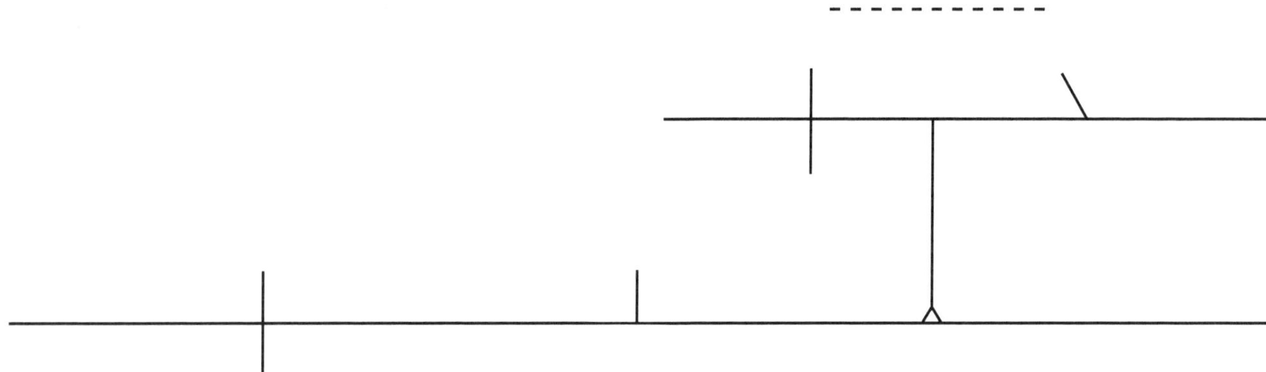

b. I can't remember what I bought for Aunt Mary Ann.

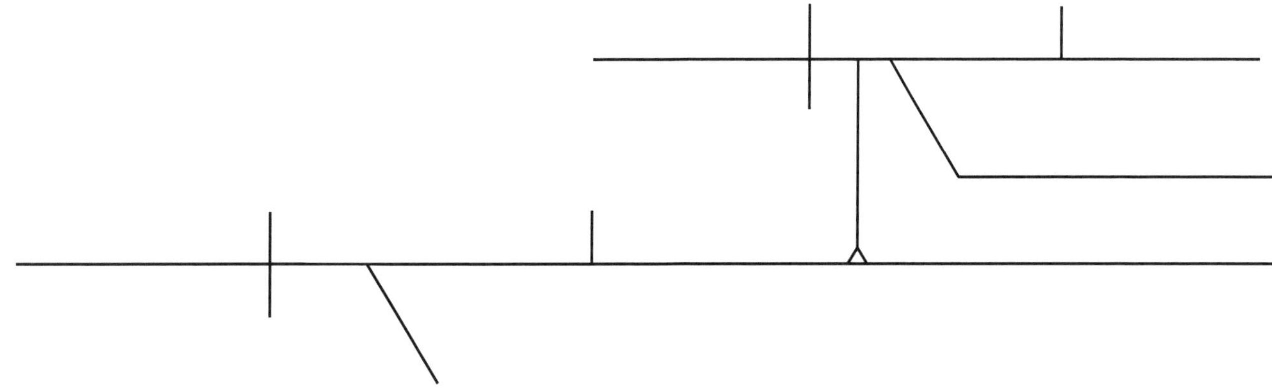

c. Does Mom know where you are going?

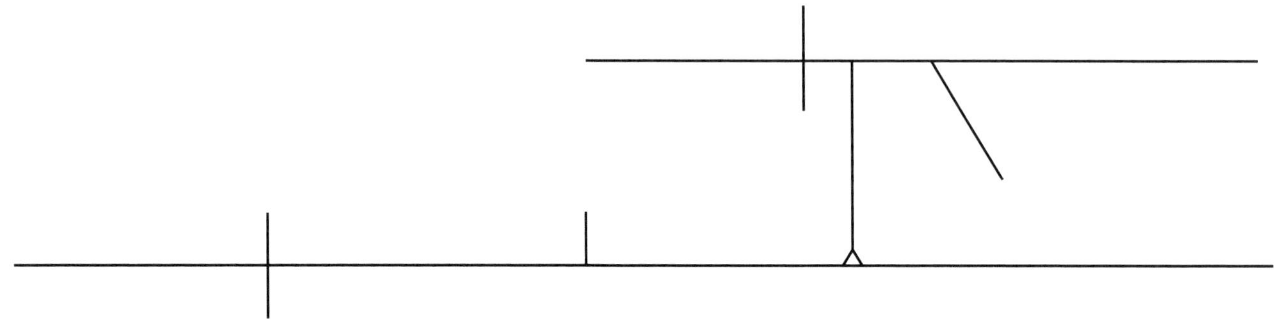

d. He said that I broke the clock!

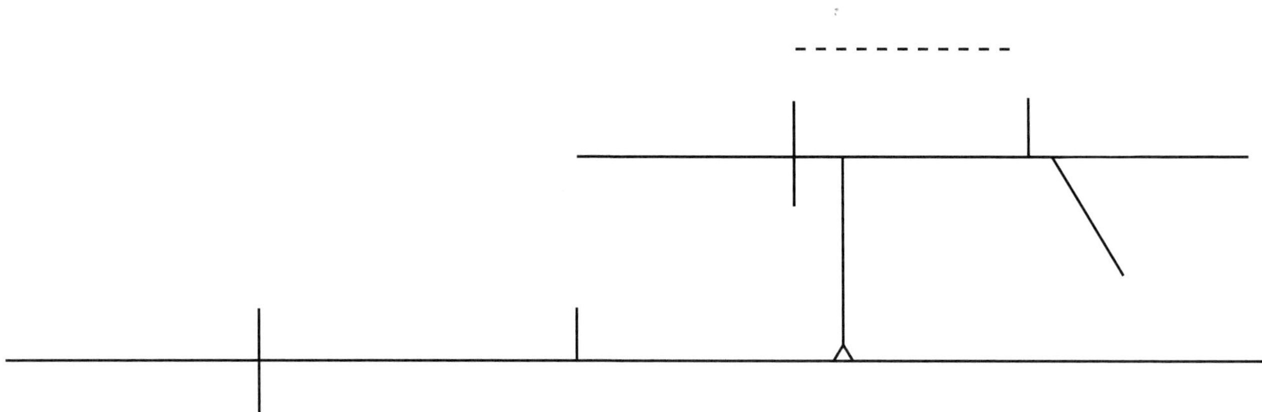

e. Tell Harry that you will be late.

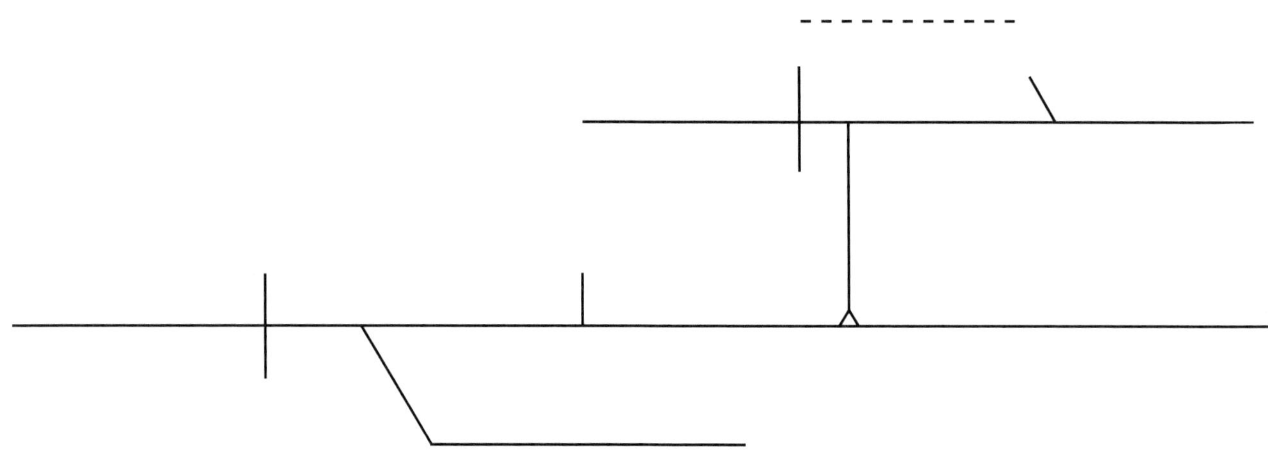

A **noun clause** can be the subject of the sentence or a subjective complement (the adjective, noun, or pronoun) that follows a *linking verb*.

Subject of the sentence: **How you dress for a job interview** is important.

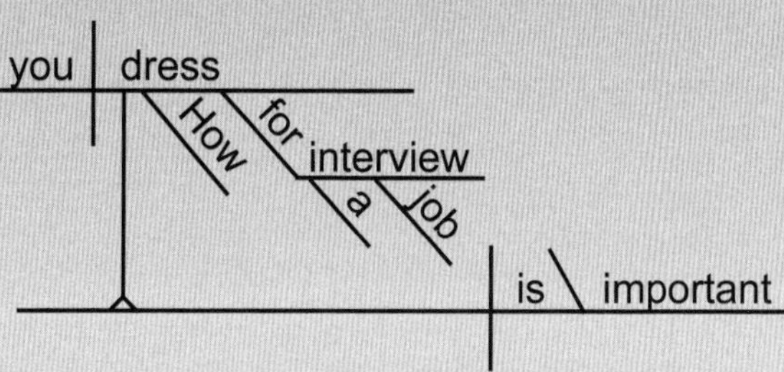

Subjective Complement: You *are* **what you eat**.

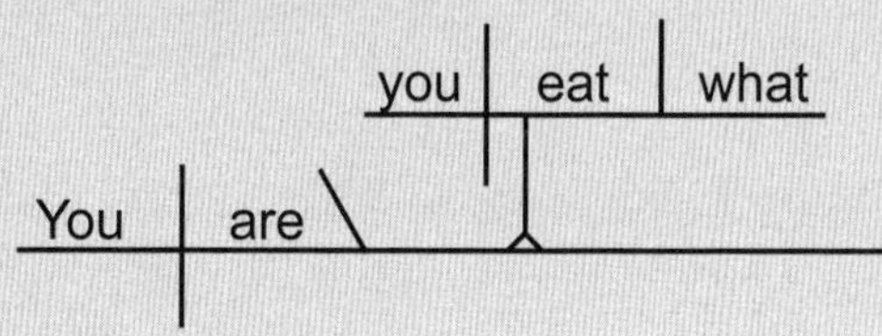

3. Write a sentence, using the prompt, to match each diagram. Then complete the diagram.

a. ....

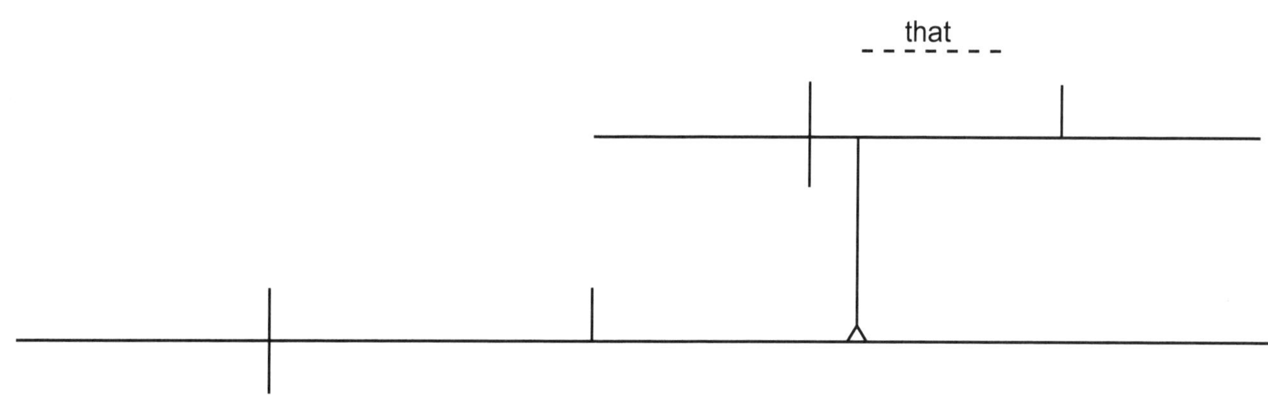

b. ....

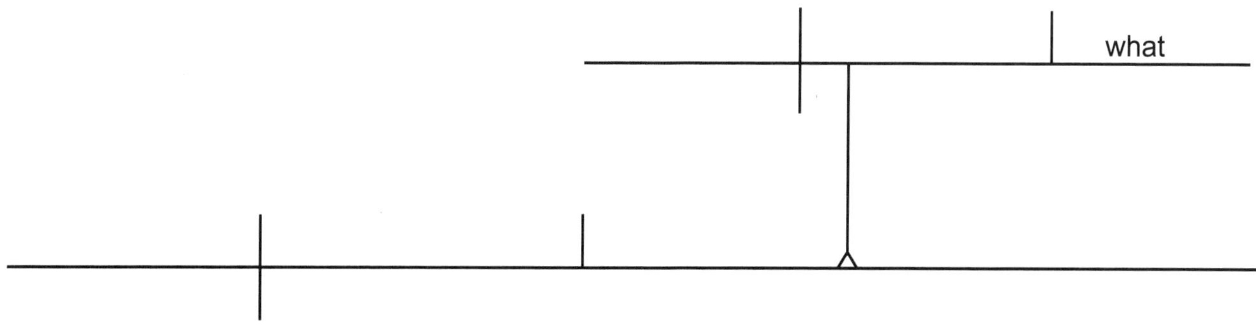

c. ....

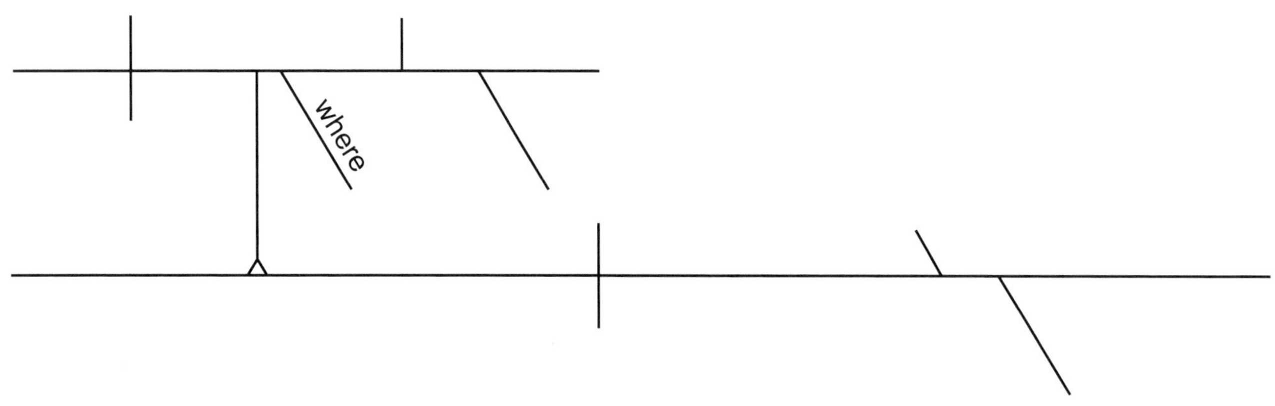

d. ....

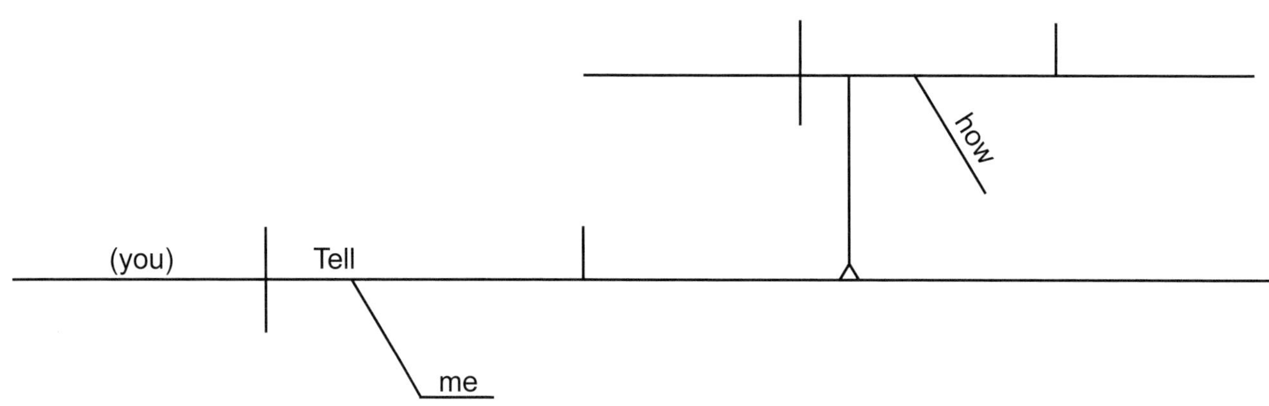

Sometimes a **noun clause** does not start with one of the main signal words:

that who what where when why how

We can only hope **it's not too late**.

Insert "that" before "it." Now it sounds like a noun clause.

We can only hope that **it's not too late**.

It is diagrammed the same way but without the word "that."

We can only hope **it's not too late**.

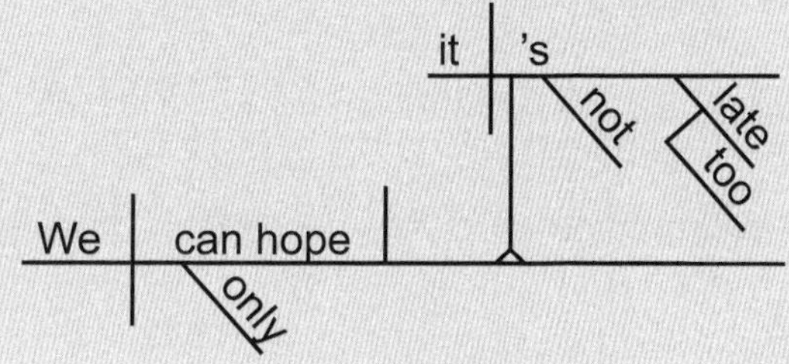

4. Diagram each sentence.

   a. What she did surprised me.

   b. You are where you should be.

c. Does the chef know I'm allergic to peanuts?

d. Did you know that George Washington didn't want to be the president?

e. That tomatoes are fruit is news to me!

Lesson 9: Adjective Clauses

An **adjective clause** is a dependent clause, complete with a subject and a verb, which modifies a noun or pronoun. It begins with a relative pronoun immediately following the noun it is describing. The dependent clause is diagrammed on its own main line under the independent clause. The relative pronoun is diagrammed as the subject of the dependent clause and is connected to the noun it describes by a dotted line.

Common Relative Pronouns		
who	which	that

The player **who scored the last goal** is my son.

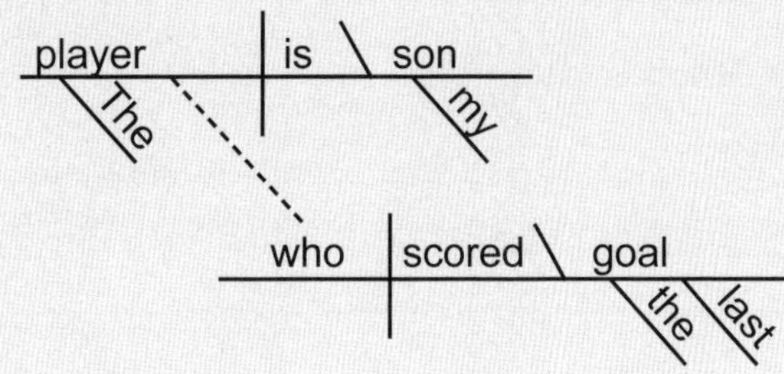

1. Each sentence diagram below has an error. Diagram each sentence correctly.

a. The girl who is eating a taco is my sister.

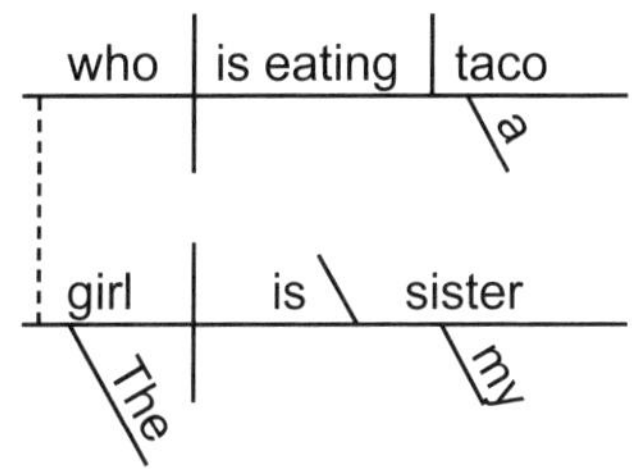

b. The boys who ran across the street are fifth-graders.

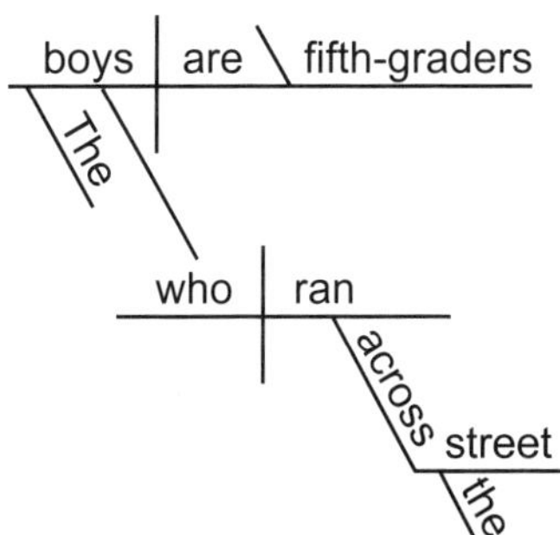

An **adjective clause** can function as the direct object beginning with the word "which."

The Easter Bunny gave me gumdrops, **which are my favorite candy**.

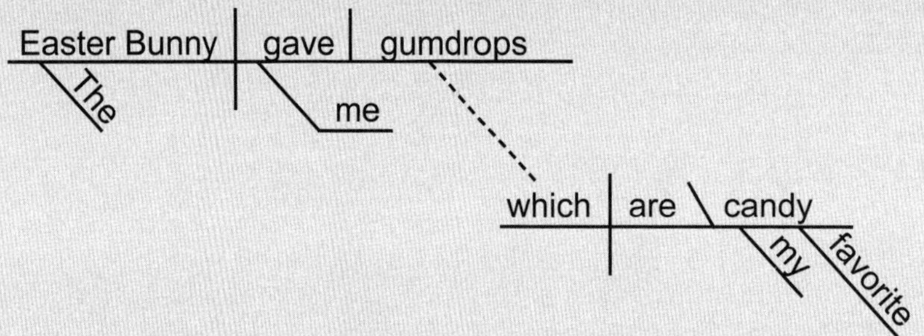

2. Fill in the diagram for each sentence.

a. The bottle of soda, which had fallen off the shelf, exploded violently.

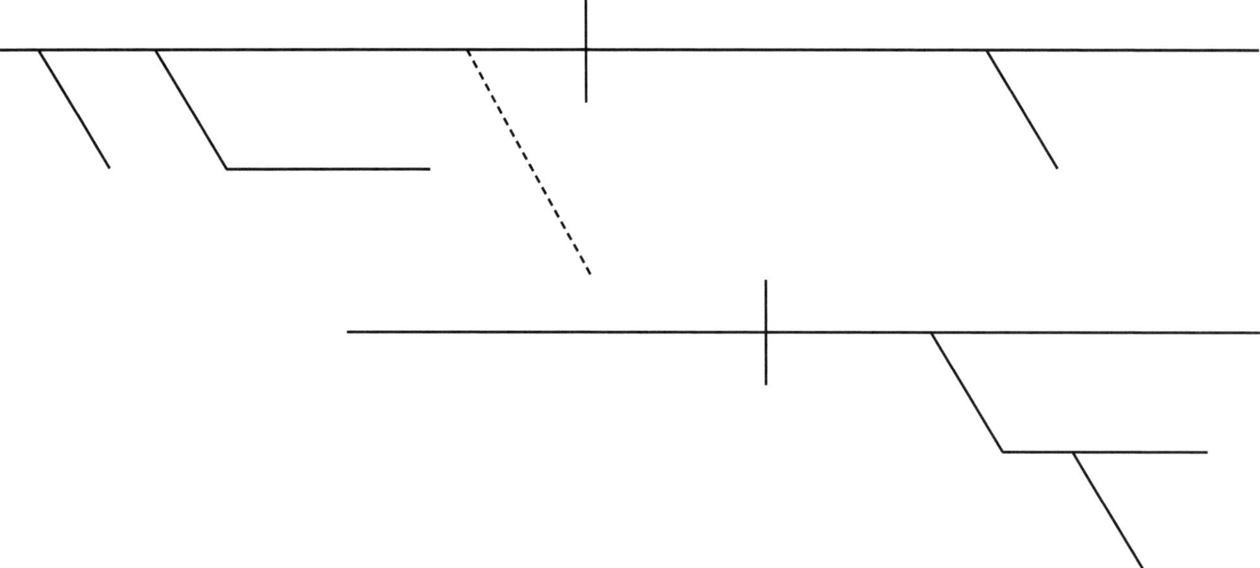

b. Three birds landed on the birdbath, which was empty.

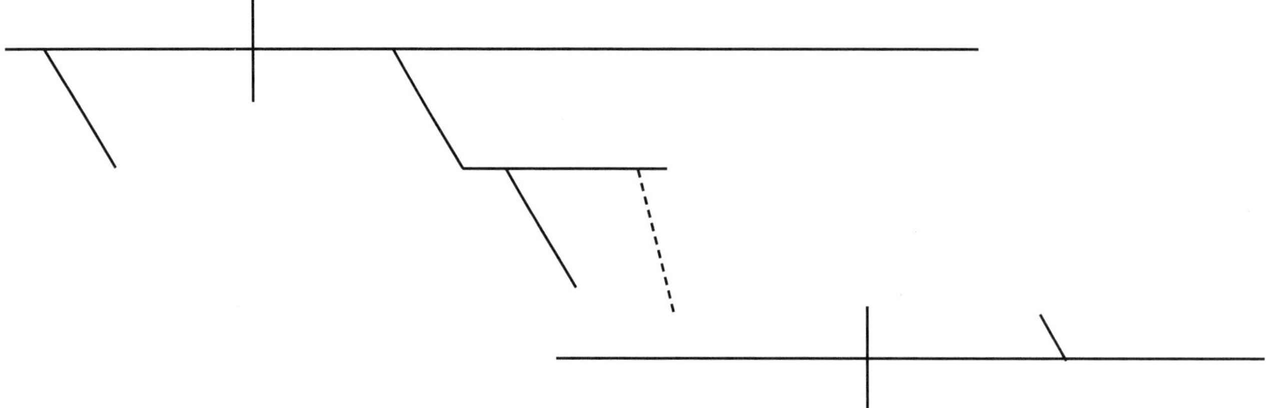

c. Aslan gave Lucy a magic potion which would heal Edmund.

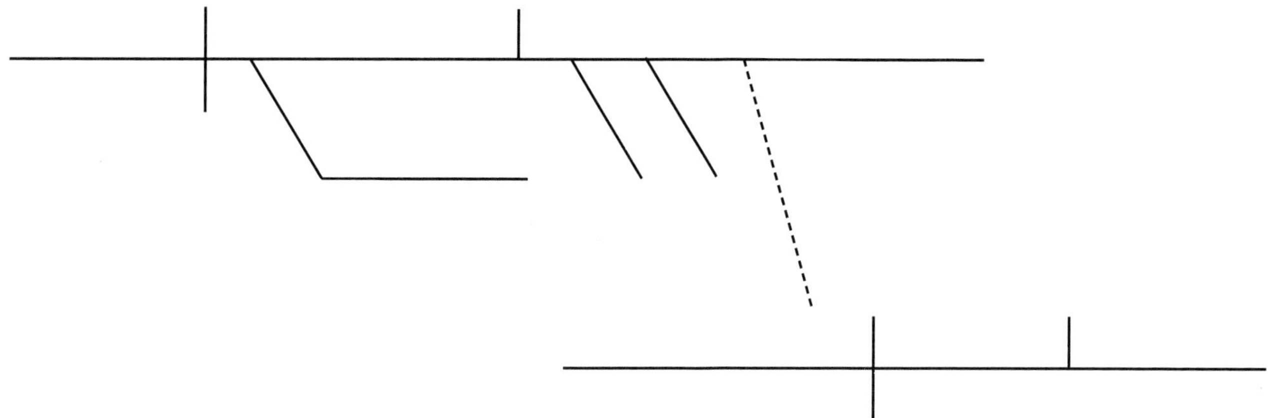

d. The tooth fairy, who was a novice, forgot to take my tooth.

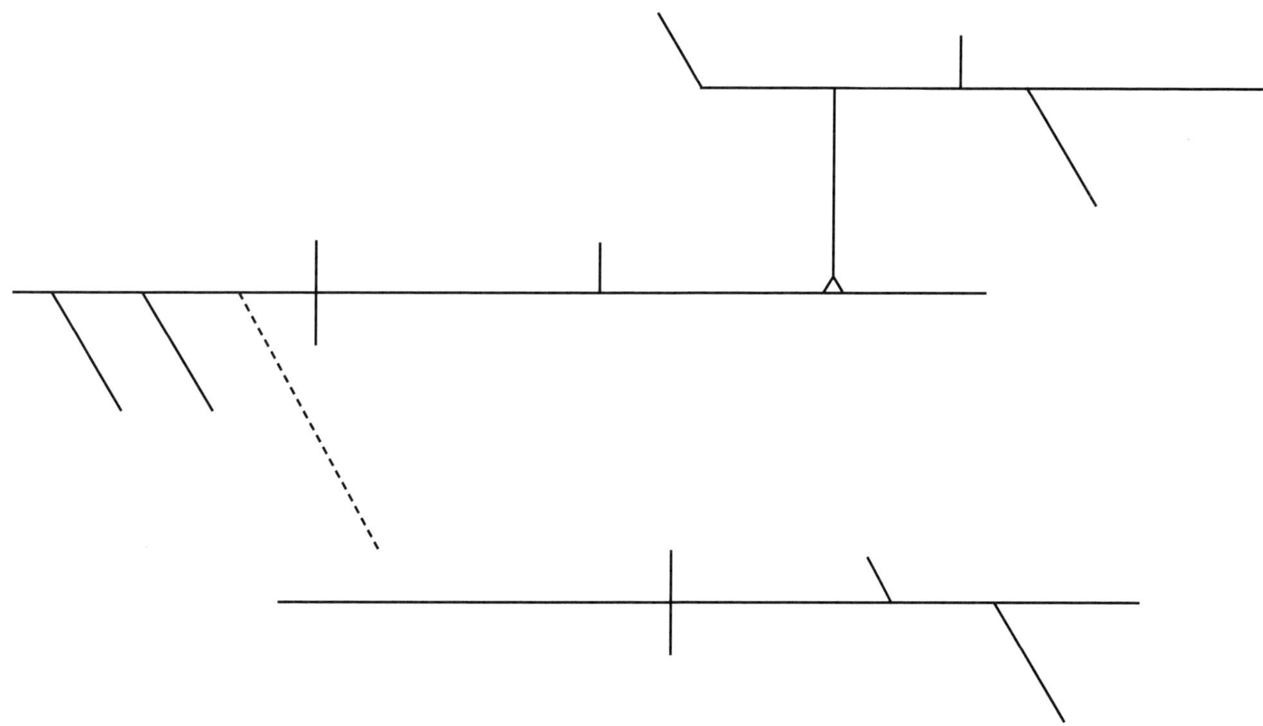

An **adjective clause**, like a noun clause, can also begin with the word "that."

Noun clause: I know **that I want a pet lizard**.

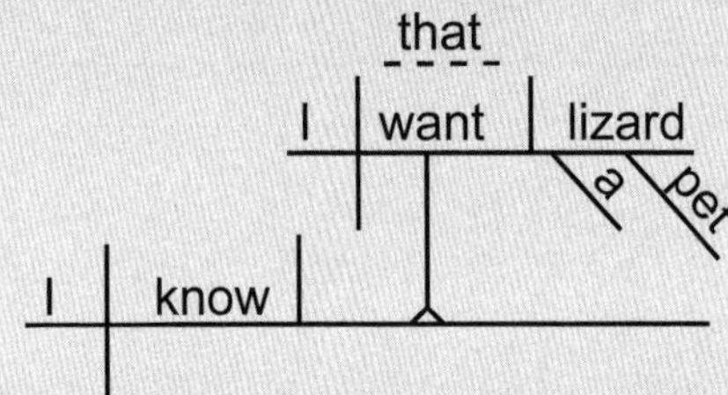

Adjective clause: I do not want a pet **that eats other animals**.

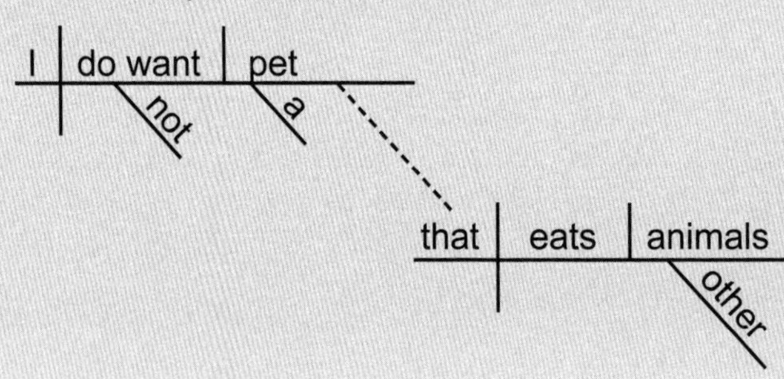

3. Write a sentence to match each diagram. Then complete the diagram.

a. ....

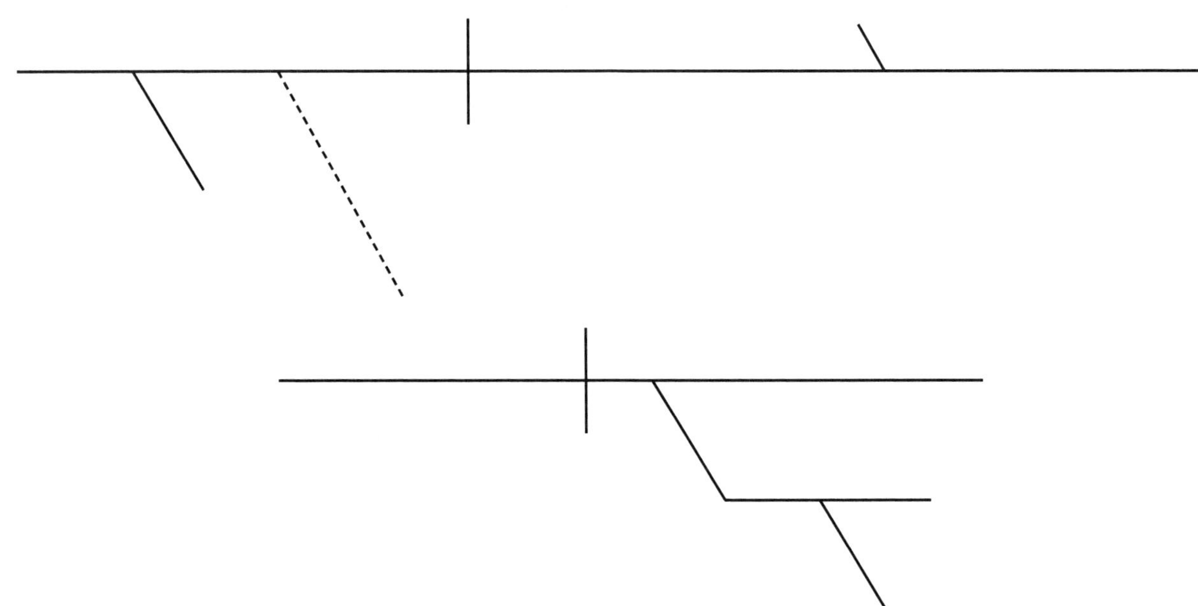

b. ....

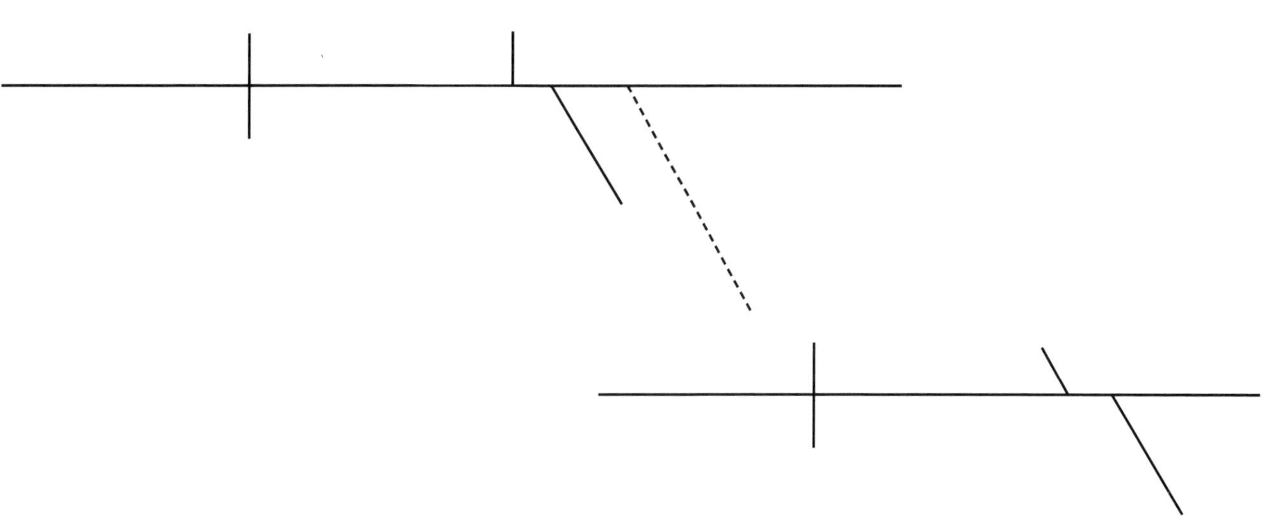

c. ....

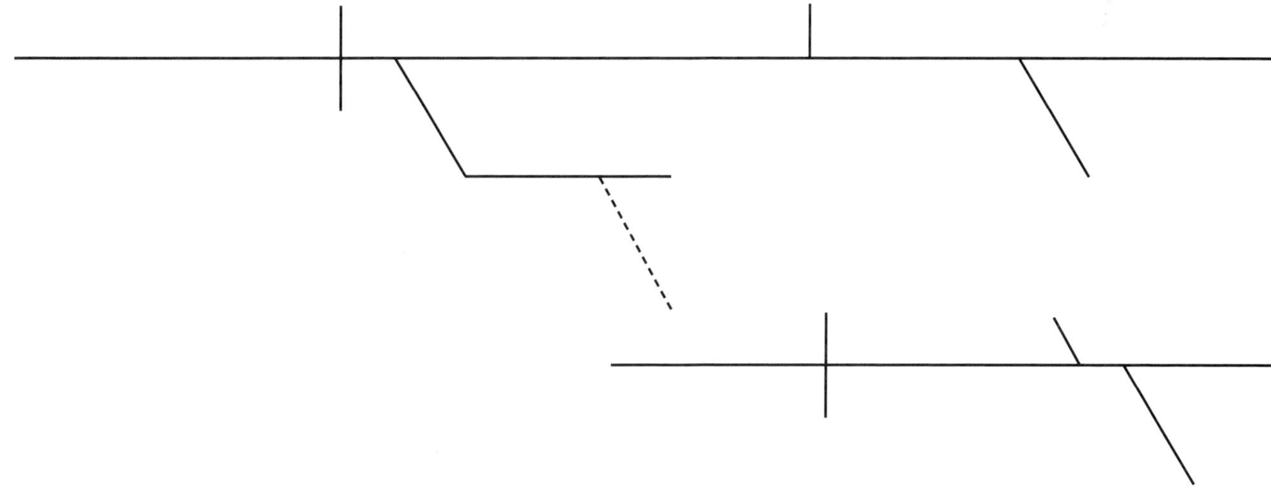

d. ....

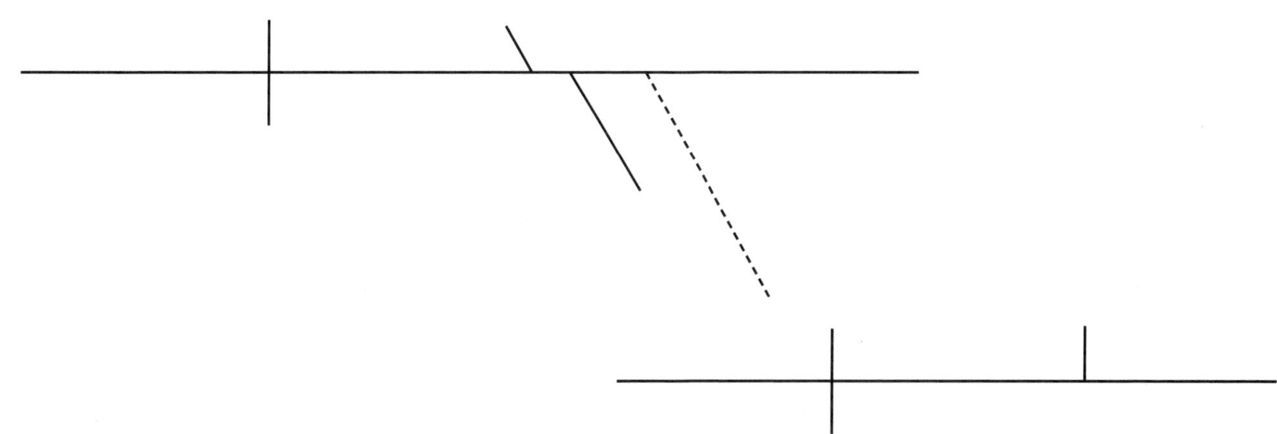

4. Diagram each sentence.

   a. Mangoes, which aren't in season, are my favorite fruit.

   b. This card game is for Nikolai, who hates role-playing games.

c. Did you see the cow that jumped over the moon?

d. This is the house that was built by Jack, who is a builder.

Lesson 10: Adverbial Clauses

An **adverbial clause** is a dependent clause, complete with a subject and a verb, which modifies a verb, adjective, or adverb. (In this lesson, it will only be modifying verbs.) It begins with a subordinating conjunction.

Subordinating Conjunctions										
when	where	while	as	since	if	although	because	after	before	until

The **adverbial clause** is diagrammed on its own main line under the independent clause. A dotted line connects the verb of the independent clause with the verb of the dependent clause. The subordinating conjunction is written on that dotted line.

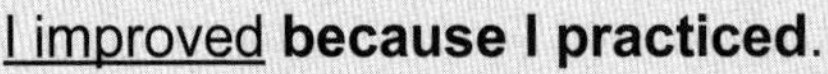

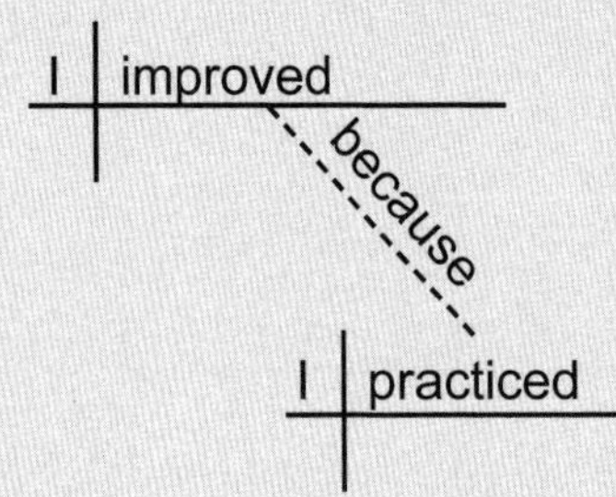

1. Each sentence diagram below has an error. Diagram each sentence correctly.

   a. I will call when I get there.

I | will call
when
I | get
there

   b. Cindy listens to music while she runs.

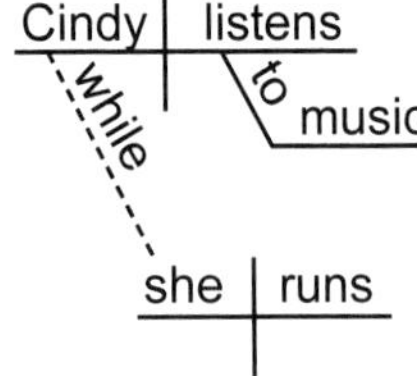

Even if the **adverbial clause** comes before the independent clause, it is diagrammed underneath the dependent clause.

Because I practiced piano daily, I improved greatly!

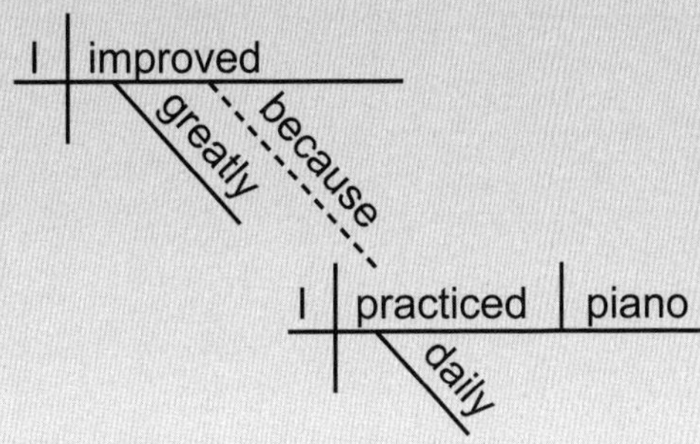

2. Fill in the diagram for each sentence.

   a. I laughed when he tripped.

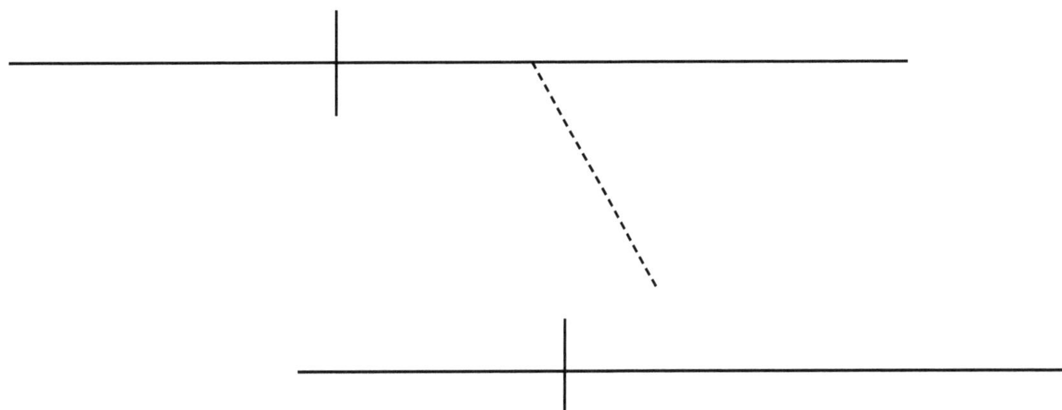

   b. Josh sneezed after he sniffed pepper.

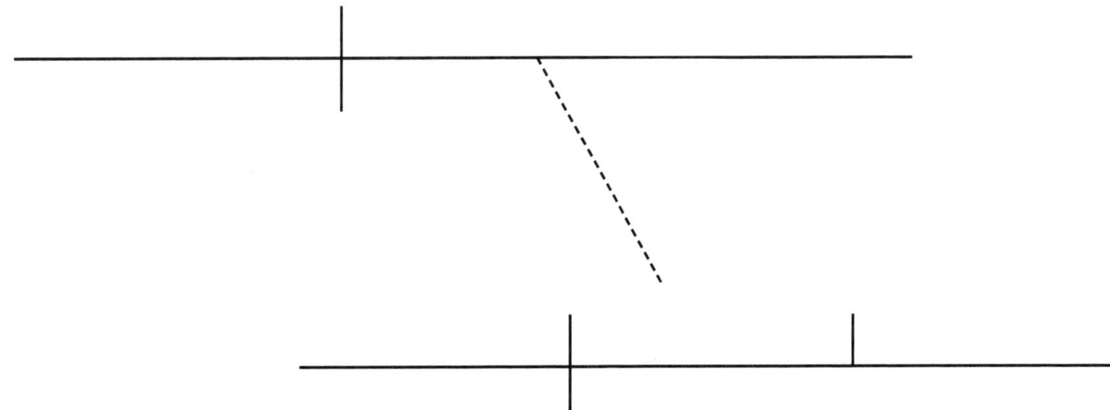

c. After I ran for three hours, I was tired!

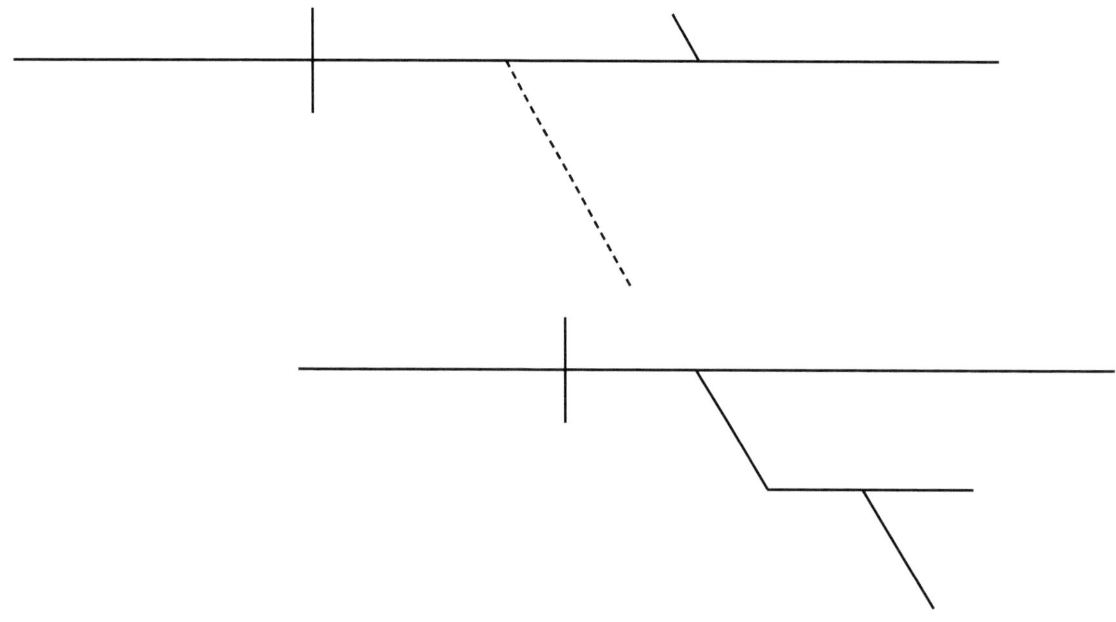

d. Before you go to school, take out the trash.

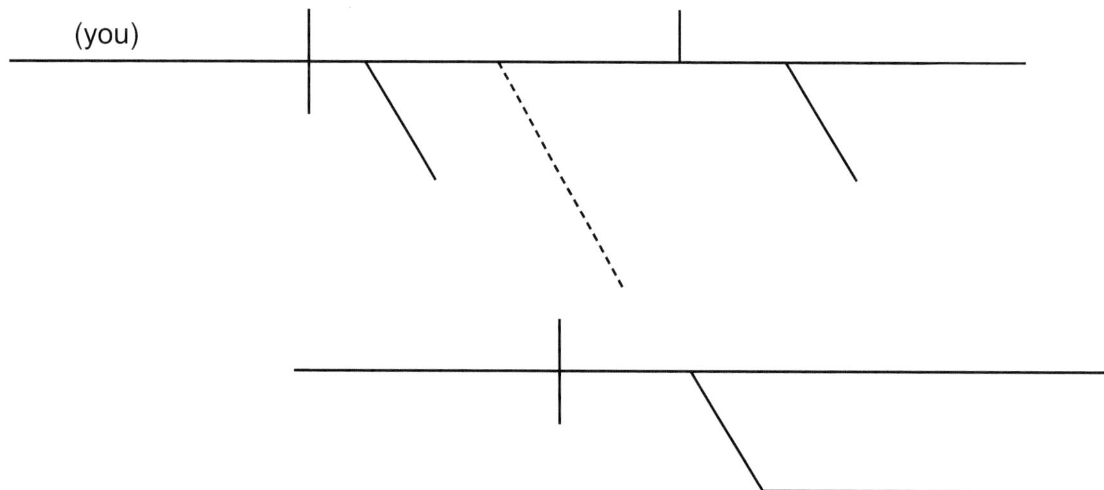

Some subordinating conjunctions can also be prepositions beginning a *prepositional phrase*. The preposition is followed by a noun and its modifiers. An **adverbial clause** (dependent clause) begins with a subordinating conjunction.

Prepositional Phrase: I will complete my homework *before dinner.* ("Before" is a preposition followed by a noun.)

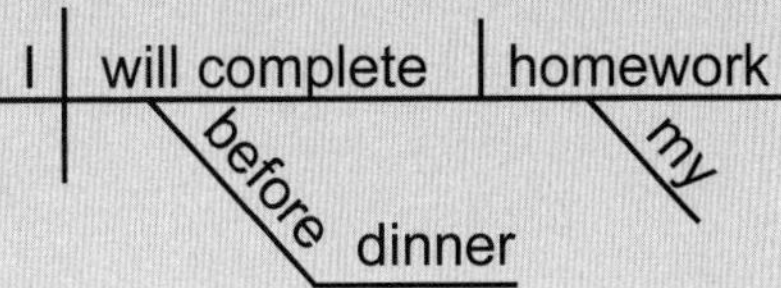

Adverbial Clause: I will complete my homework **before we eat dinner**. ("Before" is a subordinating conjunction followed by a clause.)

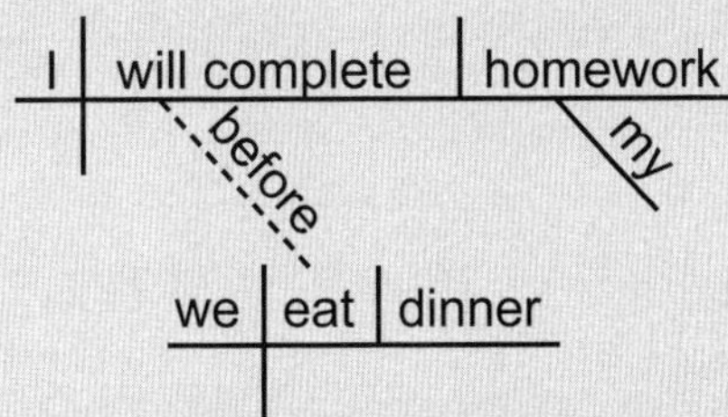

3. Write a sentence using the target word to match each diagram. Then complete the diagram.

a. ("after" as a preposition)

....

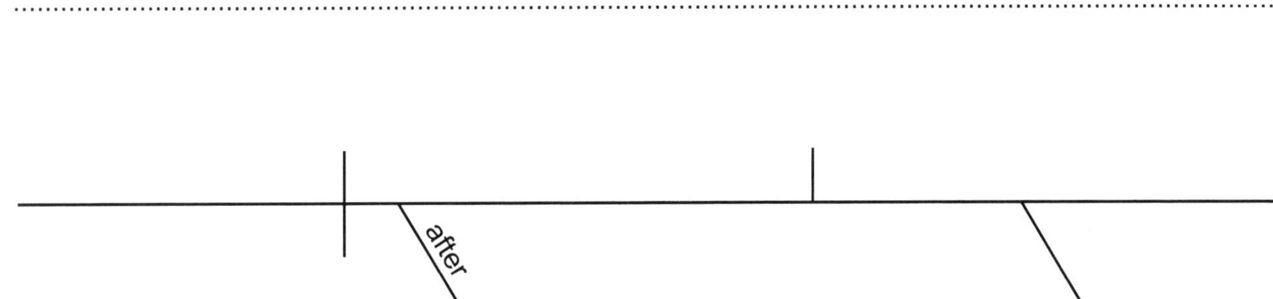

b. ("after" as a subordinating conjunction)

after

c. ("when" as a subordinating conjunction)

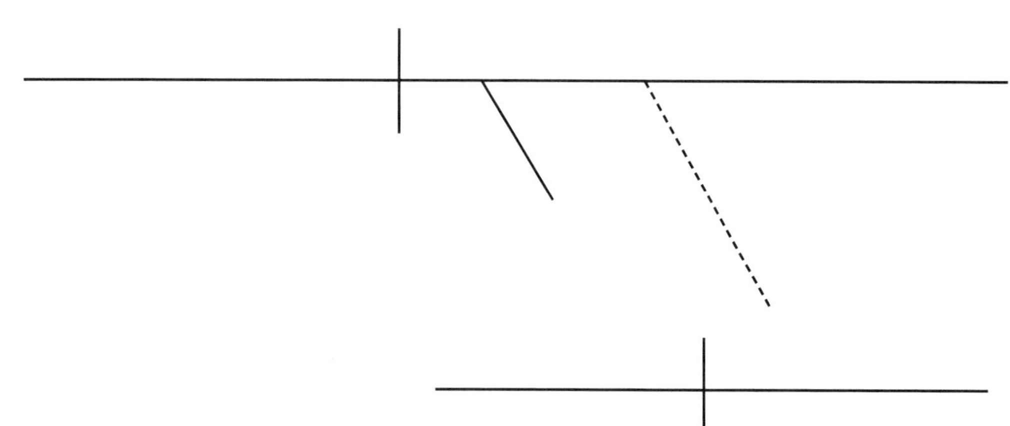

4. Diagram each sentence.

   a. Aunt Silvia made meatballs because you like them so much.

   b. Eat some carrots while you wait for dinner.

c. I can't concentrate when the music is loud.

d. After Johanna fell in the mud puddle, she took a long, hot shower!

Lesson 11: Comparisons and Elliptical Clauses

Many sentences that **compare** things have understood words (not in the sentence) that are inserted into the diagram in parentheses.

Patrick **is taller than** his brothers.

This sentence is comparing how tall Patrick "is" with how tall his brothers "are." Add the understood words *are* and *tall* at the end in order to diagram it correctly.

Patrick **is taller than** his brothers (*are*) (tall).

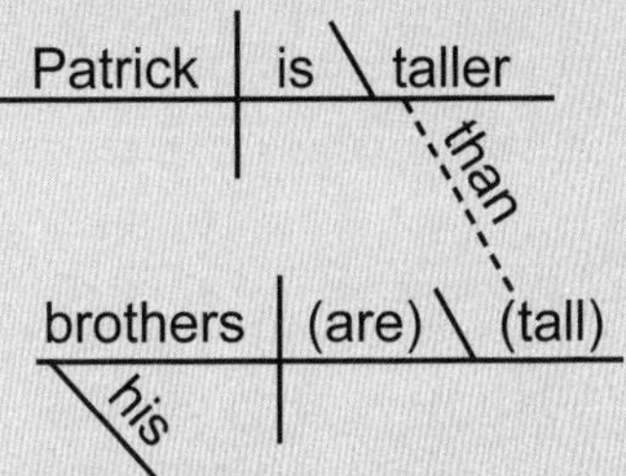

Because we are comparing Patrick's tallness with his brothers' tallness, the dotted line connects the two forms of the word "tall."

1. Each sentence diagram below has errors. Diagram each sentence correctly.

a. Porpoises are smaller than dolphins.

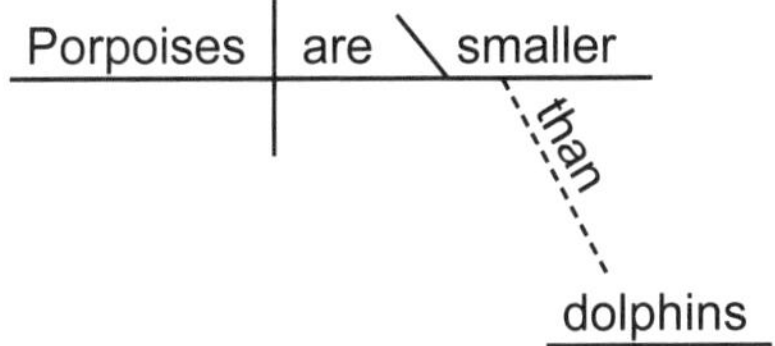

b. African elephants are bigger than Asian elephants.

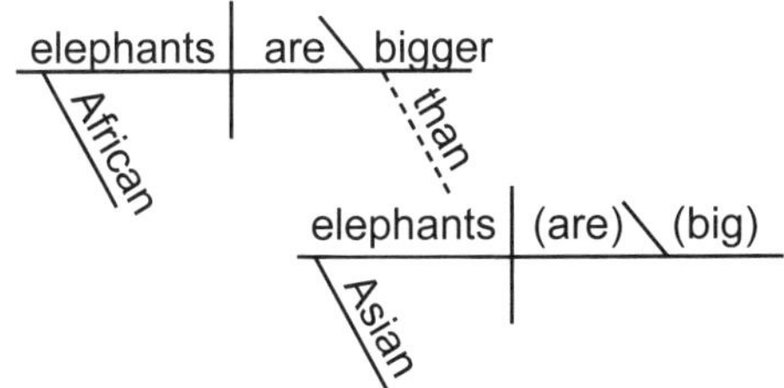

c. The Atlantic Ocean is slightly warmer than the Pacific Ocean.

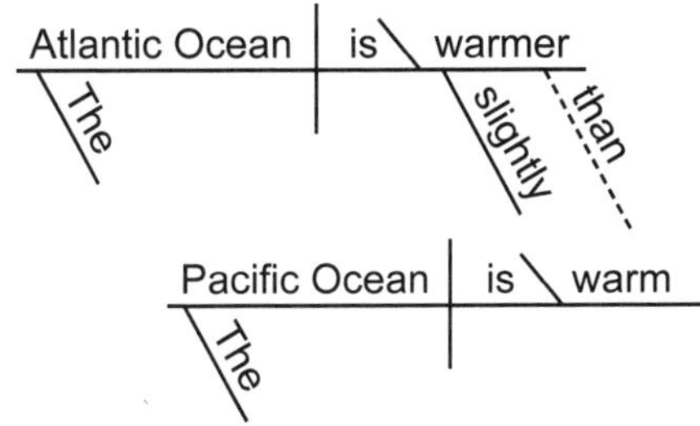

Clauses with *inserted* understood words are called **elliptical clauses**.

I like vanilla **more than chocolate**.

I like vanilla **more than (*I like*) chocolate**.

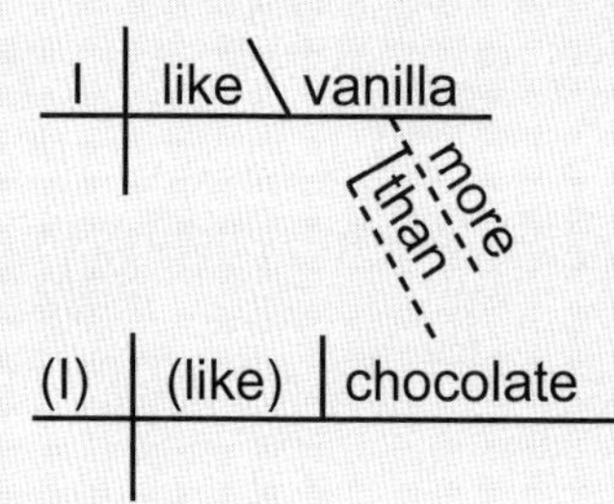

2. Fill in the diagram for each sentence.

a. Snakes are scarier than spiders.

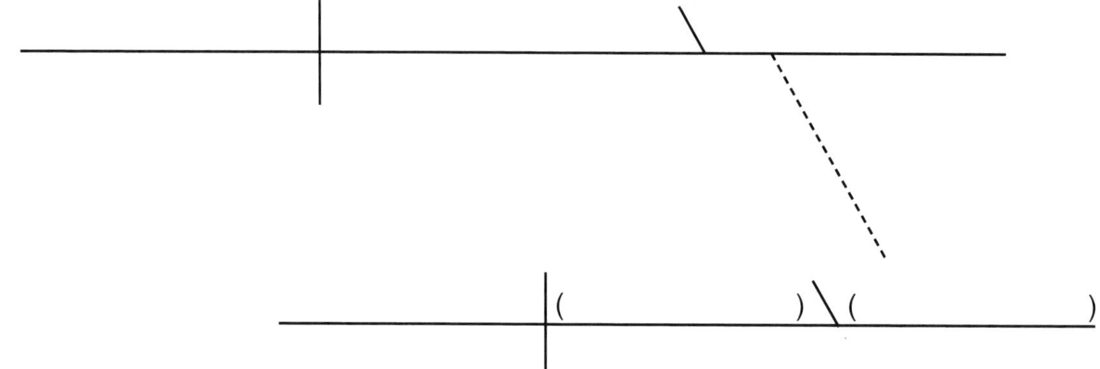

b. I like Shakespeare's comedies more than his tragedies.

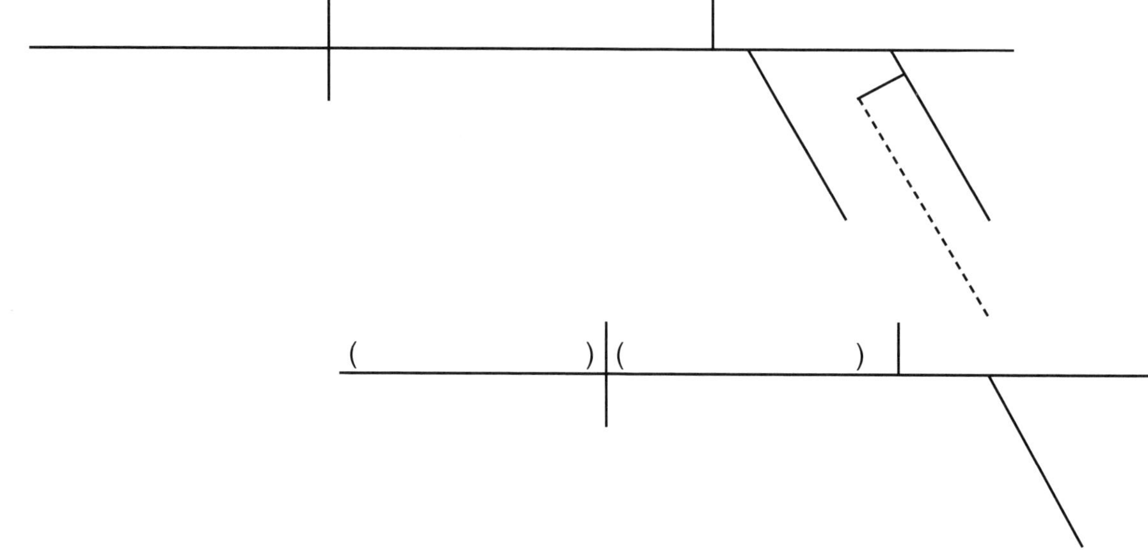

c. Is Gandalf's beard longer than Dumbledore's?

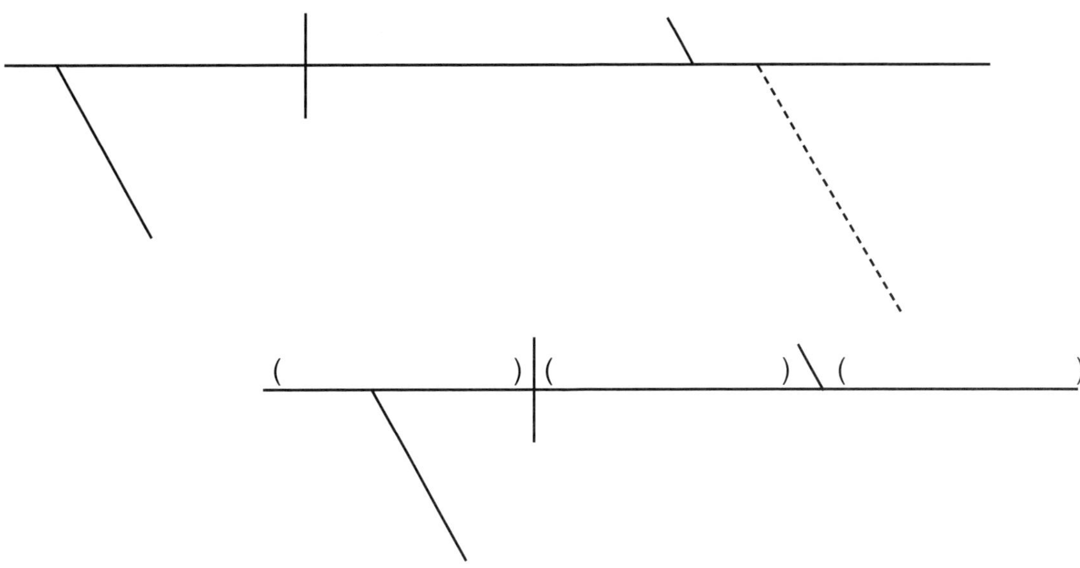

d. Bacterial infections are usually more dangerous than viral infections.

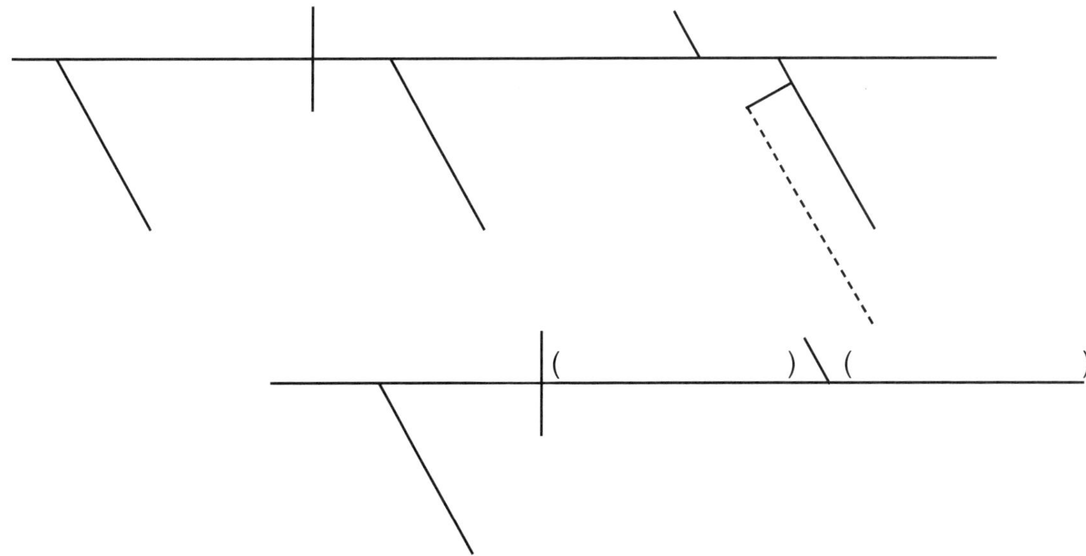

Phrases such as "as many as," "as much as," and "as well as" create **elliptical clauses**.

I can draw as well as you!

I can draw **as well as you (*can draw*)**.

In this sentence, "well" is an adverb modifying the verb "draw." The first "as" is also an adverb, modifying the adverb "well." The second "as" is a subordinating conjunction connecting the main clause "I can draw" with the dependent clause "you (can draw)."

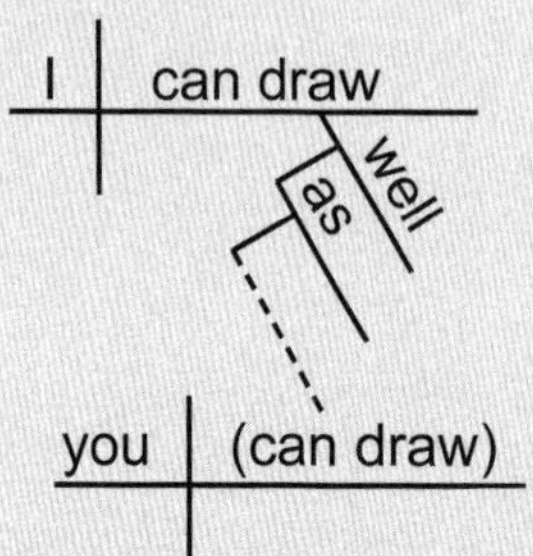

3. Fill in the diagrams for each of the sentences below.

a. I can see as far as you.

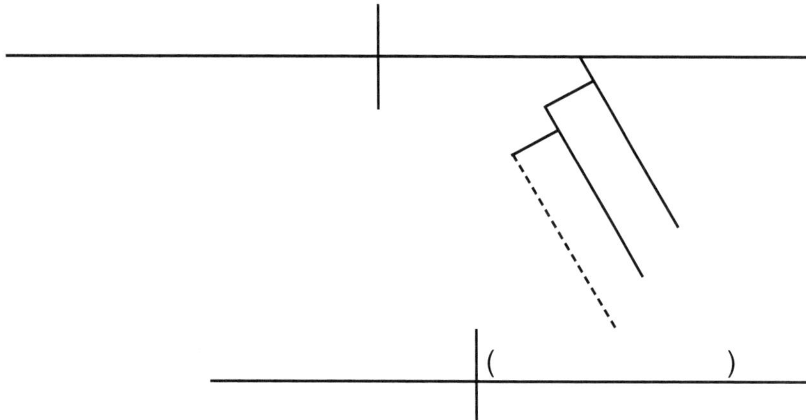

b. Does Michael weigh as much as Timothy?

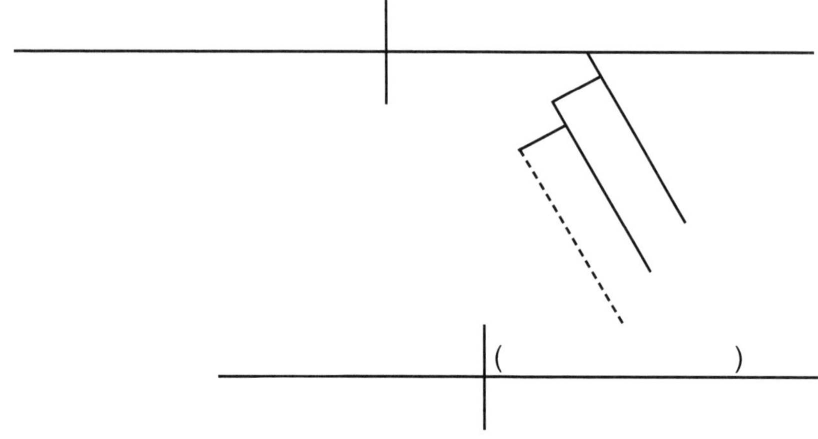

Write a sentence, using the prompts, for each diagram. Then complete the diagram.

c. ....

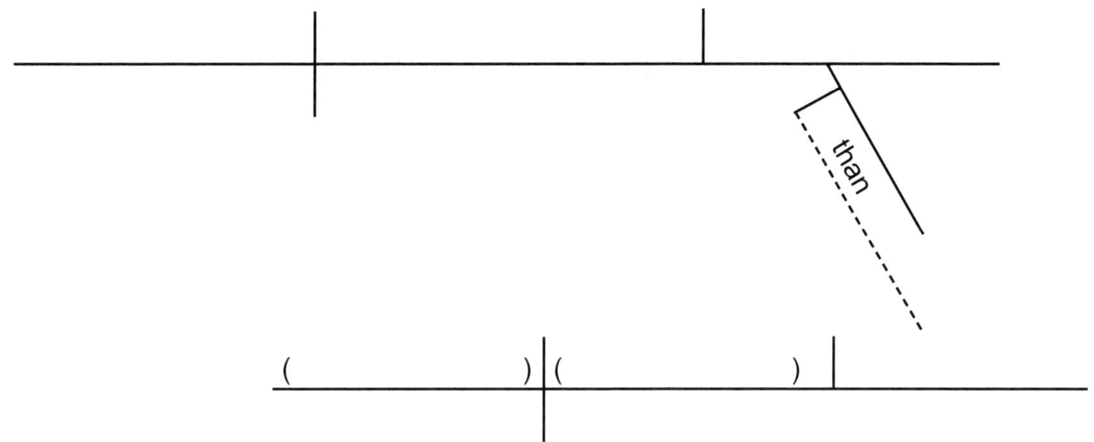

d. ....

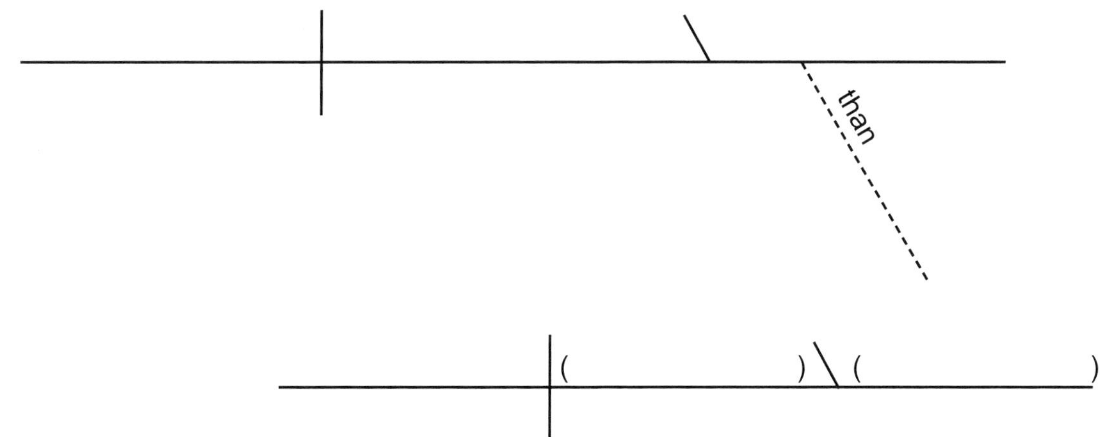

An "X" can be used in the diagram in place of the inserted words in parenthesis for **elliptical phrases**.

Dad likes *Star Wars* more than (*he likes*) *Star Trek*.

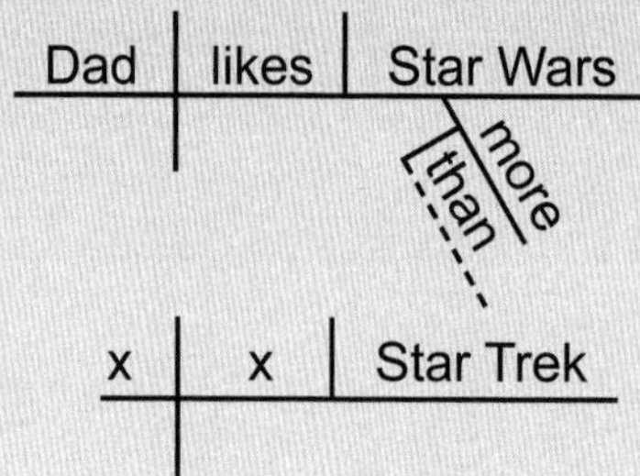

4. Diagram each sentence using the words in parenthesis or an "X."

   a. He likes movies better than TV.

   b. Honey is better for you than white sugar.

c. I don't read as often as I should.

d. Taryn, my little sister, sings as well as Jacob, my older brother.

Lesson 12: Compound Sentences

A **compound complex** sentence has two independent clauses joined by a *coordinating conjunction* (and, but, for, yet, so, or, nor) and at least one dependent clause.

When you finish this book, you will have completed all the diagramming lessons *and* you will impress your friends with your mad diagramming skills!

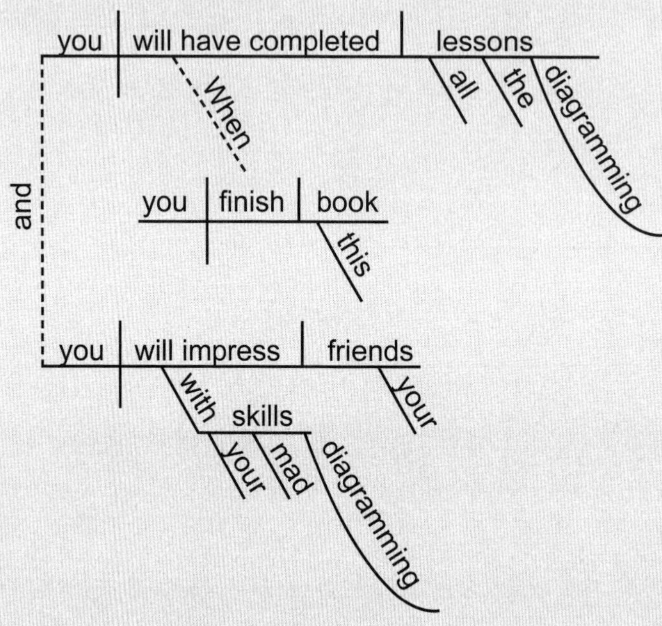

1. This sentence diagram below has an error. Diagram the sentence correctly.

I'll make a chocolate soufflé before we eat dinner, and we can eat it for dessert.

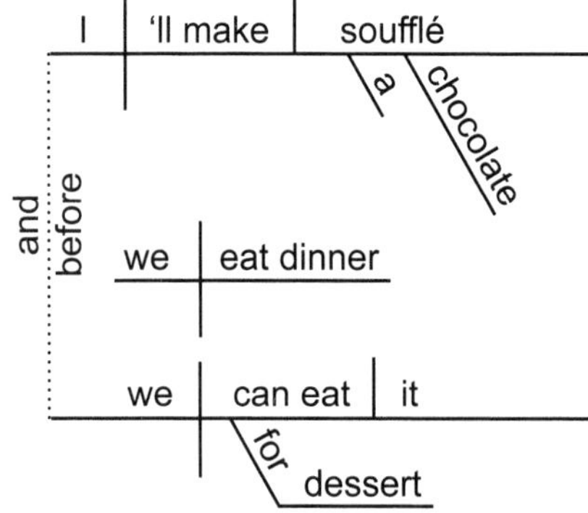

2. Fill in the diagram for each sentence.

   a. Koalas, which are not bears, eat leaves from those very fragrant trees, eucalyptus, and pandas, which also are not bears, eat leaves from bamboo, a tall grass.

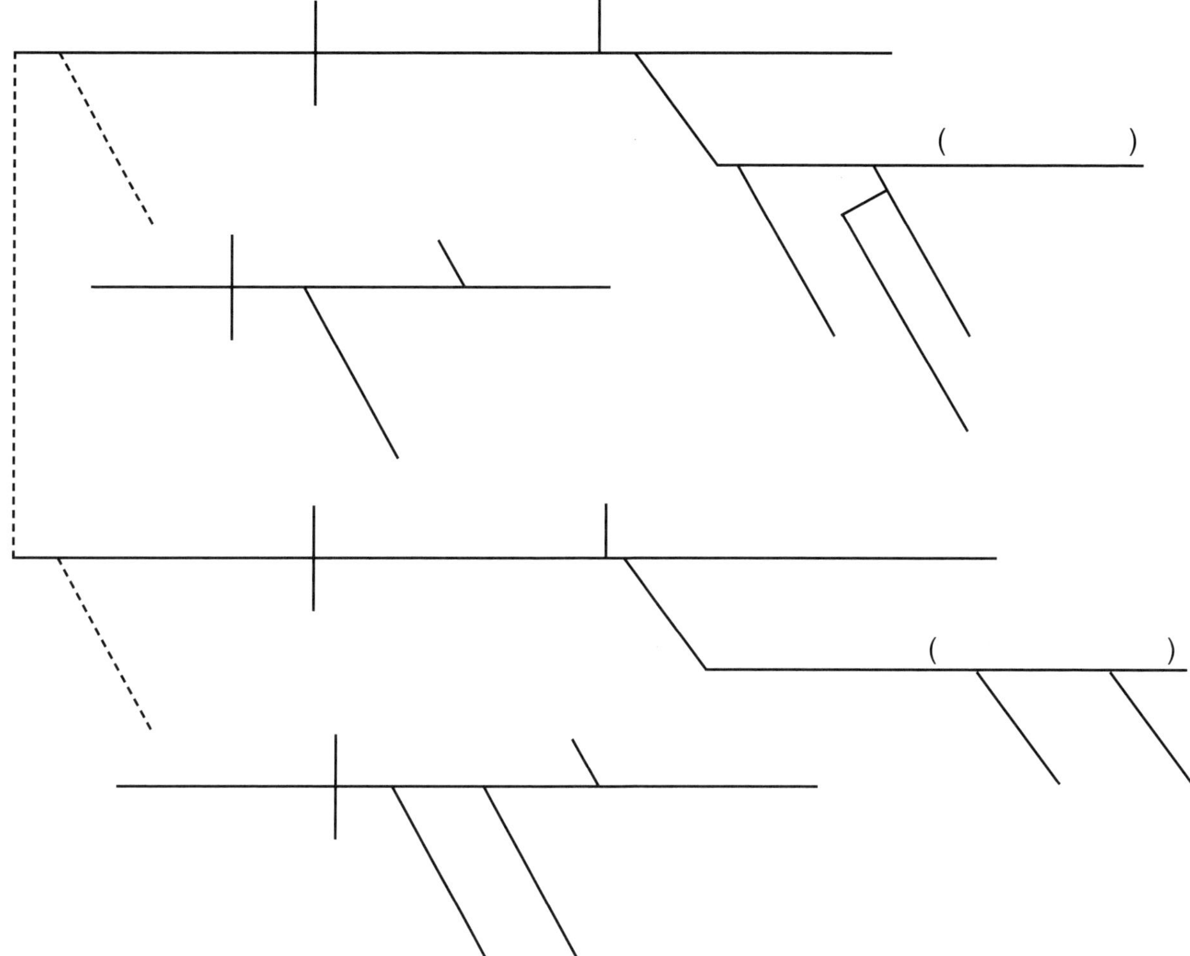

b. Walking down the busy street, the young woman paused whenever a bus stopped, but she never boarded one.

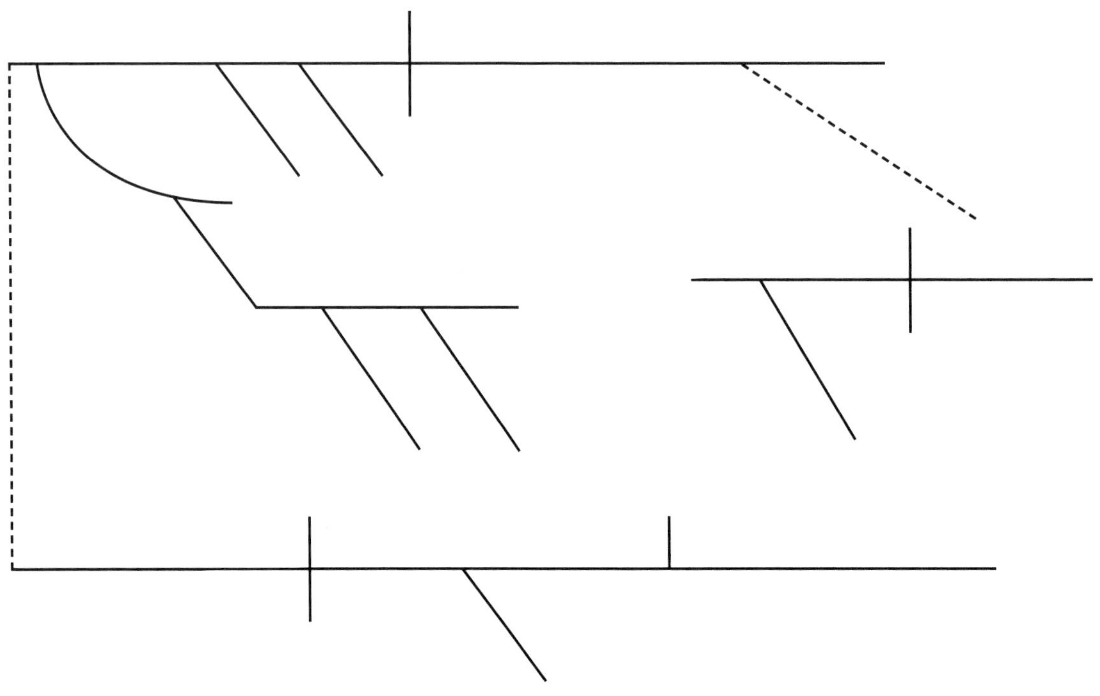

c. Chemistry was my best subject in high school, although I hated attending class, but in college I did poorly and loved going to class.

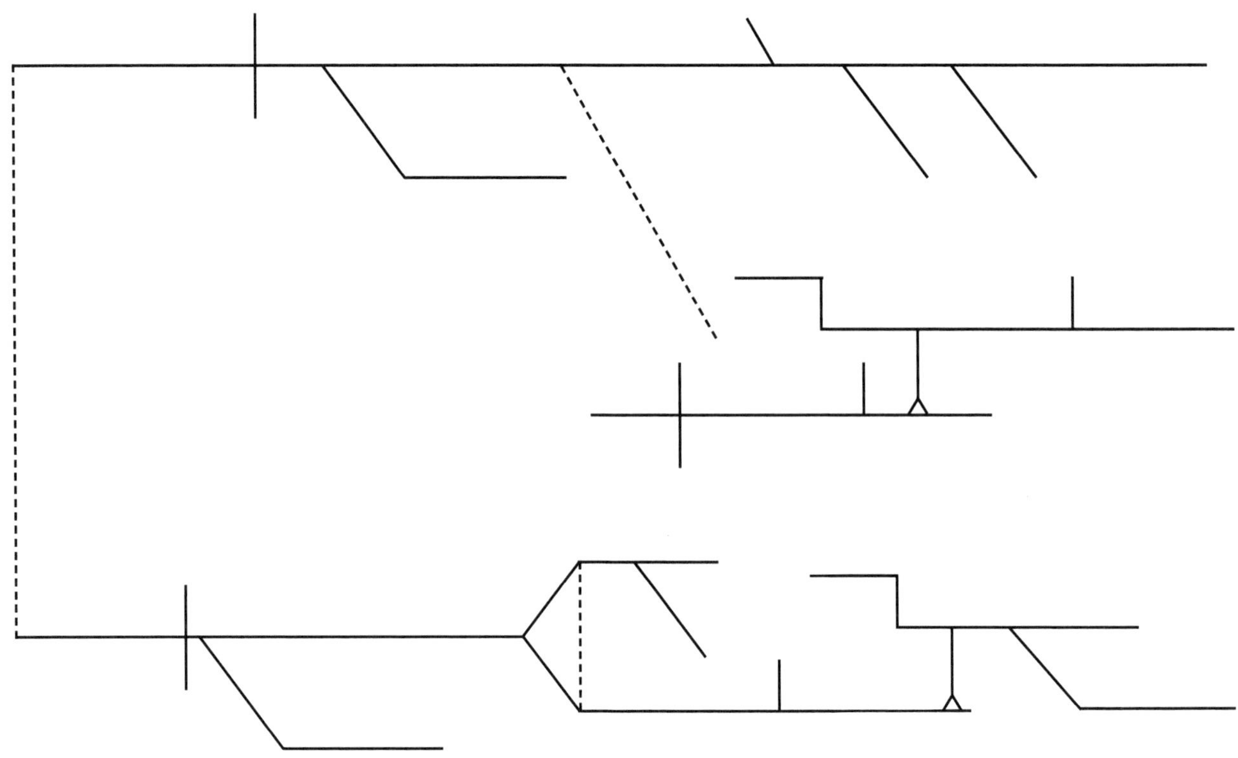

d. If you assemble the pizzas now, we can cook them as soon as we return from church, but if you wait 'til later, dinner won't be ready until 8:00.

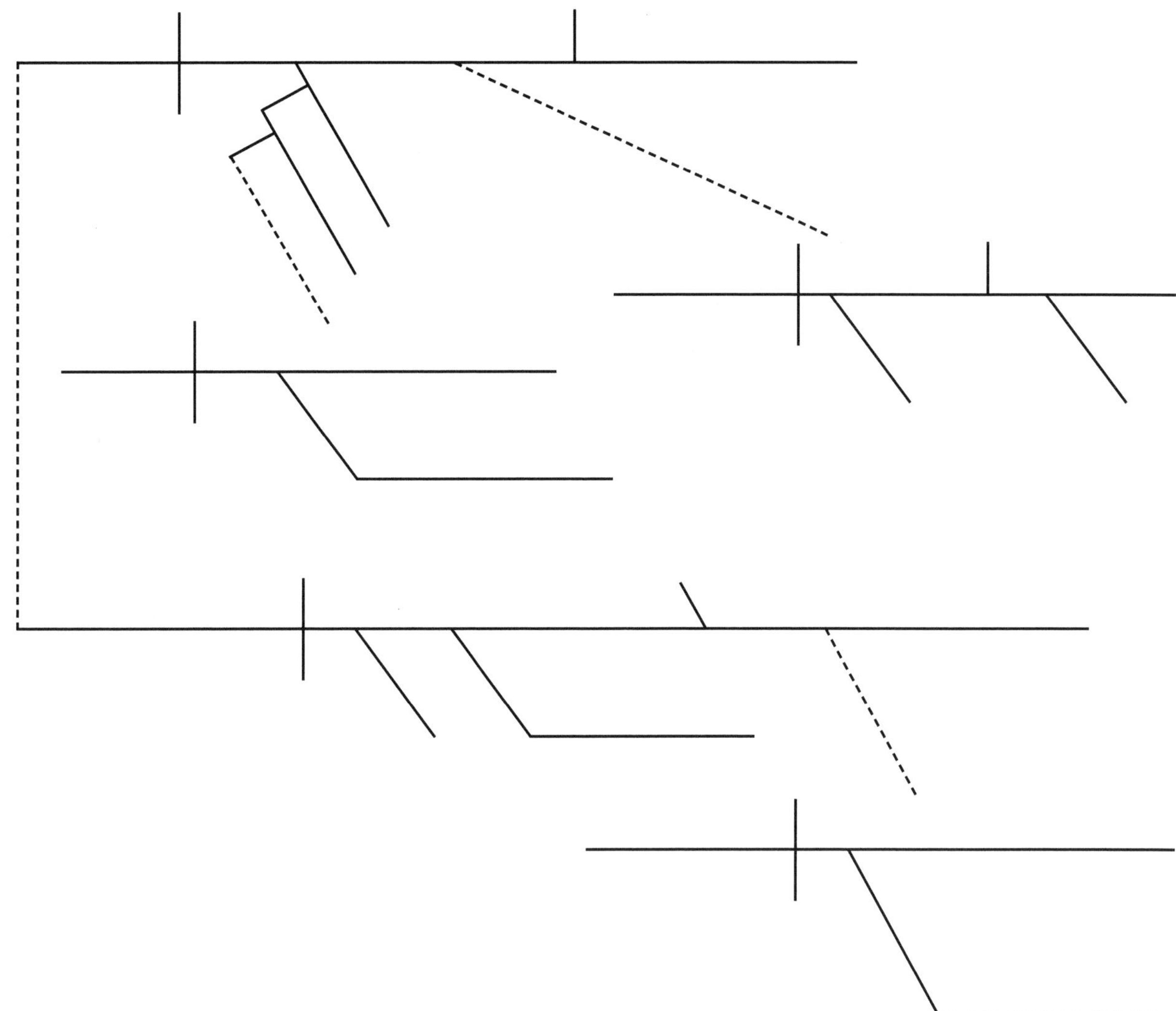

3. Write a sentence, using the prompts, for each diagram. Then complete the diagram.

a. ....

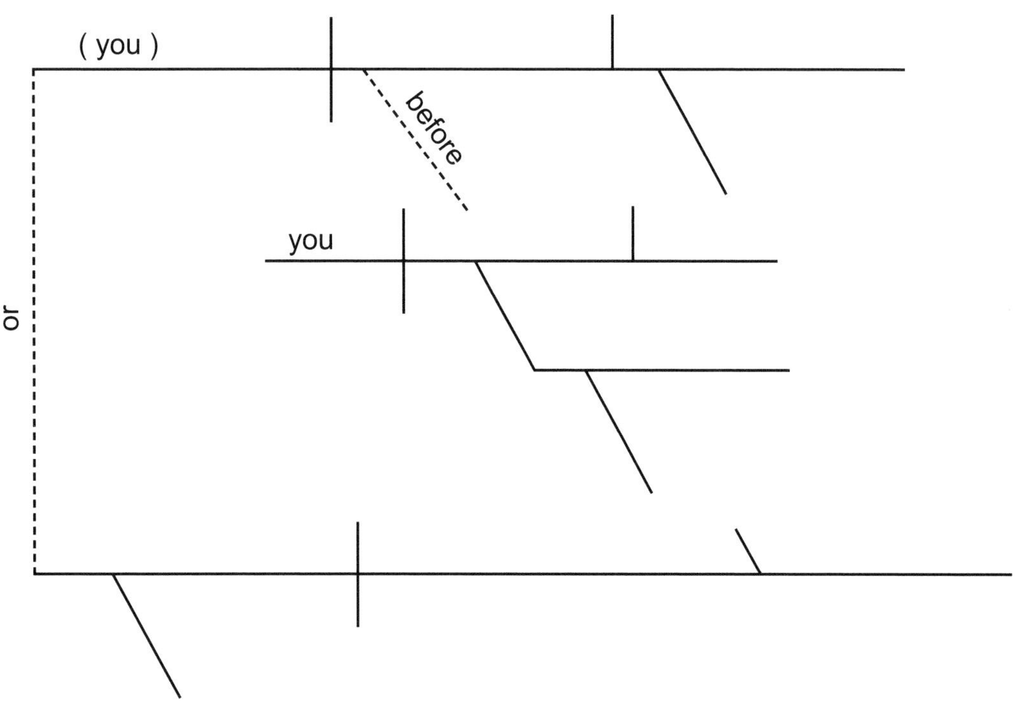

b. ....

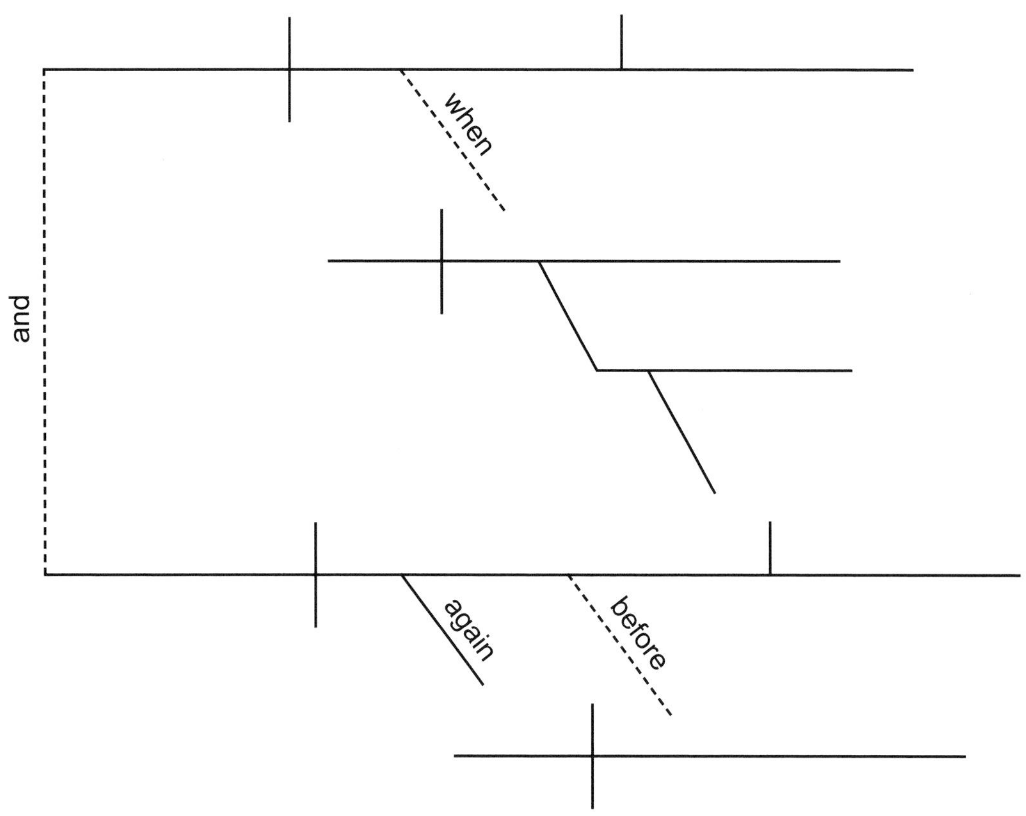

c. ....

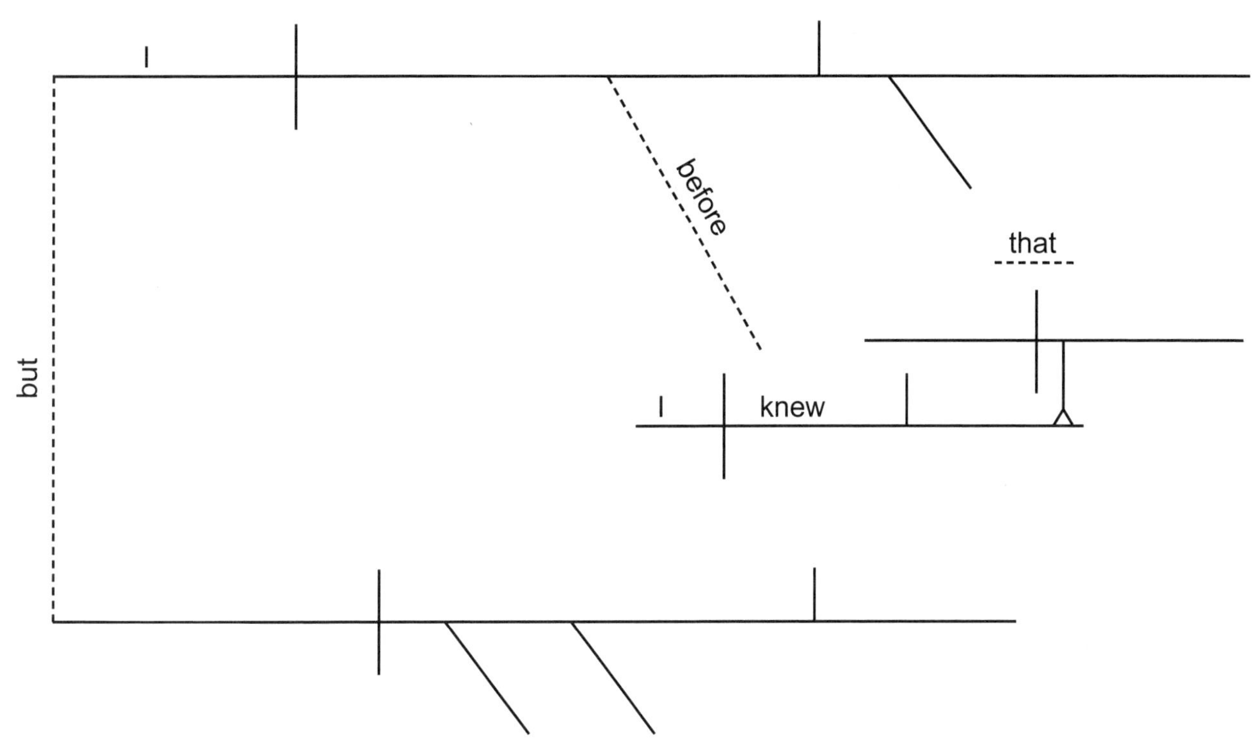

d. ....

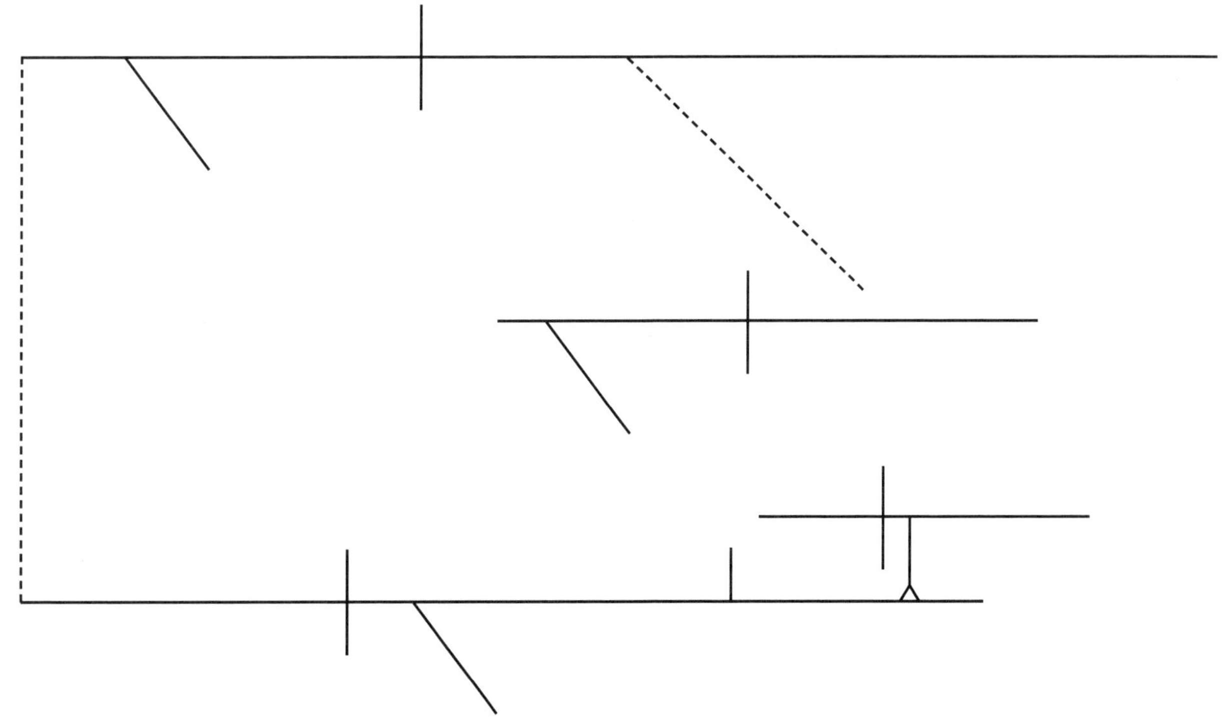

4. Diagram each sentence.

   a. Either Dad will shovel the driveway when he gets home from work, or he will pay the neighbor who owns a snowblower.

   b. Sleeping Beauty and Snow White woke up when their princes kissed them, but when the frog was kissed, he turned into a prince.

c. The madly rushing river, which dried up last summer, is now in danger of flooding, but men are diligently working on building a sand-bag wall.

d. The girl swinging on the swing set every day after school usually stays there until 4:00 when she likes to walk home, but yesterday her dad picked her up in a pick-up truck bigger than yours.

Review

Diagram each of these sentences.

1. The most popular sport in the U.S.A., football, is not in the Olympics.

2. Many of our county's ash trees have been destroyed by the Emerald Ash Borer, an invasive green beetle from Asia.

3. I will paint my bedroom a pale shade of green.

4. They named the twins Bert and Nan.

5. Jumping on a trampoline is great fun!

6. The kind, young nurse is very good at comforting young children.

7. Last night I finally saw a shooting star!

8. A flock of geese sat carelessly on the frozen lake.

9. Loudly whining and mournfully moaning, the persistent puppy begged for a treat.

10. Cuddling her new kitten under a fleece blanket, Emmie listened to the storm outside but felt safe and warm.

11. Would you like to dance?

12. To know me is to love me.

13. Katrina wants to see a concert this summer.

14. I need to give my dog vitamins every morning.

15. The doctor says that I have allergies.

16. We don’t know where Kitty is hiding.

17. The hat, which has my team logo, is my favorite.

18. My favorite performer was the girl who played guitar and wore pink cowboy boots.

19. She can't play the guitar tonight because she broke her arm.

20. If the dog begs at the back door, please let him out.

21. Uncle Brian is older than Uncle Patrick.

22. Nobody snores as loud as Grandpa!

23. After the rain stopped, a beautiful rainbow appeared, and we ran outside to take pictures!

24. Swinging between buildings is Spider-Man's signature move, but taking down criminals is what impresses me.

25. The little dog laughed when the cow jumped over the moon, and the frightened dish ran away with the spoon, who was relieved to get away from the teasing fork.

Answers

Lesson 1 (pp. 1-7)

1 a.

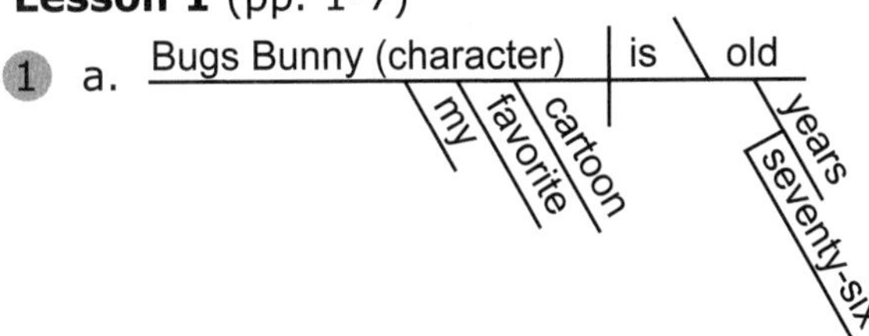

b.
I | visited | Charleston (city)
the
most
amazing

c.
You | baked | macaroons (cookie)
my
favorite

2 a.
Auntie Lola | will bring | sushi (food)
my
favorite

b.
Bobby | was drinking | milk (drink)
chocolate
a
healthy
and
delicious

c.

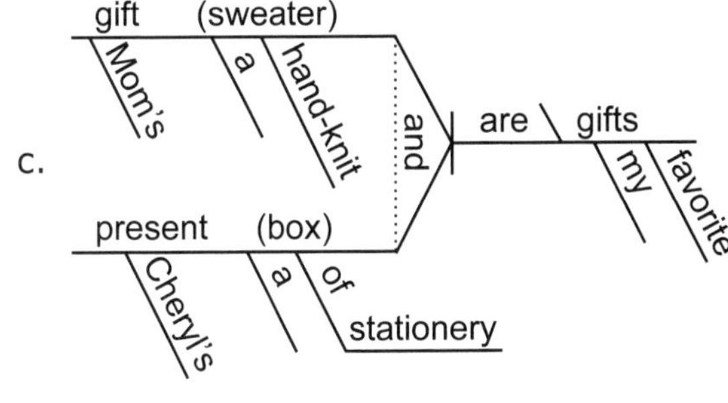

d.

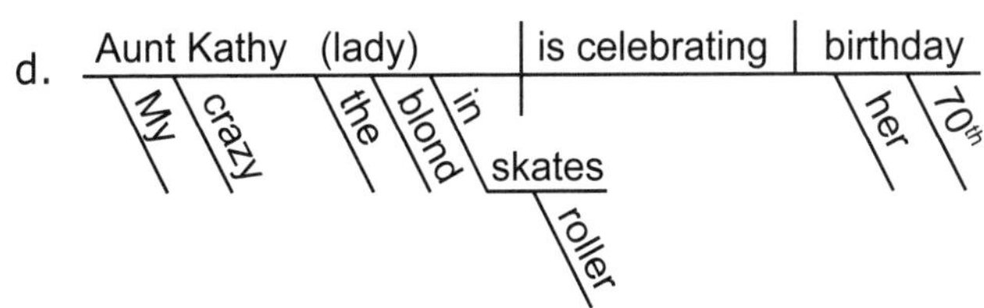

e.

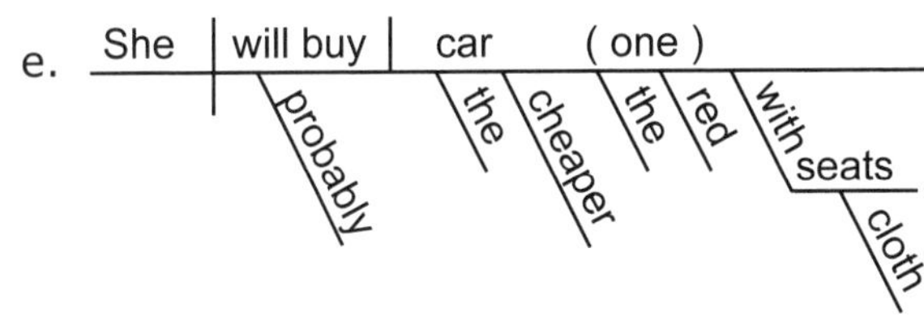

f.

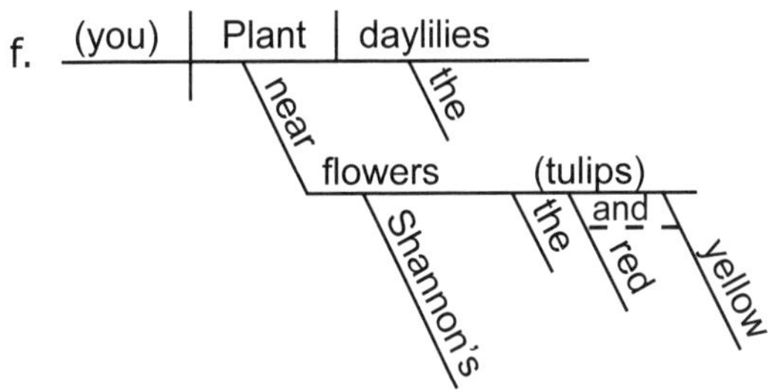

3 Sentences will vary. Examples:

a. Our science teacher, Mrs. Jacobucci, races dragsters!

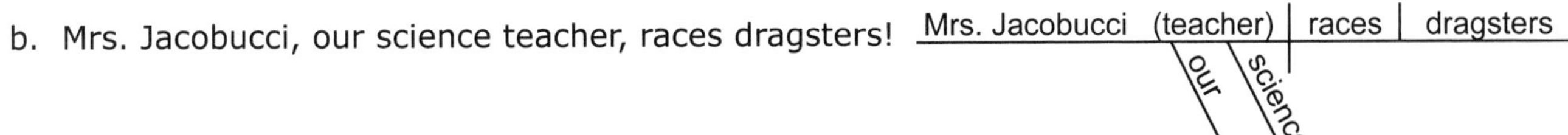

b. Mrs. Jacobucci, our science teacher, races dragsters!

Mrs. Jacobucci (teacher) | races | dragsters
our
science

c. My favorite sport is the great American pastime, baseball.

sport | is \ pastime (baseball)
My
favorite
the
great
American

d. My favorite sport is baseball, the great American pastime.

sport | is \ baseball (pastime)
My
favorite
the
great
American

e. Poppy's chair, the green leather recliner, is so comfortable!

chair (recliner) | is \ comfortable
Poppy's
the
green
leather
so

f. We won tickets for the Broncos, Eli's favorite team!

We | won | tickets
for
Broncos (team)
the
Eli's
favorite

4 a.

sister (Darla) | is leaving
My
older
much
for
college
week
next

b.

Nathan (brother) | visited | Apple (New York City)
my
oldest
the
Big

c.

Charlie (Newfoundland)
the
big
black
and
Max (beagle)
the
noisy
little
are \ dogs
my
favorite

d.

brother (Abel) | was hiding
My
in
cellar (place)
the
our
favorite
hiding

e.

Library of Congress (library) | houses
The
the
largest
in
world
the
books
16 million
and
miles
838
of
bookshelves

f.

movie (Victoria and Albert) | is
The
about
Queen Victoria
and
husband (Prince Albert)
her

Lesson 2 (pp. 8-14)

1 a. king | dubbed | him \ Sir Galahad
The

b. We | elected | Victor \ president

c. Everyone | considers | firemen \ heroes

2 a.
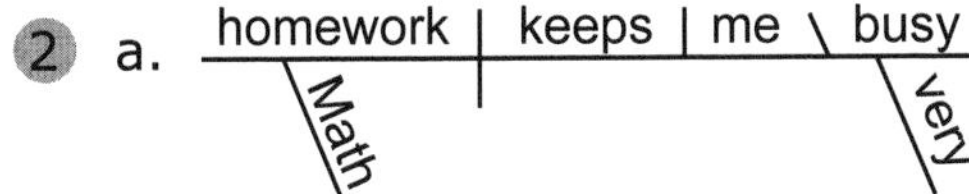

b.
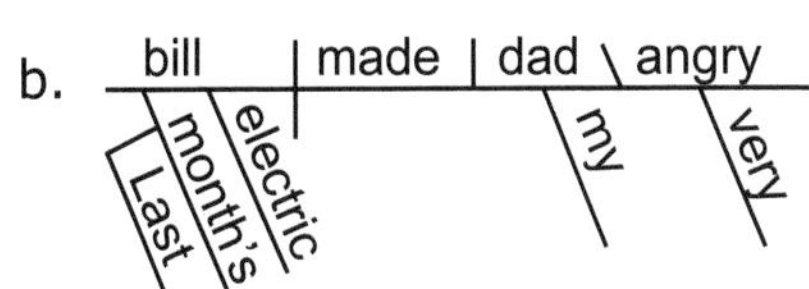

c. king | named | son \ successor
the
Surprisingly
his
youngest
his

d.
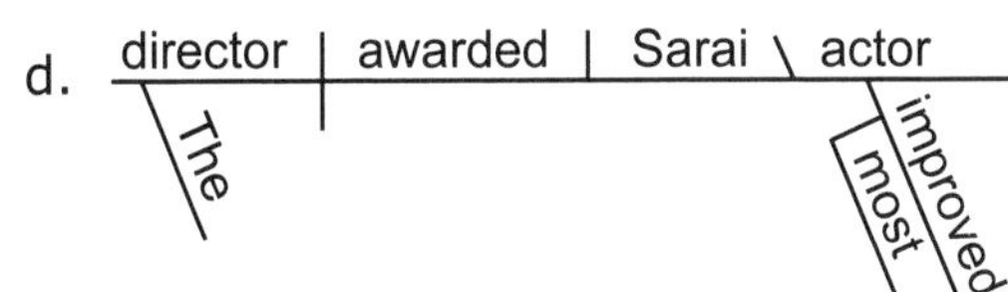

e. son | keeps | car \ clean
My
his
very

3 Sentences will vary. Examples:

a. We named our dog Bobo. We | named | dog \ Bobo
our

b. They elected Marita Salazar president. They | elected | Marita Salazar \ president

c. Who painted the walls dark blue? Who | painted | walls \ blue
the
dark

d. Therese decorated the snowflake cookies white with silver sparkles.

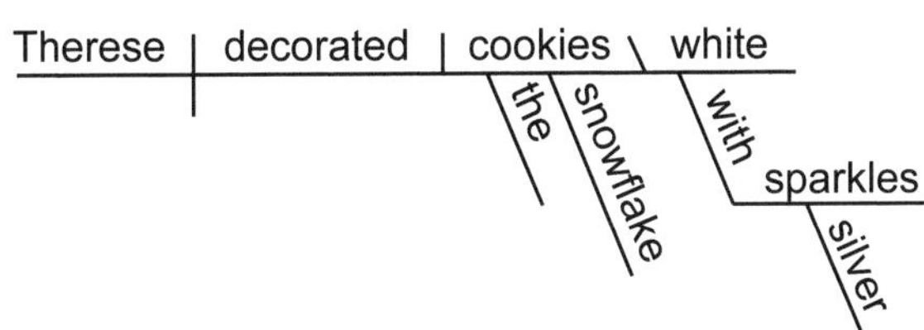

e. Don't make the dog mad. (you) | Do make | dog \ mad
n't
the

f. Our coach, Mrs. Graham, declared Andreas and Ajit most improved players.

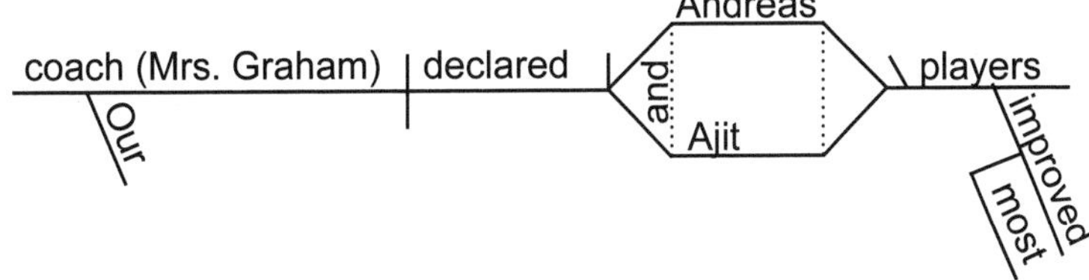

4 a.

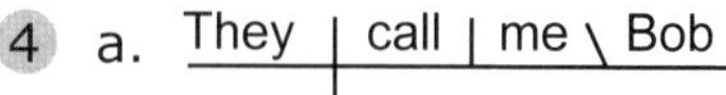

b.

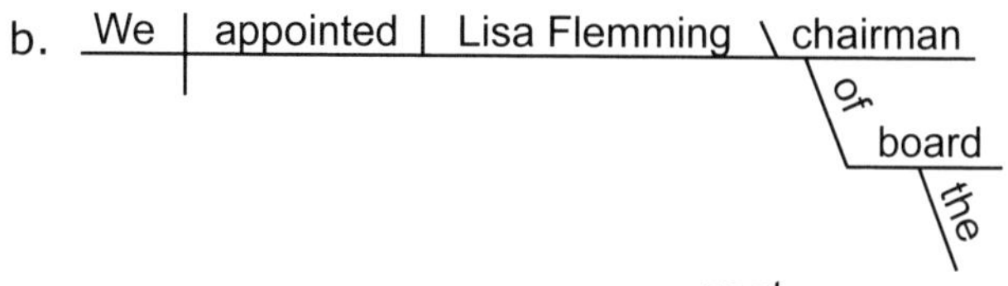

c.

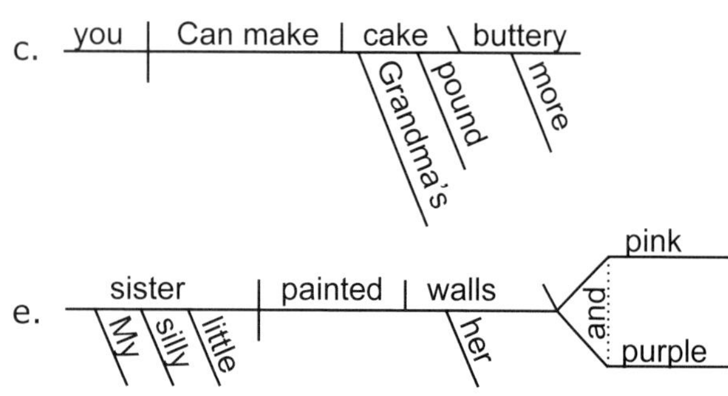

d.

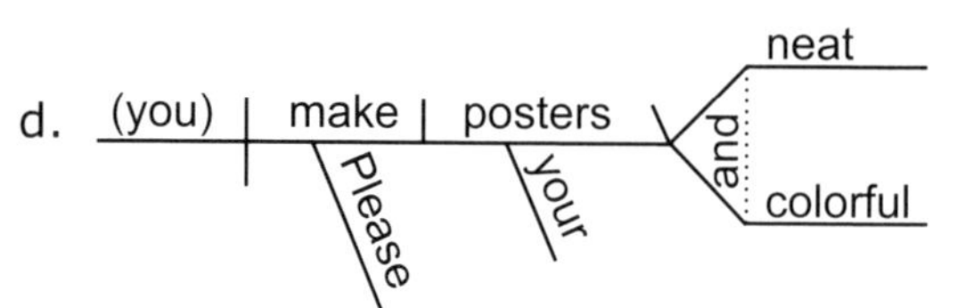

e.

Lesson 3 (pp. 15-21)

1 a.

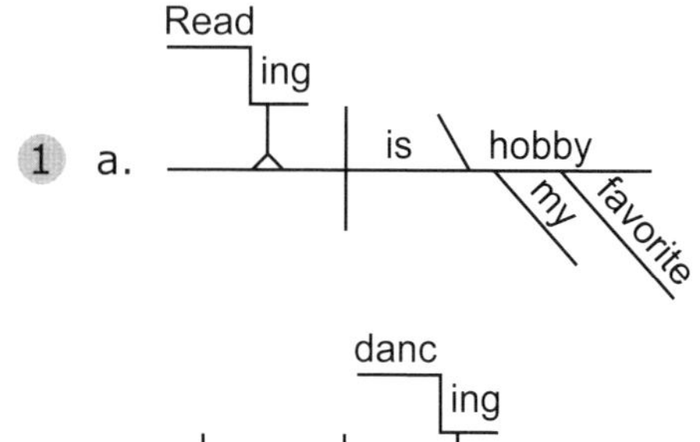

b.

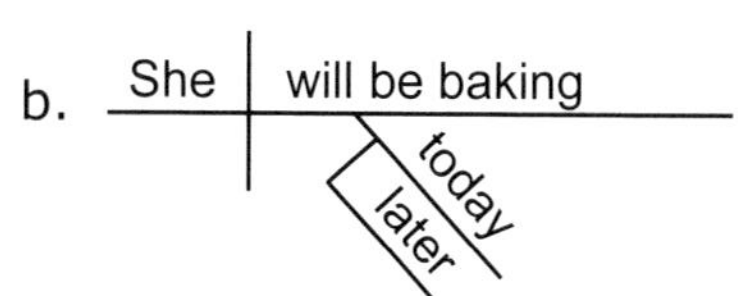

c.

danc
ing
I
enjoy
really

2 a.

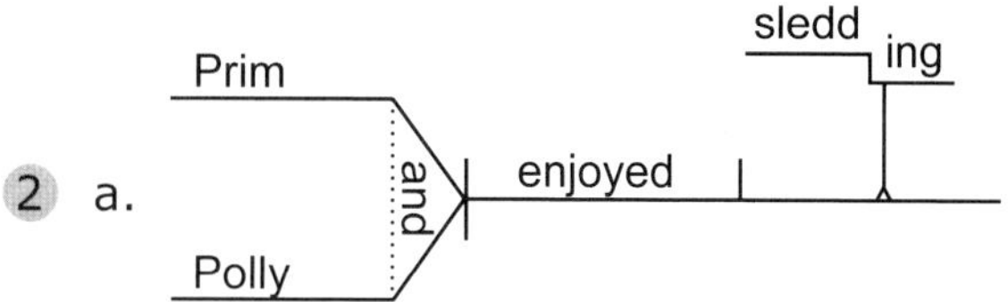

b.

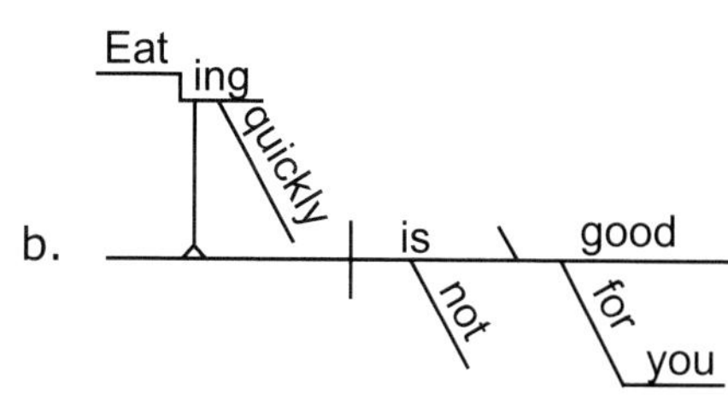

c.

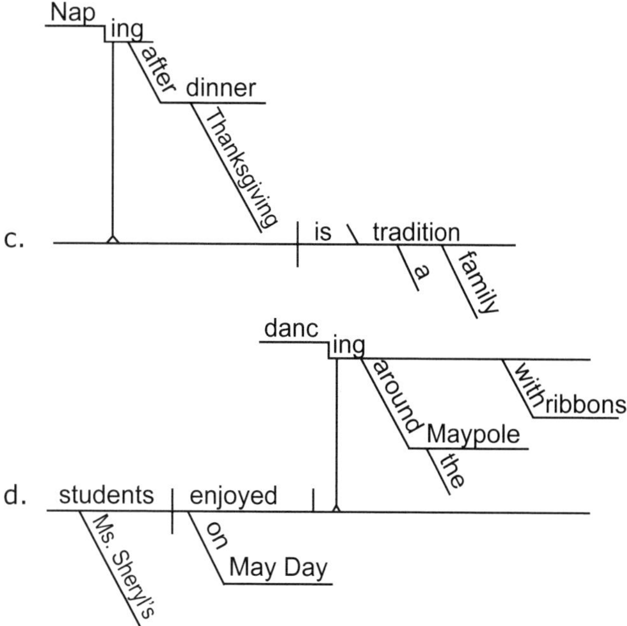

d.

3 Sentences will vary. Examples:

a. She enjoys skipping.

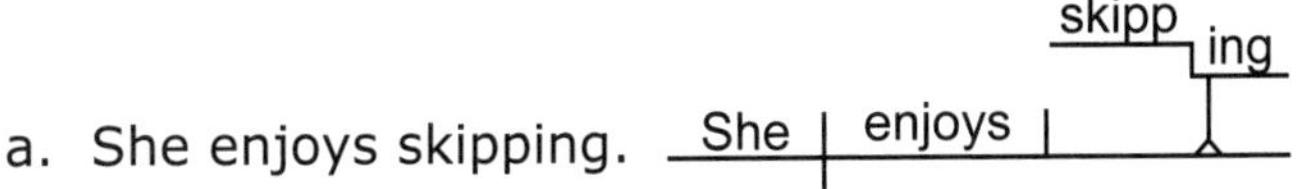

b. He finished reading the book.

read
ing | book
the
He | finished |

c. Smoking is a bad habit.

d. Eating in the bathtub is gross.

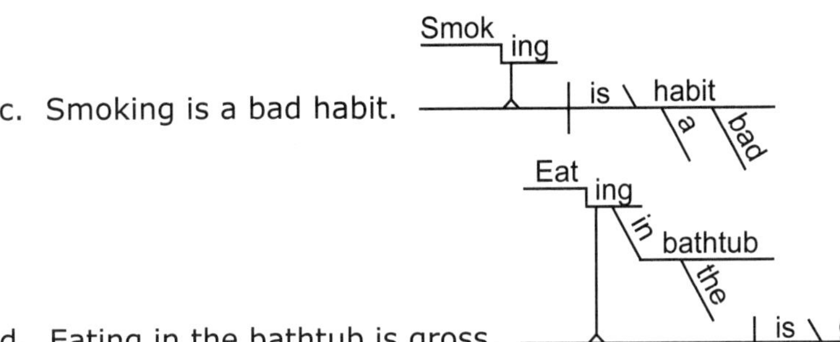

4 a.

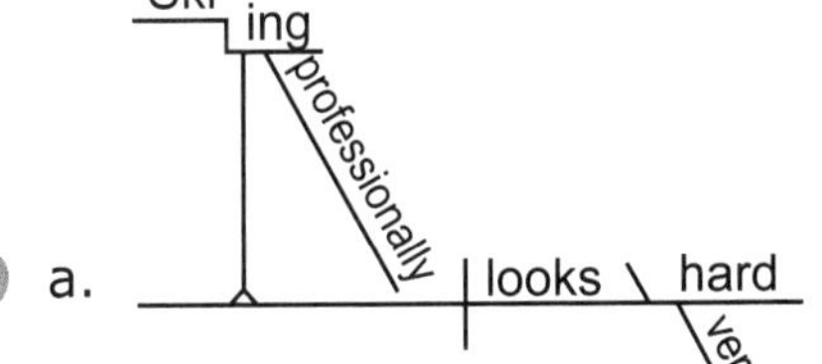

b.

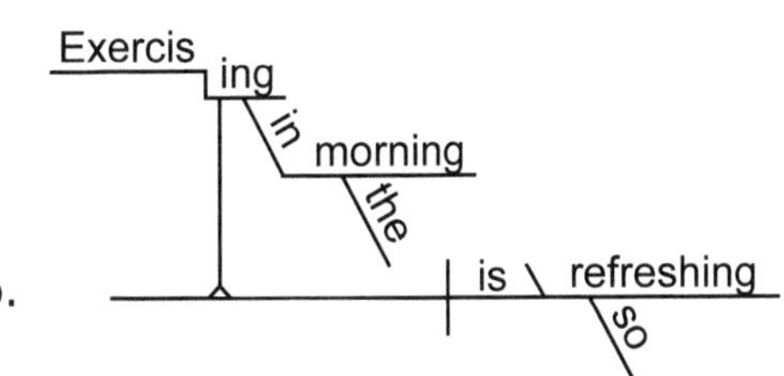

c.

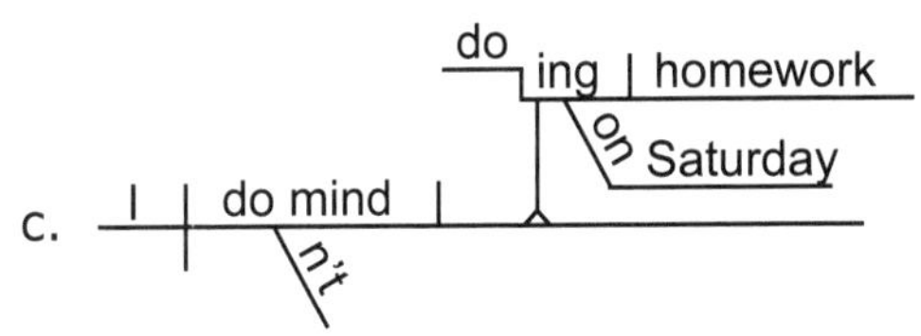

d.

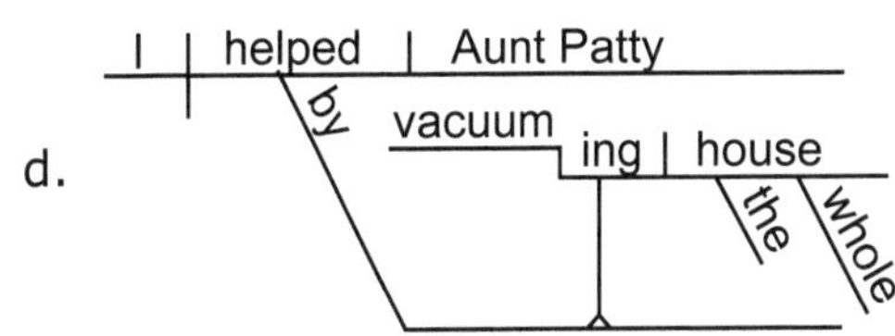

e.

Diagramm
ing | sentences
makes | me \ happy

Lesson 4 (pp. 22-28)

1 a.

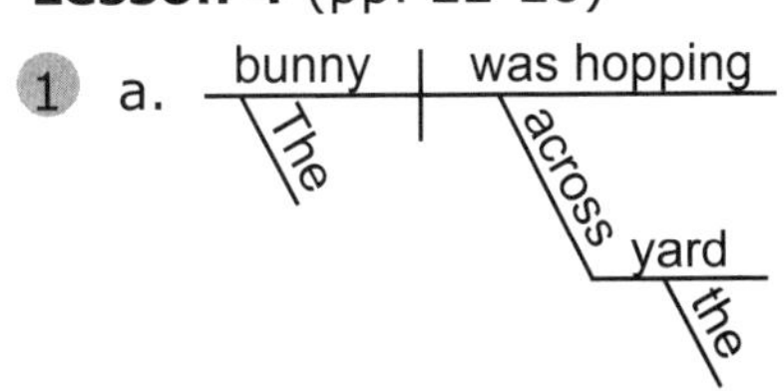

b.

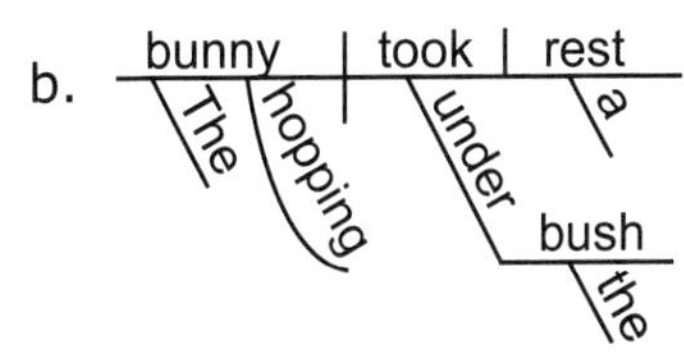

2 a.

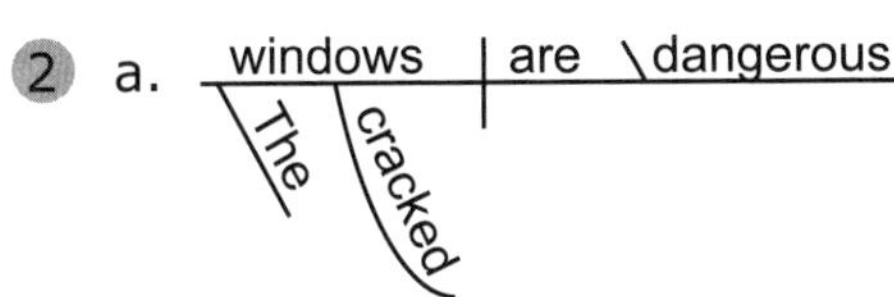

b.

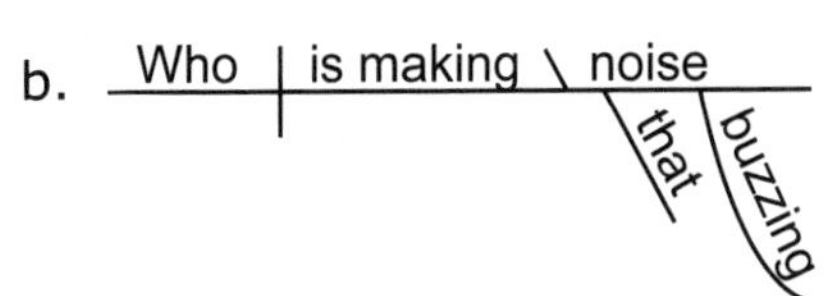

c.

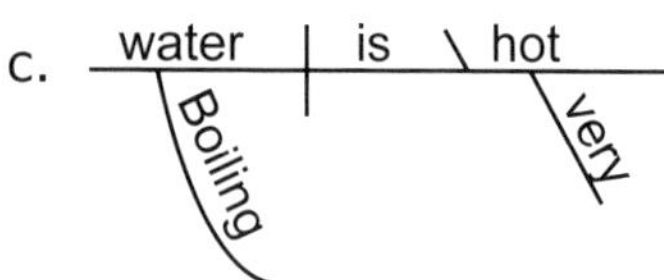

d.

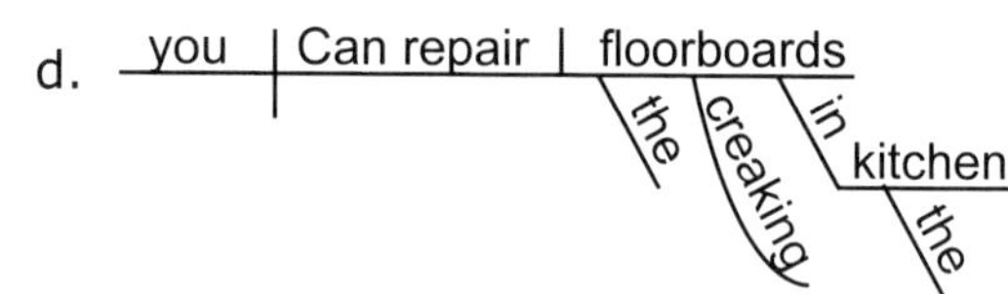

e.

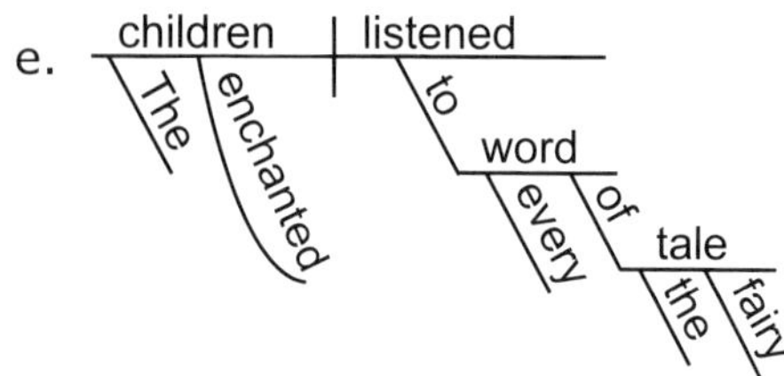

3 Sentences will vary. Examples:

a. My jumping bean died.

bean | died
My
jumping

b. The nervous actor steadied his shaking hands.

actor | steadied | hands
The
nervous
his
shaking

c. Frowning, Aidan ate his peas.

Aidan | ate | peas
Frowning
his

d. Surrounded, the small army surrendered.

army | surrendered
Surrounded
the
small

e. Washed and waxed, Dad's car looked awesome!

car | looked \ awesome
Washed and waxed
Dad's

4 a.

doll | sat
Forgotten
the
toy
on
swing set
the
for
week
a

b.

runner | jumped
The
injured
bravely
back
into
race
the

c.

Mr. Bell | repaired | teddy bear
Alice's
mangled

d.

kitten | did like | rain
The
mewing and hissing
not
the

e.

finger | looked \ painful
Bent and broken
Ronnie's

Lesson 5 (pp. 29-35)

1 a.

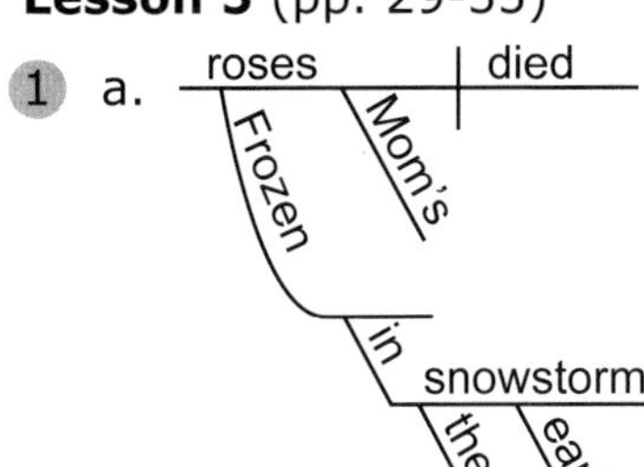

b.

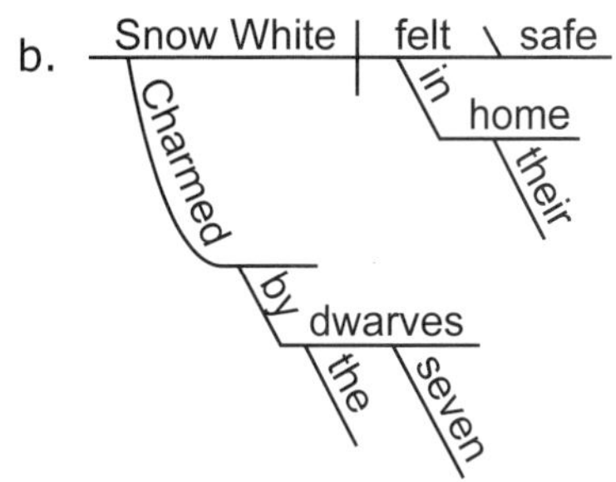

2 a.

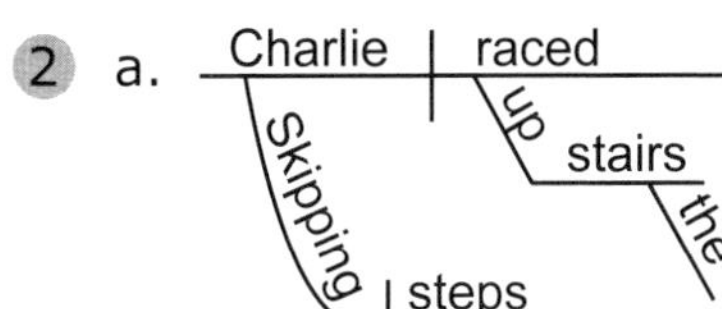

b.

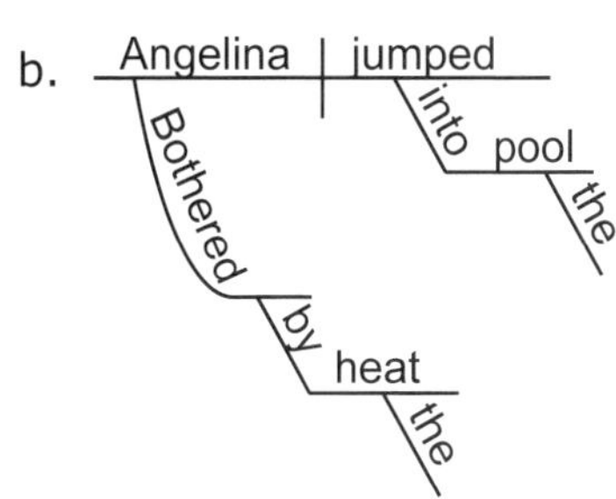

c.

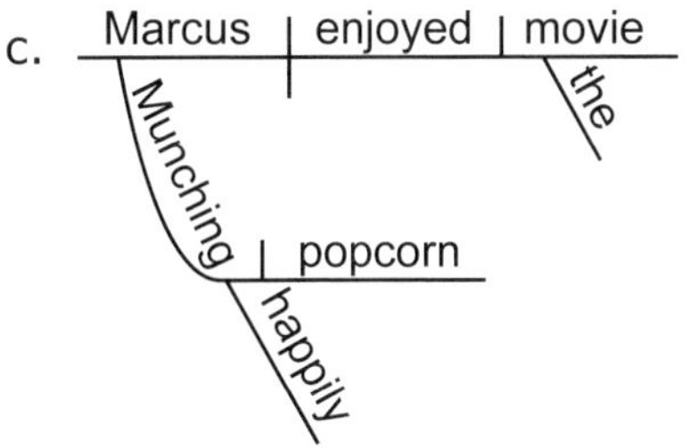

d.

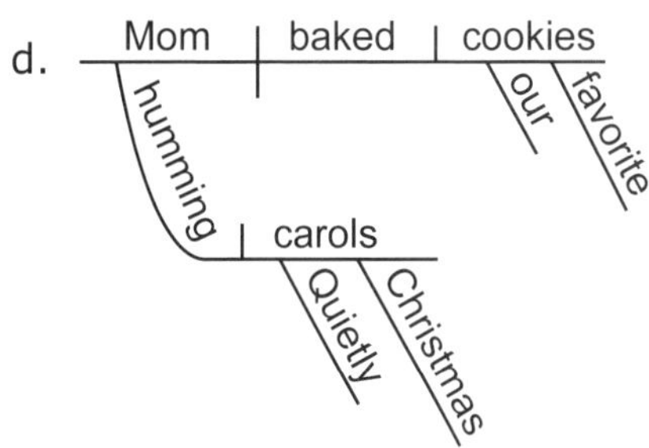

e.

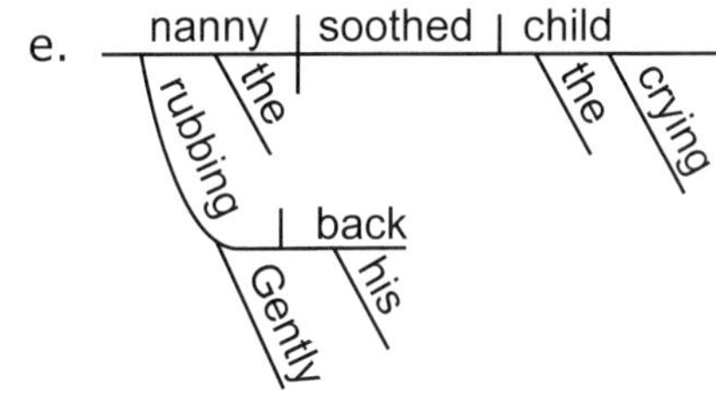

3 Sentences will vary. Examples:

a. Sipping hot tea, Emily watched the sunrise.

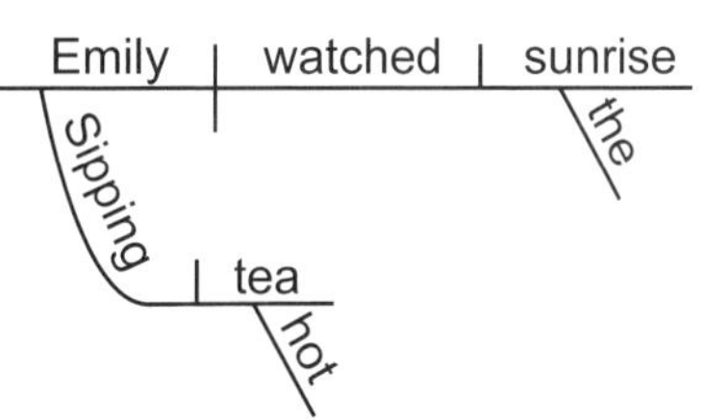

b. Yipping and yapping, our dog chased three squirrels.

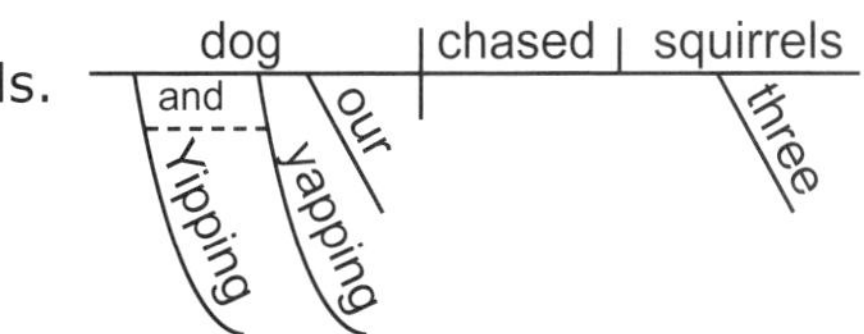

c. Alexandria, snuggled sweetly under the covers, slept peacefully.

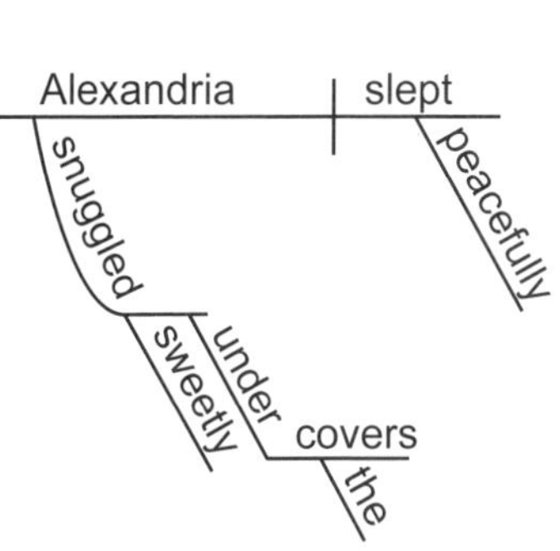

d. I took pictures of Tyler jumping on the trampoline.

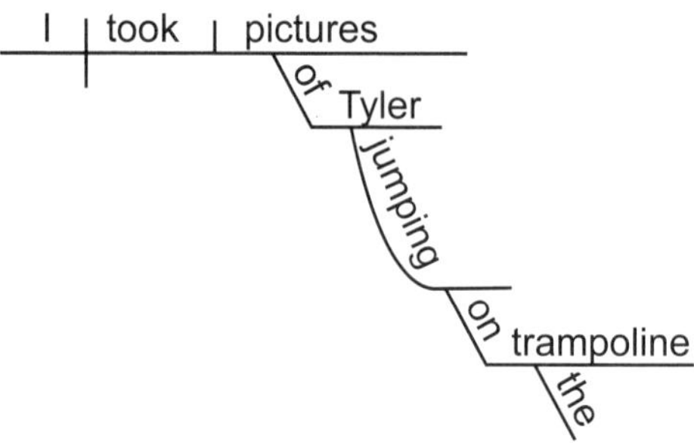

4 a.

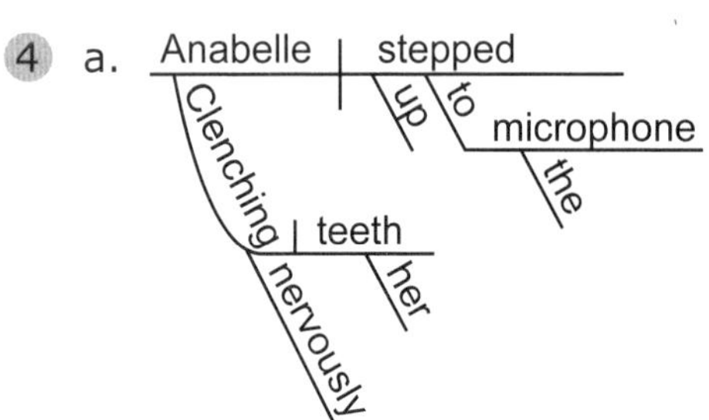

b.

lifeguard | watched | swimmers
The
twirling
whistle
her
mindlessly
carefully
the

c.

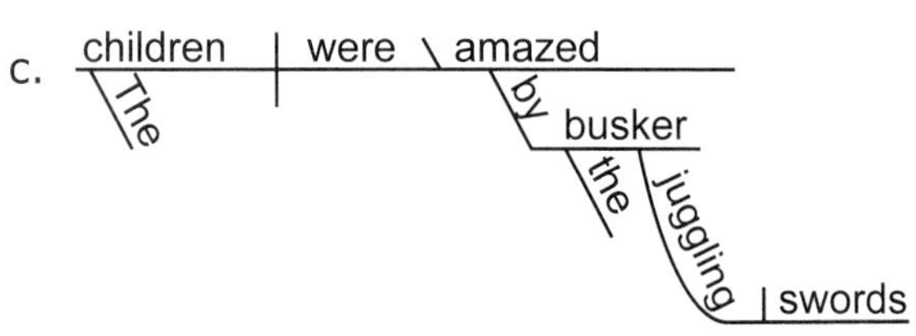

d.

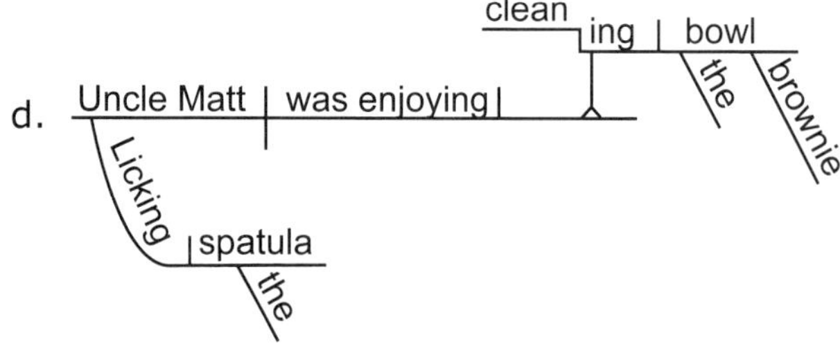

Lesson 6 (pp. 36-42)

1 a.

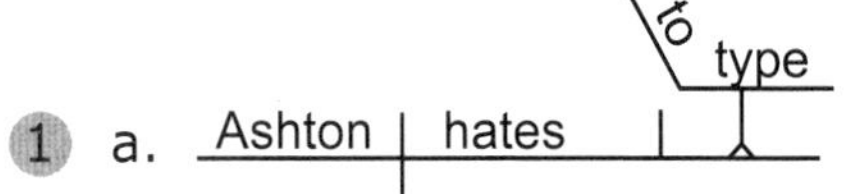

b.

to
email
Mrs. Jones | prefers

c.

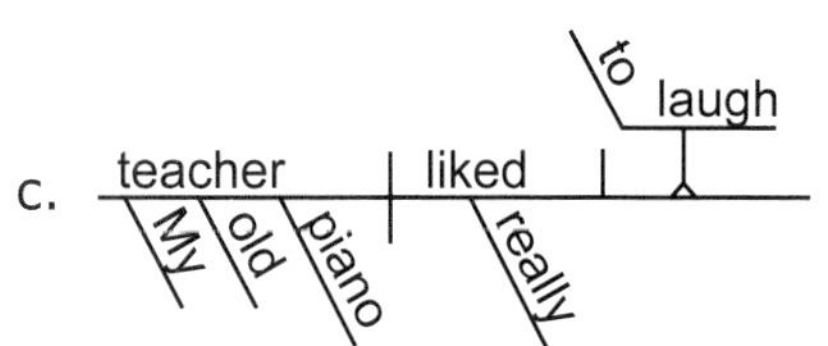

d.

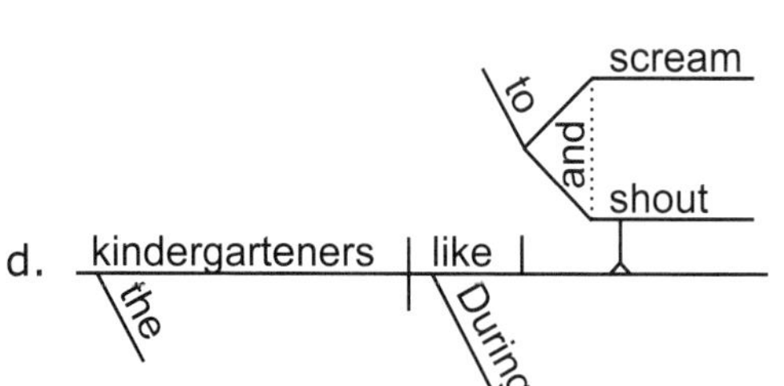

2 a.

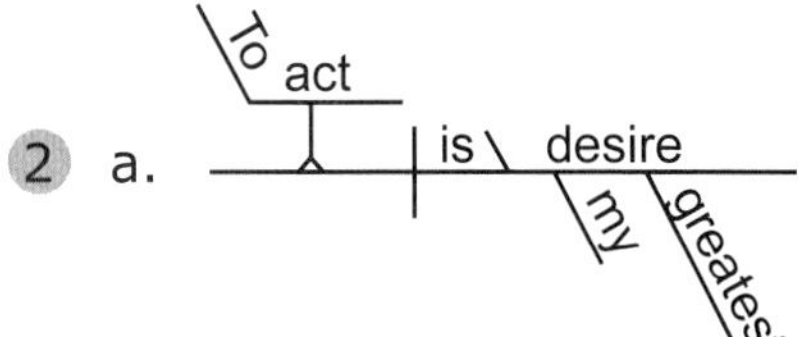

b.

to
leave
I | want

c.

To
fail
is
to
learn

d.

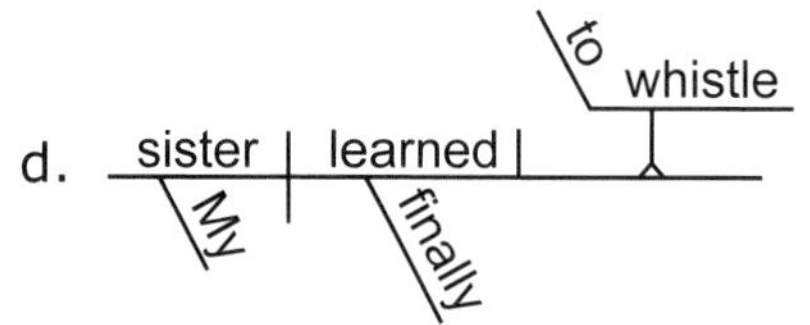

e.

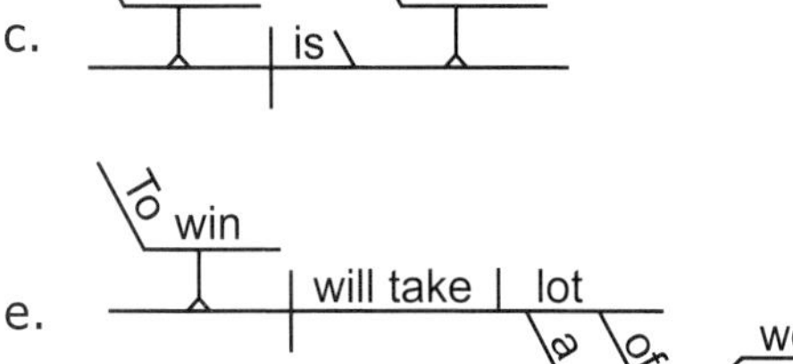

3 Sentences will vary. Examples:

a. The boys hate to lose.

boys | hate | to lose
The

b. To fly would be divine.

To fly | would be \ divine

c. The tired baby does not want to sleep.

baby | does want | to sleep
The tired not

d. To love is to live.

To love | is \ to live

e. The mama bird soon returned to the nest.

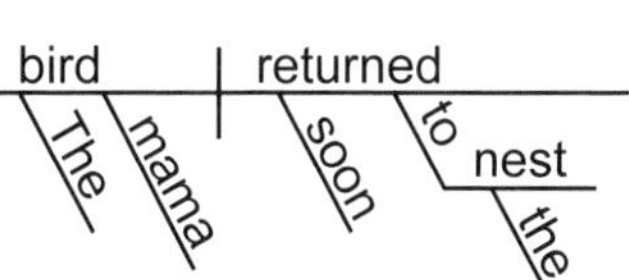

4 a.

children | like | to whine
Tired often

b.

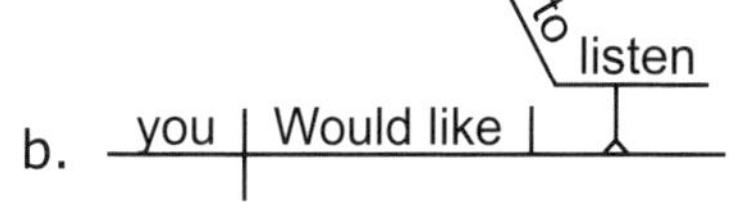

c.

(you) | Tell | to hurry
Lucy

d.

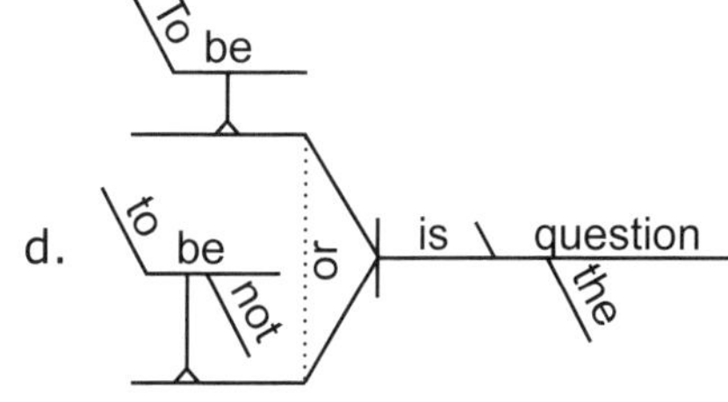

e.

(you) | teach | to ski
Please me

f.

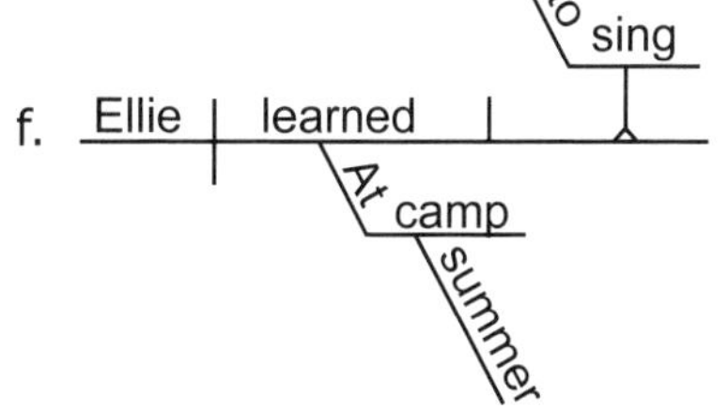

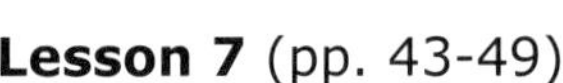

Lesson 7 (pp. 43-49)

1 a.

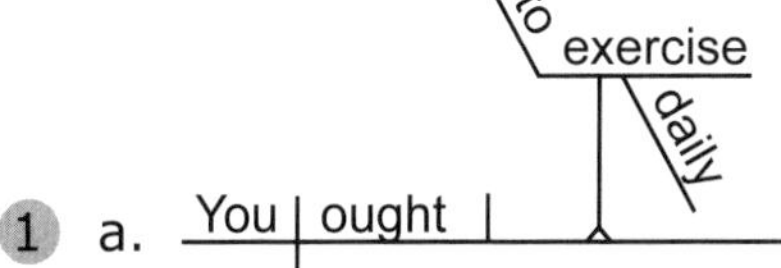

b.

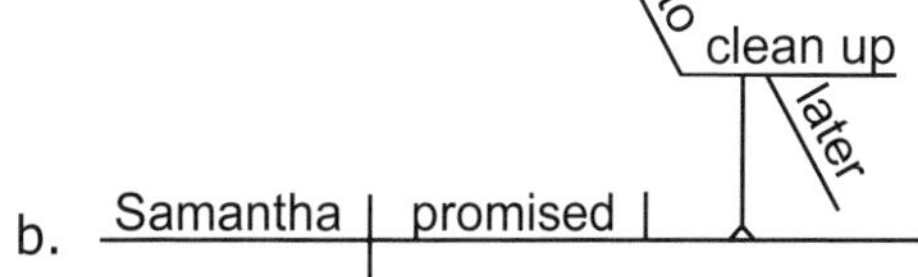

c.

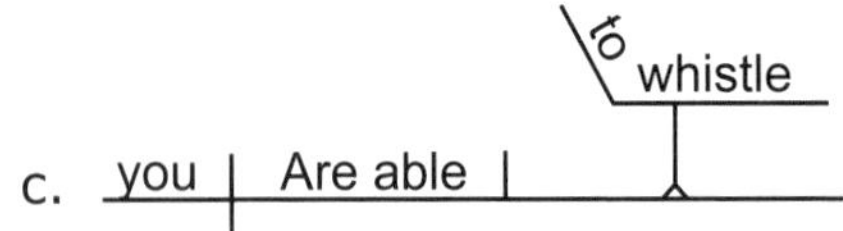

2 a.

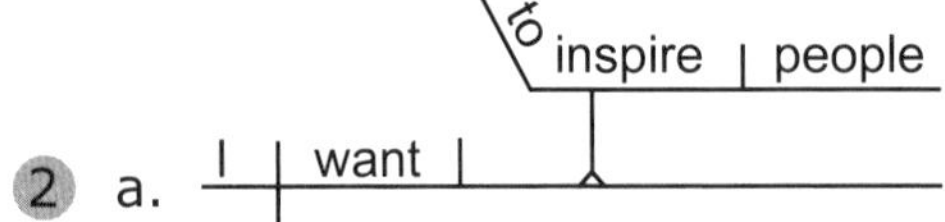

b.

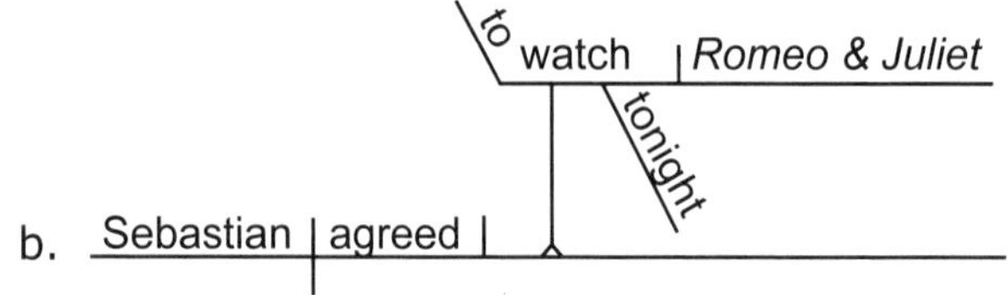

c.

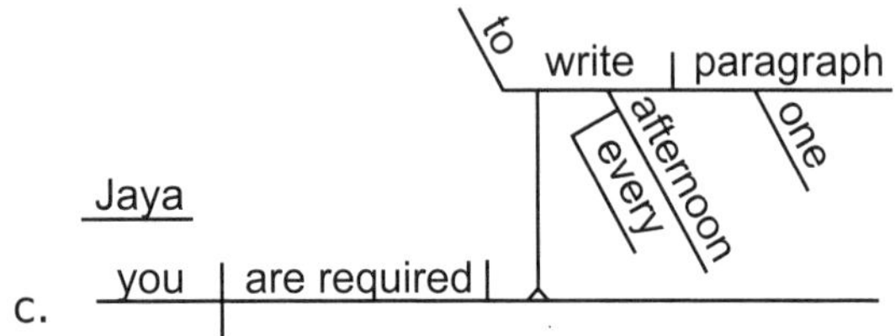

d.

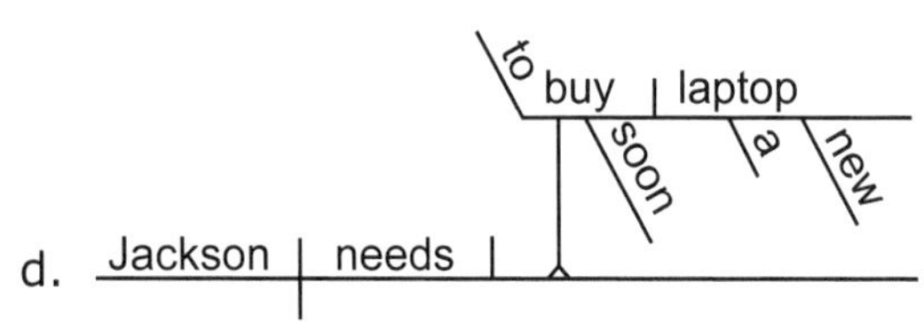

e.

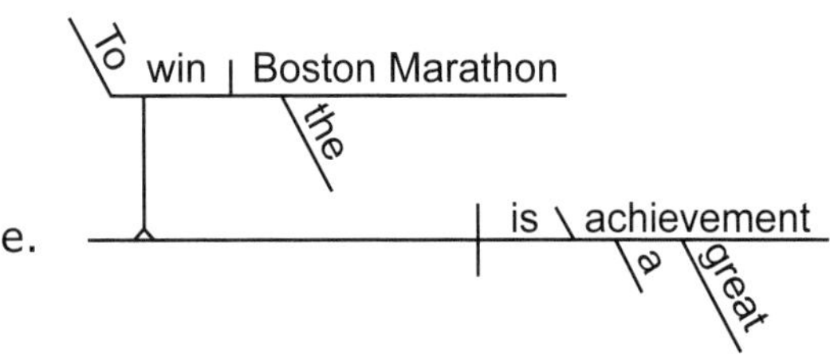

3 Sentences will vary. Examples:

a. Jim wants to sleep longer.

b. Buddy likes to bask in the sun.

c. Evie learned to ride a bicycle.

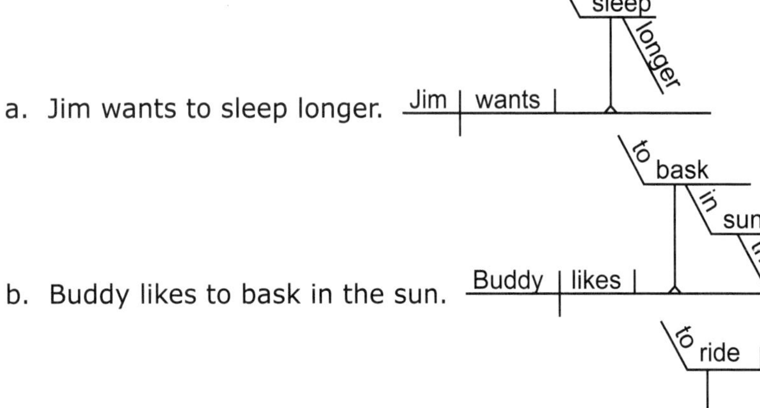

d. I like to eat bagels for breakfast.

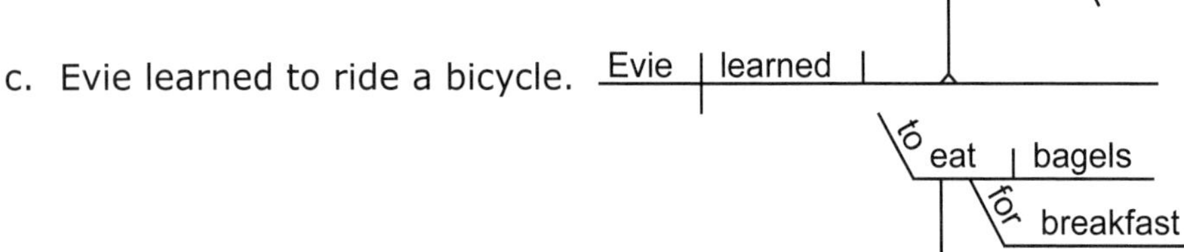

e. To fight for freedom was a great honor.

4 a. 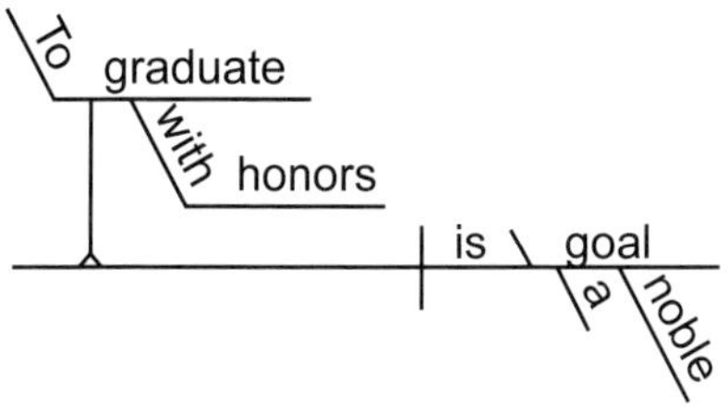 To graduate with honors | is \ goal a noble

b. 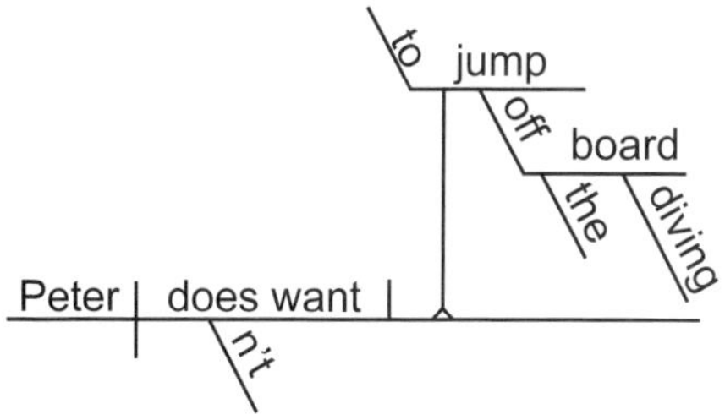 Peter | does want n't | to jump off board the diving

c. 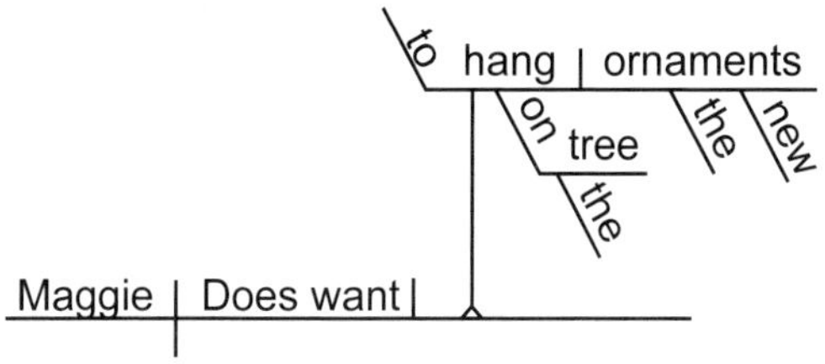 Maggie | Does want | to hang | ornaments the new on tree the

d. 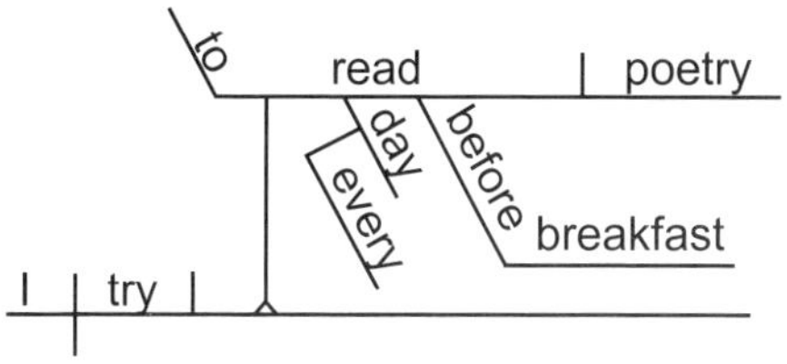 I | try | to read | poetry every day before breakfast

e. 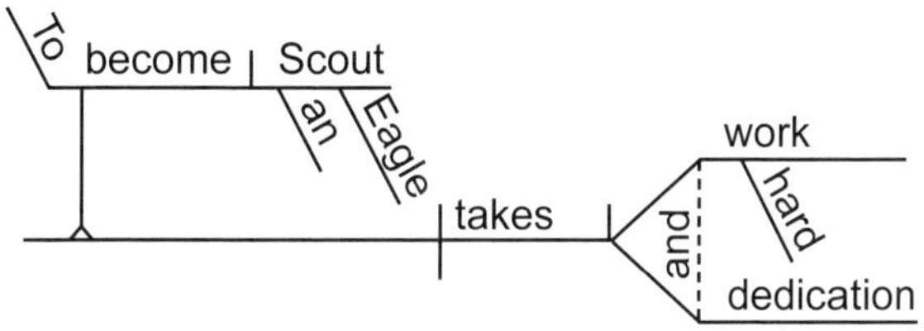 To become | Scout an Eagle | takes | work hard and dedication

f. 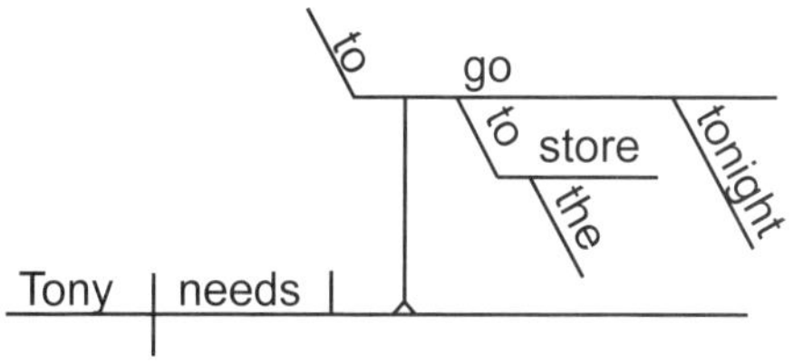 Tony | needs | to go to store the tonight

Lesson 8 (pp. 50-56)

1 a. 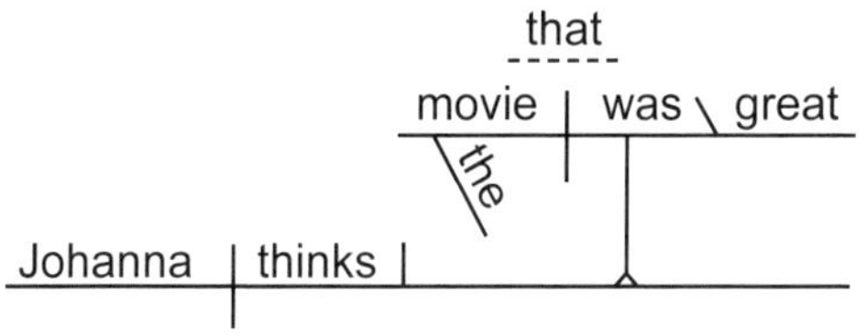 Johanna | thinks | that movie the | was \ great

b. 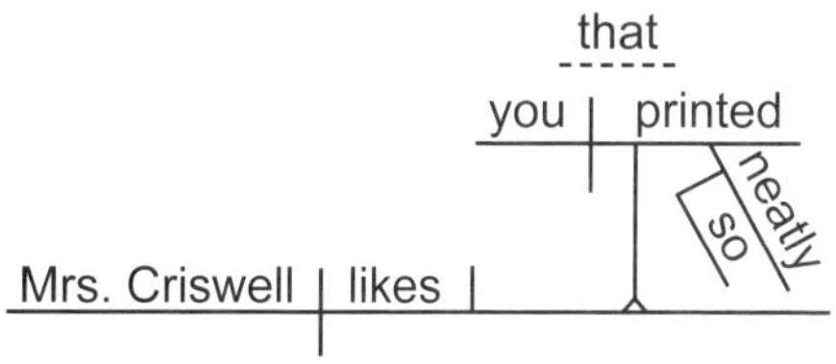 Mrs. Criswell | likes | that you | printed neatly so

c. 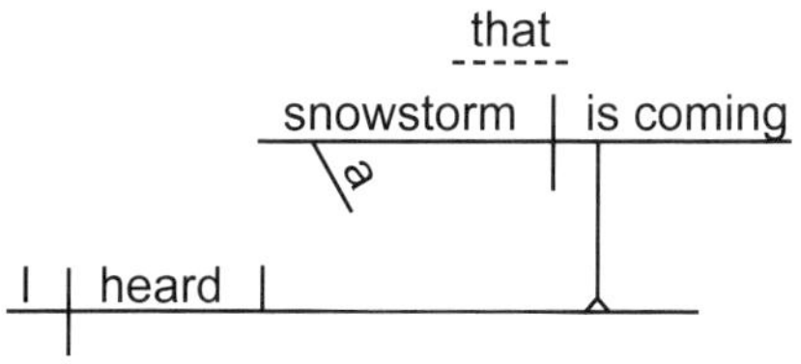 I | heard | that snowstorm a | is coming

2 a. 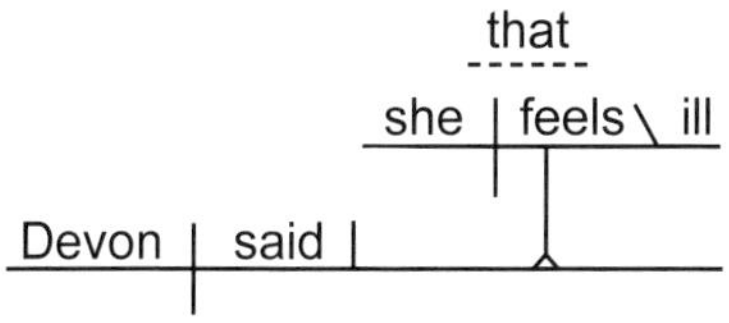 Devon | said | that she | feels \ ill

b. 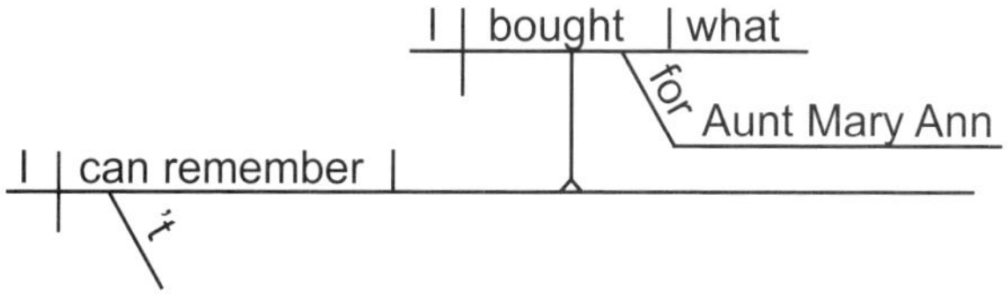 I | can remember 't | I | bought | what for Aunt Mary Ann

c. 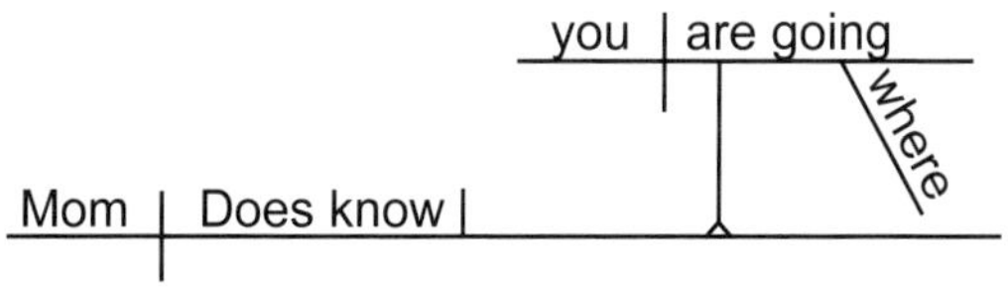 Mom | Does know | you | are going where

d. 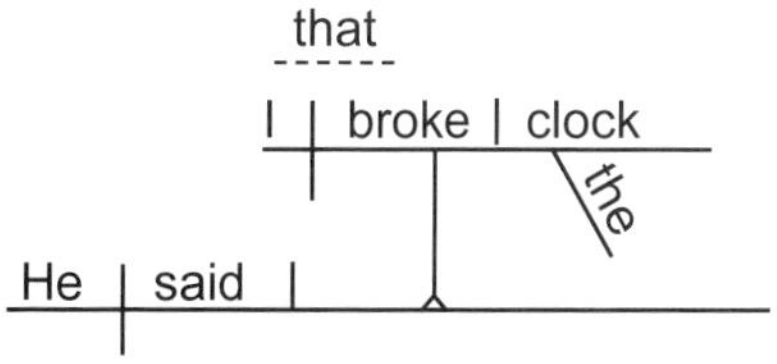 He | said | that I | broke | clock the

e. 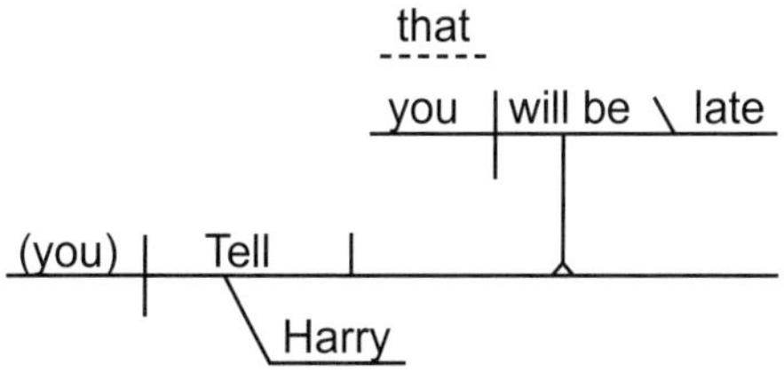 (you) | Tell Harry | that you | will be \ late

3 Sentences will vary. Examples:

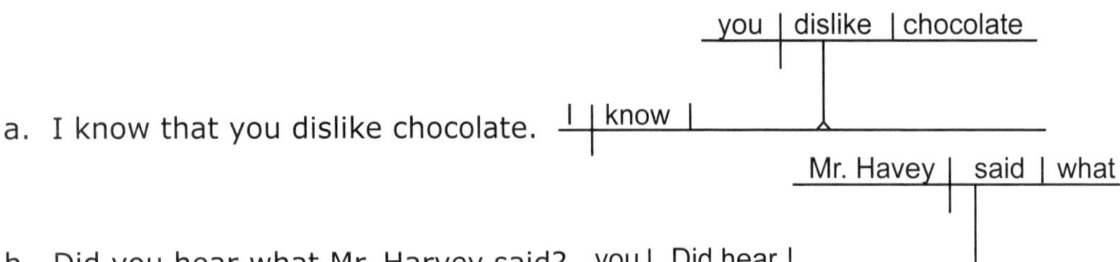

a. I know that you dislike chocolate.

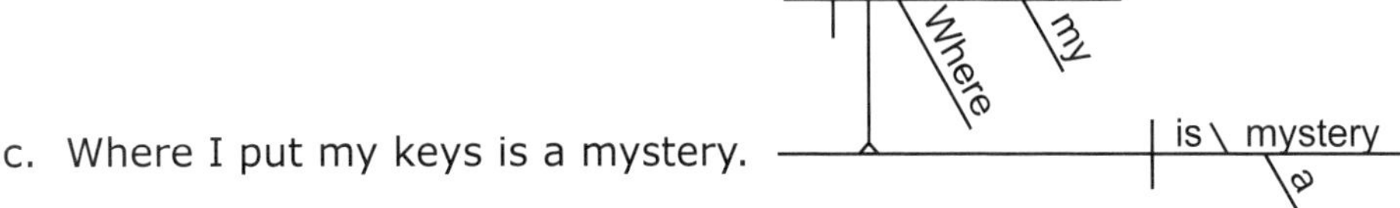

b. Did you hear what Mr. Harvey said?

c. Where I put my keys is a mystery.

d. Tell me how you make sausage.

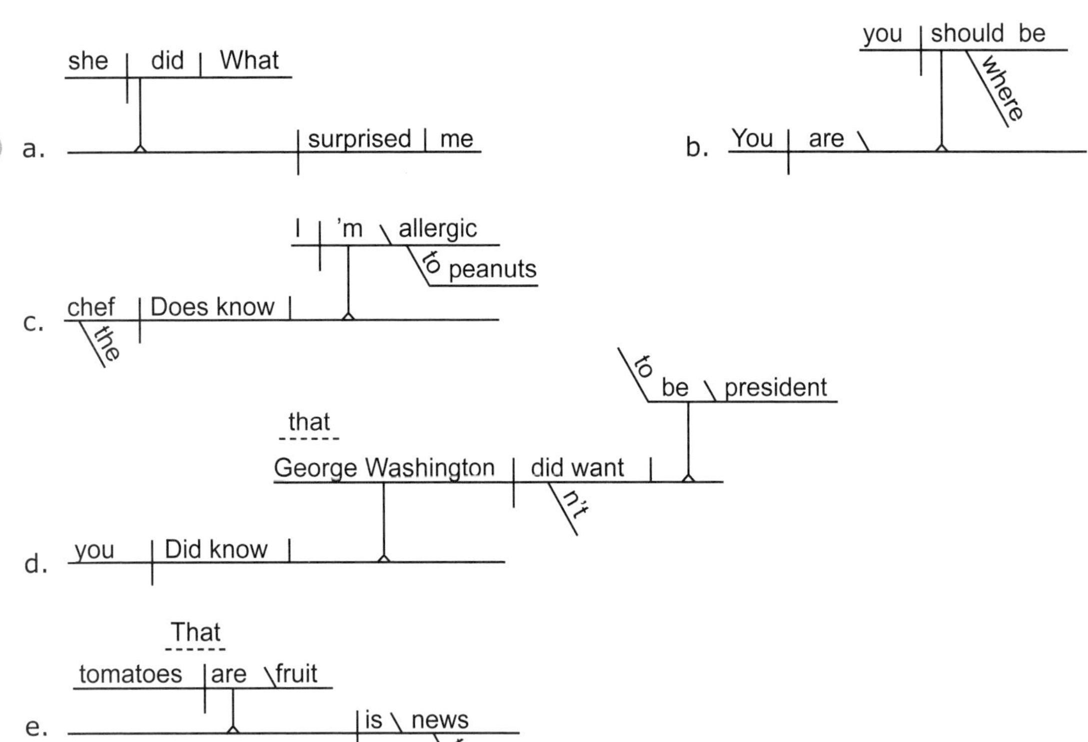

4 a.

b.

c.

d.

e.

Lesson 9 (pp. 57-63)

1 a.

b.

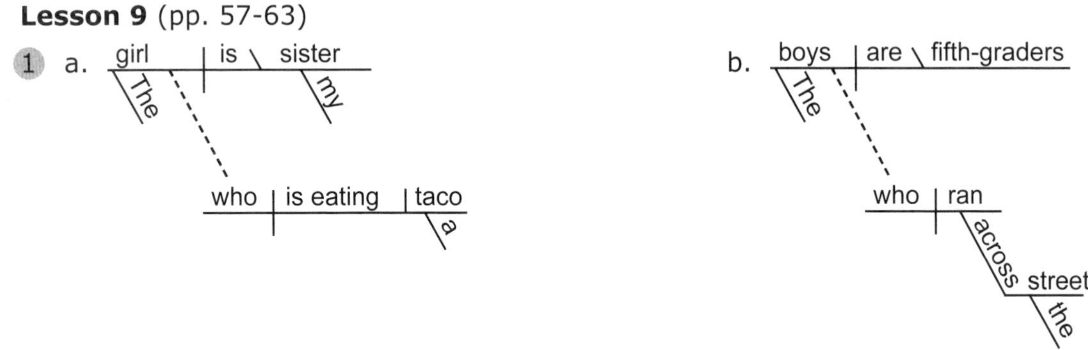

2 a.

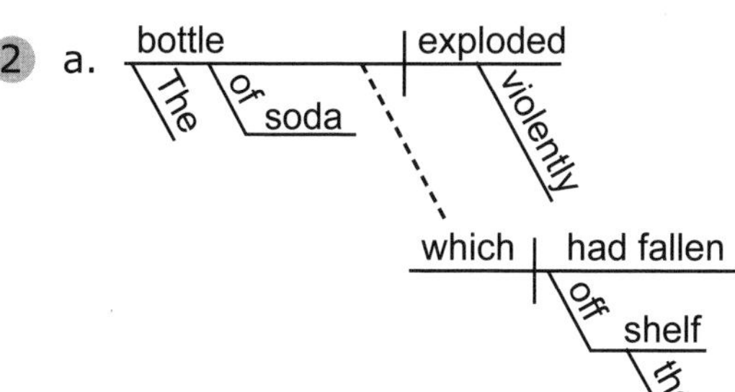

b.

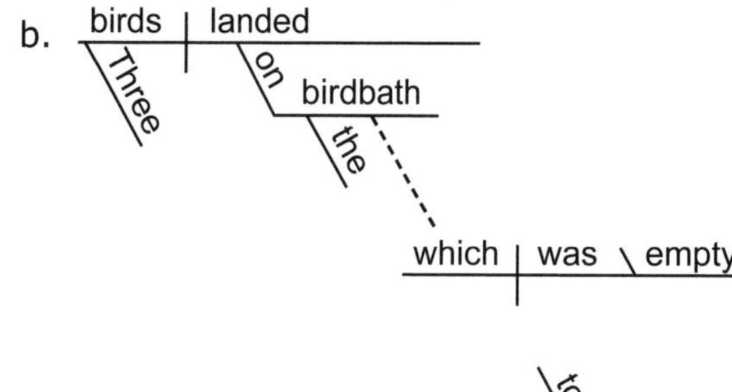

c.

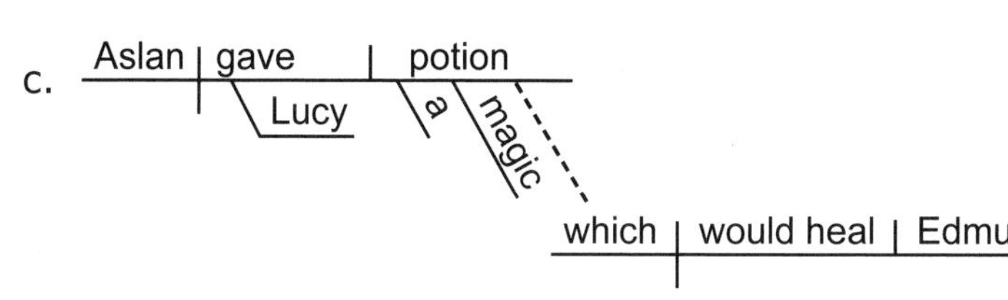

d.

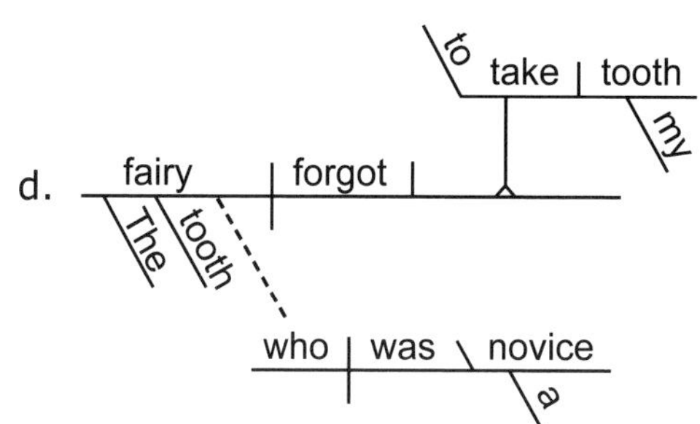

3 Sentences will vary. Examples:

a. The meatball, which rolled off the table, was delicious!

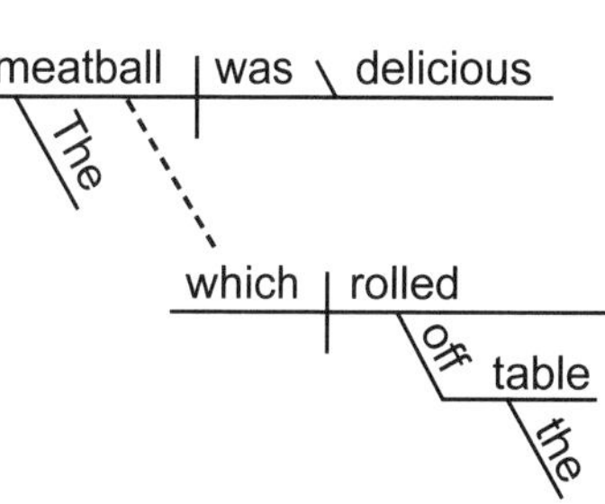

b. Uncle Frank bought a bicycle that looks really old.

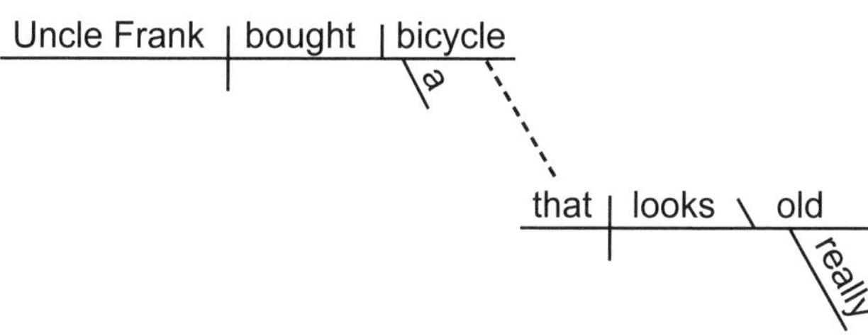

c. Mom sewed a quilt for Mrs. Harris, who is our neighbor.

Mom | sewed | quilt
a
for
Mrs. Harris
who | is \ neighbor
our

d. He is the teacher who teaches chemistry.

He | is \ teacher
the
who | teaches | chemistry

4 a.

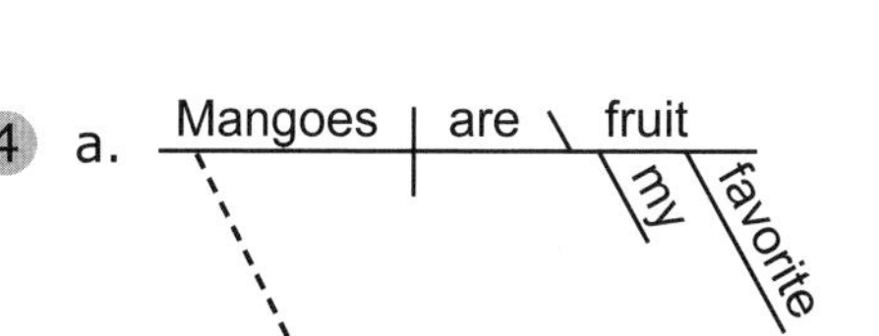

b.

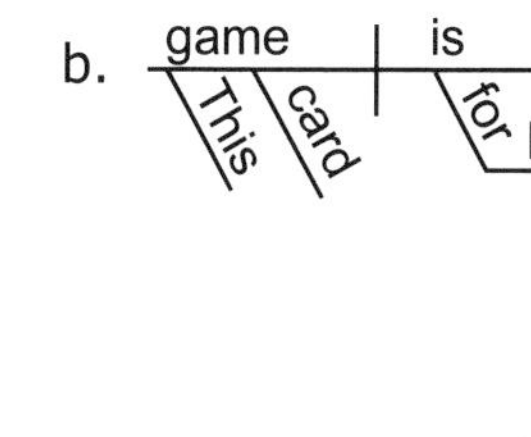

c.

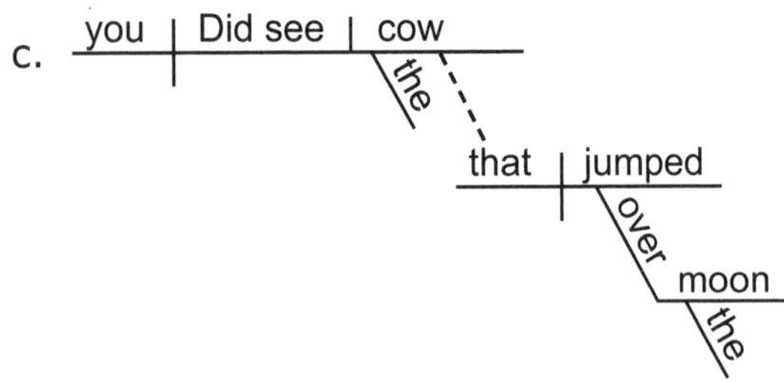

d.

This | is \ house
the
that | was built
by
Jack
who | is \ builder
a

Lesson 10 (pp. 64-70)

1 a.

I | will call
when
I | get
there

b.

Cindy | listens
to
music
while
she | runs

2 a.

I | laughed
when
he | tripped

b.

Josh | sneezed
after
he | sniffed | pepper

c.

I | was \ tired
After
I | ran
for
hours
three

d.

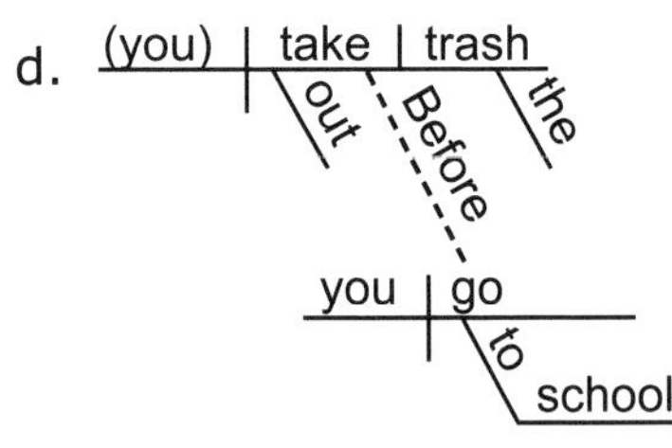

3 Sentences will vary. Examples:

a. David will play video games after school.

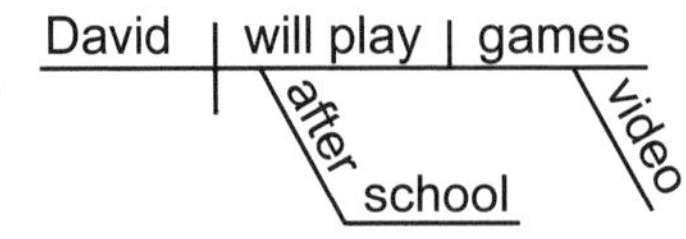

b. The monkeys were happy after the zookeepers fed them.

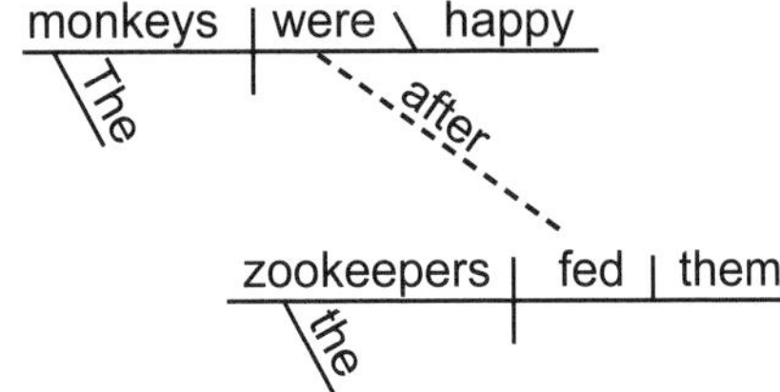

c. Grandpa usually snores when he sleeps.

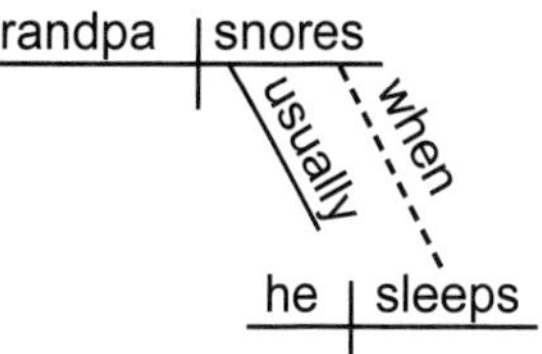

4 a. Aunt Silvia | made | meatballs
because
you | like | them
much
so

b. (you) | Eat | carrots
some
while
you | wait
for
dinner

c. I | can concentrate
't
when
music | is \ loud
the

d. she | took | shower
a
long
hot
After
Johanna | fell
in
puddle
the
mud

Lesson 11 (pp. 71-77)

1 a. Porpoises | are \ smaller
than
dolphins | (are) \ (small)

b. elephants | are \ bigger
African
than
elephants | (are) \ (big)
Asian

c. Atlantic Ocean | is \ warmer
The
slightly
than
Pacific Ocean | (is) \ (warm)
the

2 a. Snakes | are \ scarier
than
spiders | (are) \ (scary)

b. I | like \ comedies
Shakespeare's
more
than
(I) | (like) | tragedies
his

c.
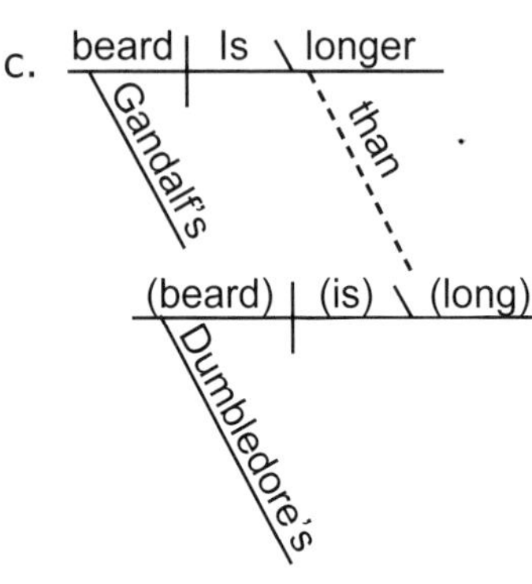

d.
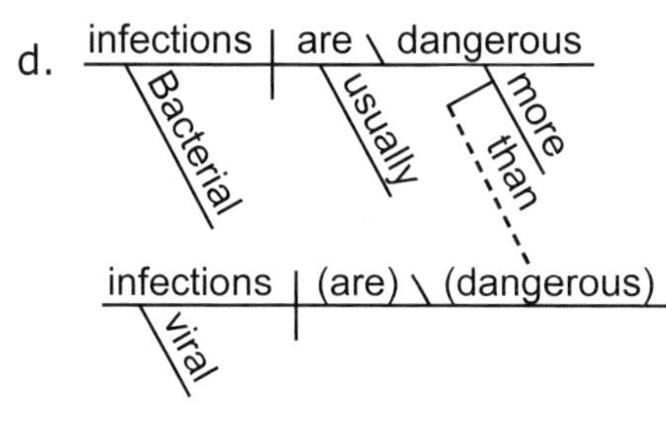

3 a.
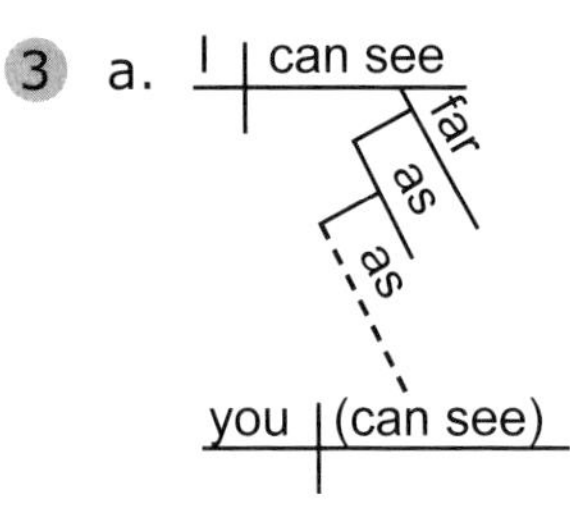

b.
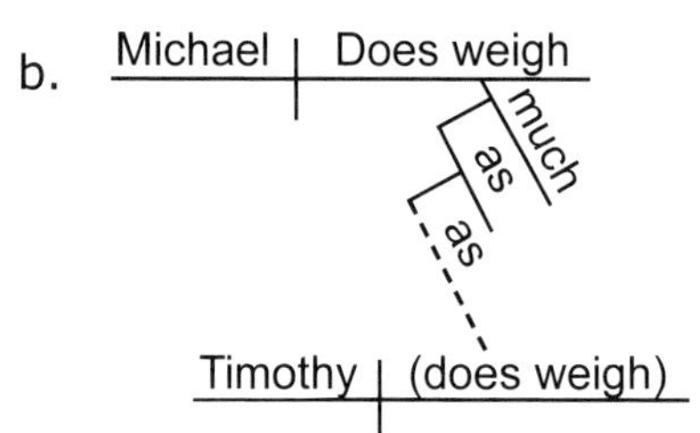

Sentences will vary. Examples:

c. I like Pepsi more than Coke.

I | like | Pepsi
more
than
(I) | (like) | Coke

d. Gelato tastes better than ice cream.

Gelato | tastes \ better
than
ice cream | (tastes) \ (good)

4 a.
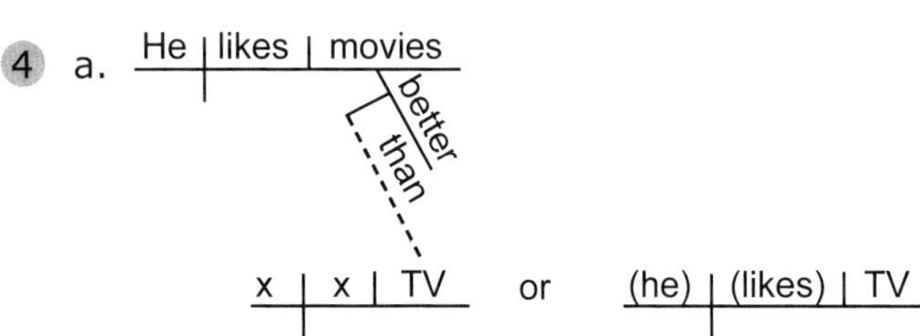

b.
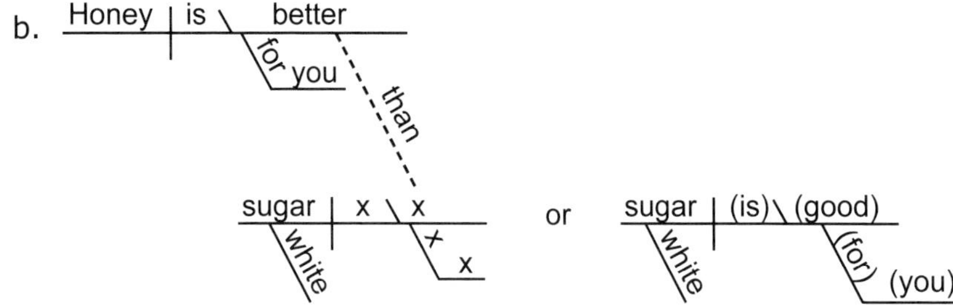

c. 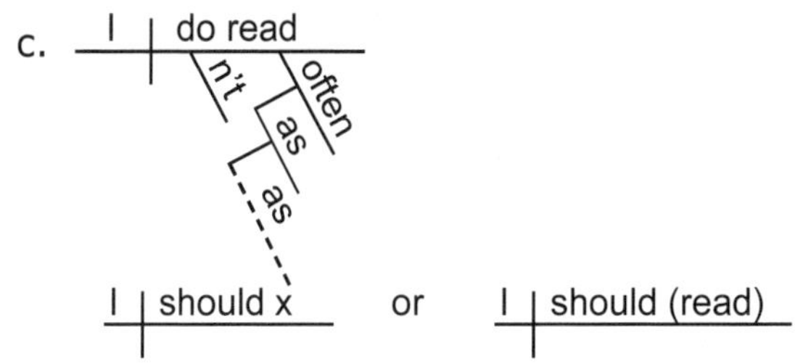

I should x or I should (read)

d. 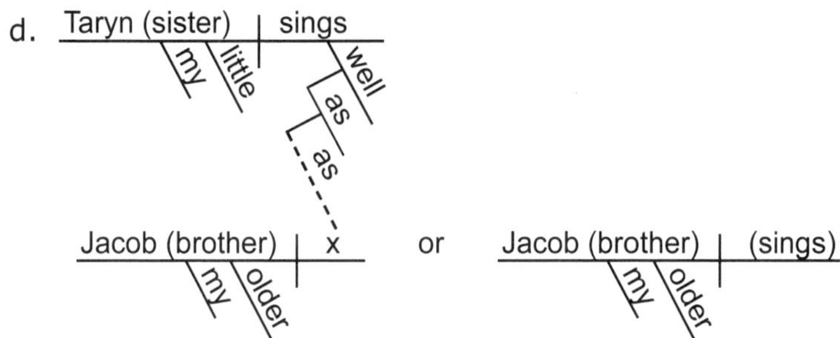

Lesson 12 (pp. 78-85)

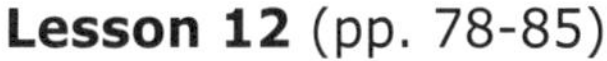

1 a. 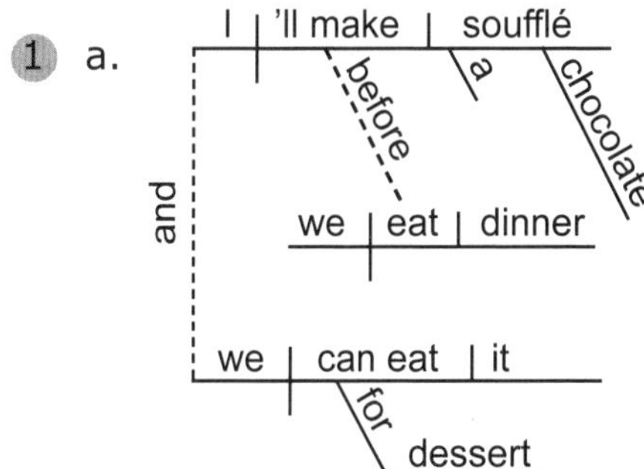

2 a. 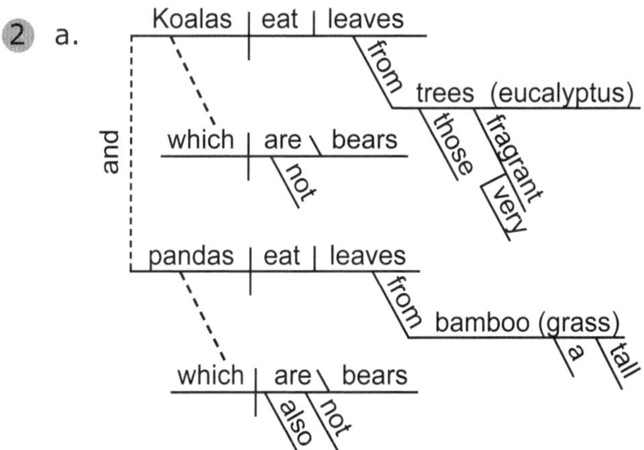

b. 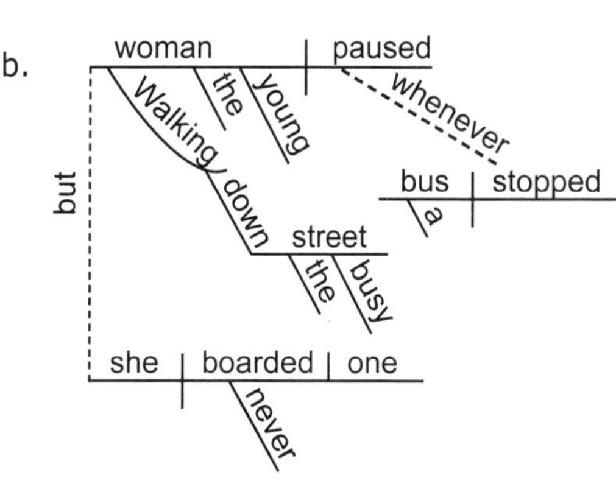

c. 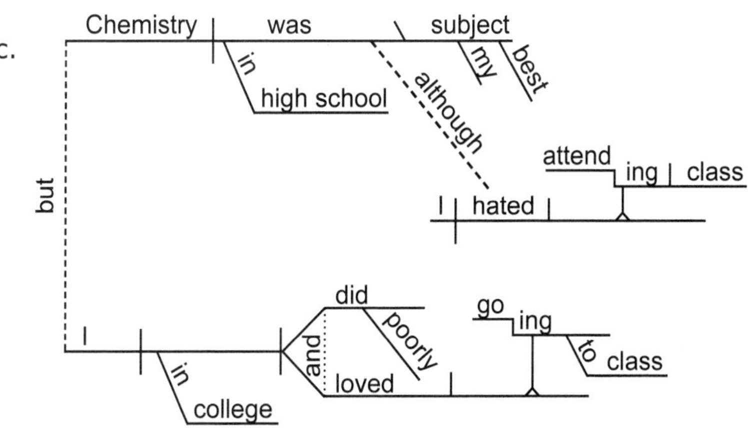

d.

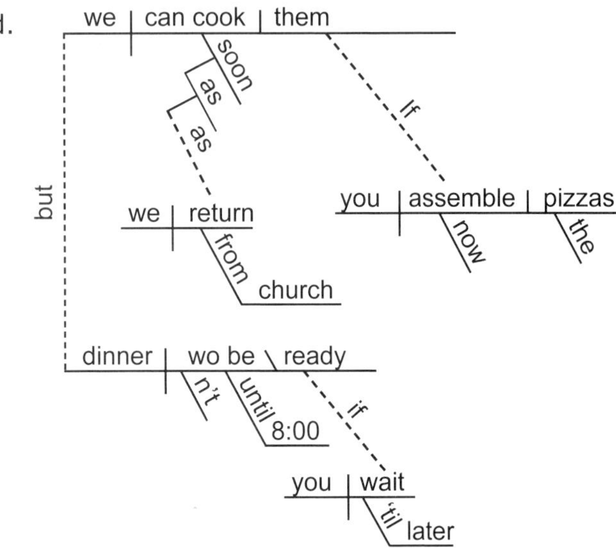

3 Sentences will vary. Examples:

a. Beat the eggs before you add them to the batter, or the brownies will taste funny.

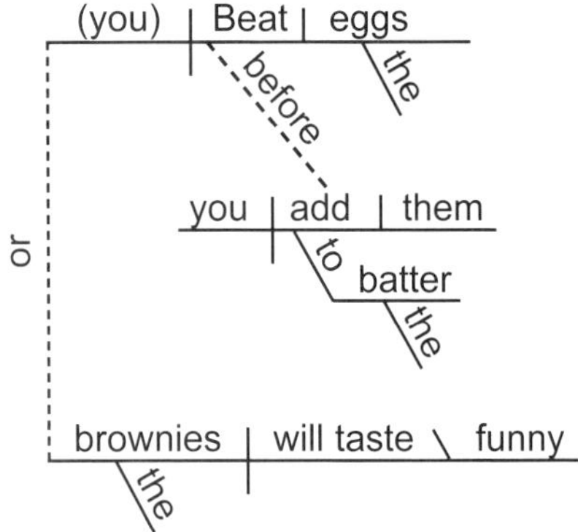

b. I will call you when I get to the party, and I will call you again before I leave.

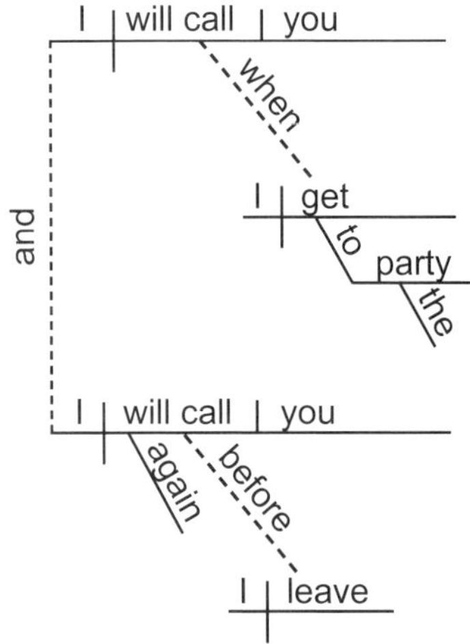

c. I bought that sweater before I knew that you did, but now I can't return it.

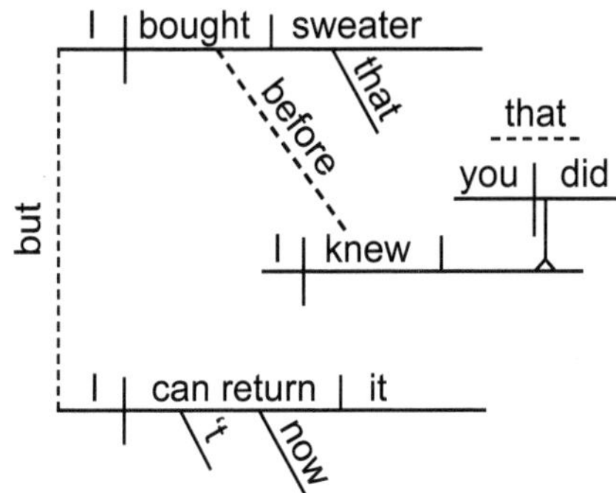

d. The Jedi rejoiced when the Death Star exploded, but they did not see Darth Vader escape.

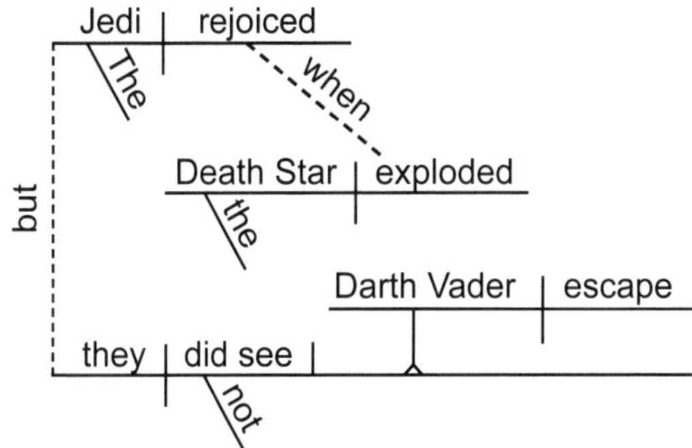

4 a.

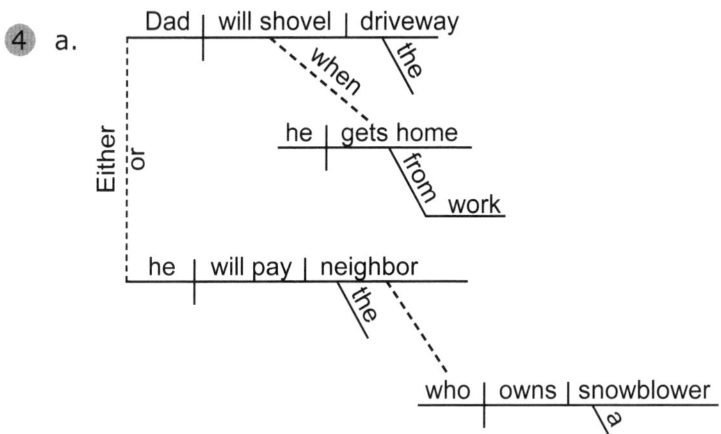

b.

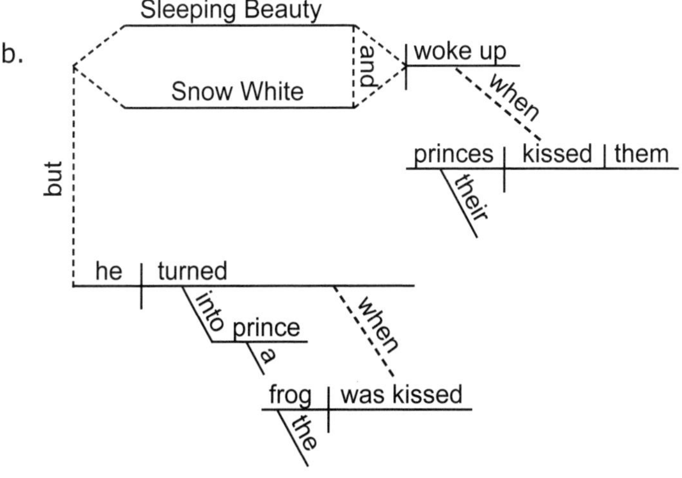

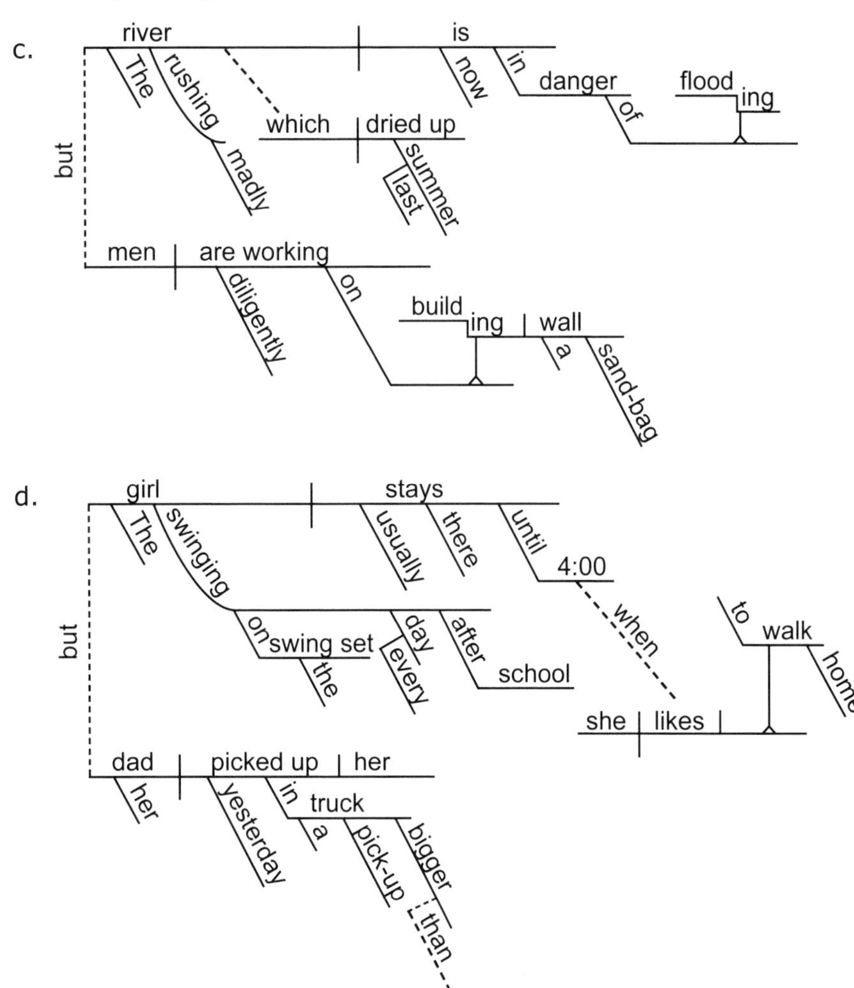

Review (pp. 86-98)

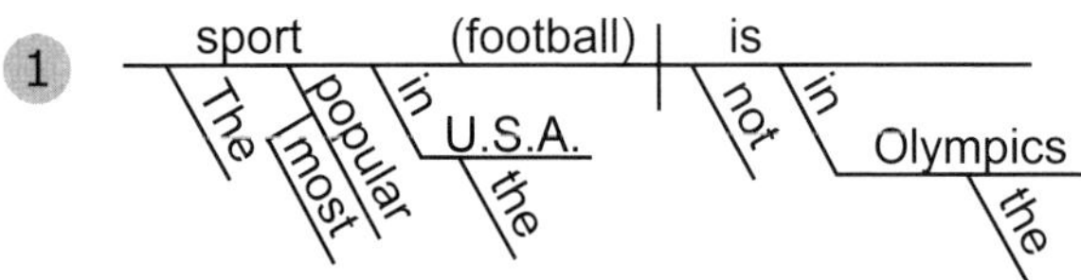

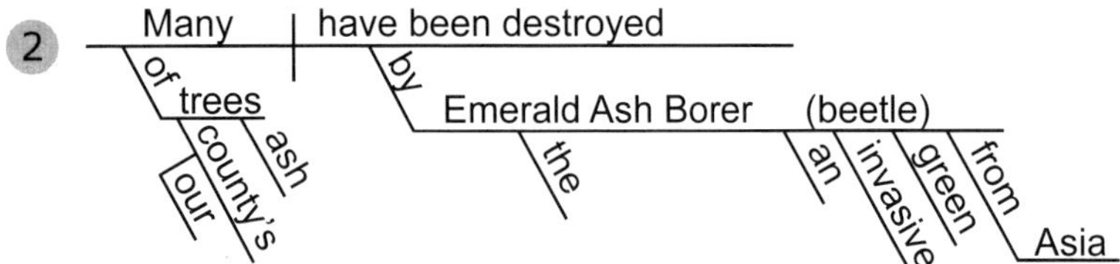

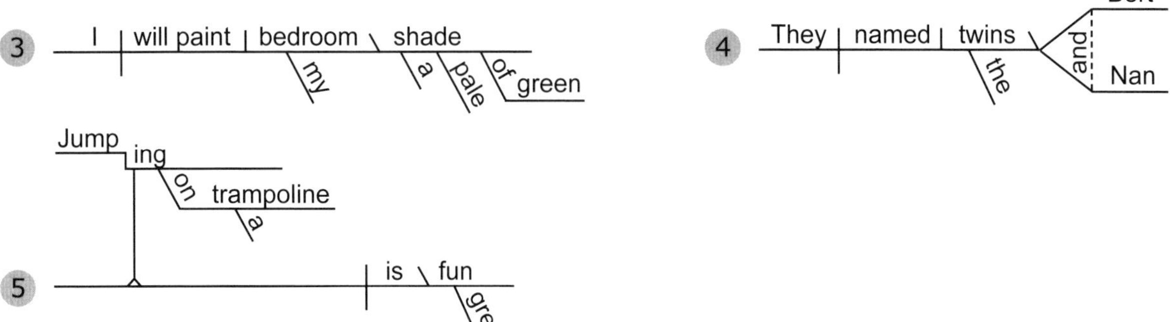

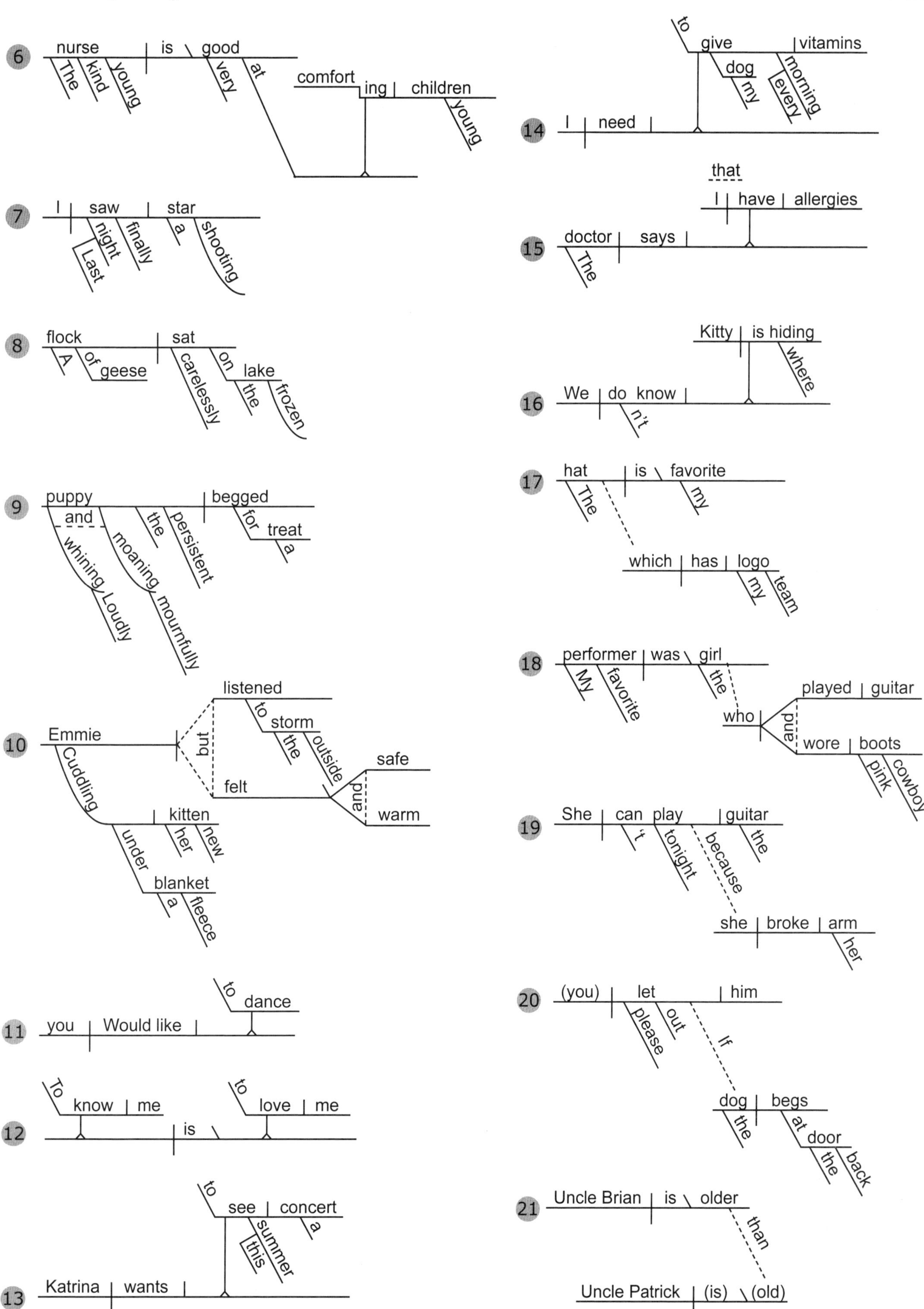

6
nurse | is \ good
The
kind
young
very
at
comfort
ing | children
young
7
I | saw | star
night
Last
finally
a
shooting
8
flock | sat
A
of
geese
carelessly
on
lake
the
frozen
9
puppy
and
whining
Loudly
moaning
mournfully
the
persistent
begged
for
treat
a
10
Emmie
Cuddling
kitten
her
new
under
blanket
a
fleece
but
listened
to
storm
the
outside
felt
and
safe
warm
11
you | Would like
to
dance
12
To
know | me
is \
to
love | me
13
Katrina | wants
to
see | concert
a
summer
this
14
I | need
to
give | vitamins
dog
my
morning
every
15
doctor | says
The
that
I | have | allergies
16
We | do know
n't
Kitty | is hiding
where
17
hat | is \ favorite
The
my
which | has | logo
my
team
18
performer | was \ girl
My
favorite
the
who
and
played | guitar
wore | boots
pink
cowboy
19
She | can play | guitar
't
tonight
the
because
she | broke | arm
her
20
(you) | let | him
please
out
If
dog | begs
the
at
door
the
back
21
Uncle Brian | is \ older
than
Uncle Patrick | (is) \ (old)

22

Nobody
snores
loud
as
as
Grandpa
(snores)

23

rainbow
appeared
a
beautiful
After
rain
stopped
the
and
we
ran
outside
to
take
pictures

24

Swing
ing
between
buildings
is
move
Spider-Man's
signature
but
tak
ing
criminals
down
what
impresses
me
is

25

dog
laughed
The
little
when
cow
jumped
the
over
moon
the
and
dish
ran
the
frightened
away
with
spoon
the
who
was relieved
to
get
away
from
fork
the
teasing

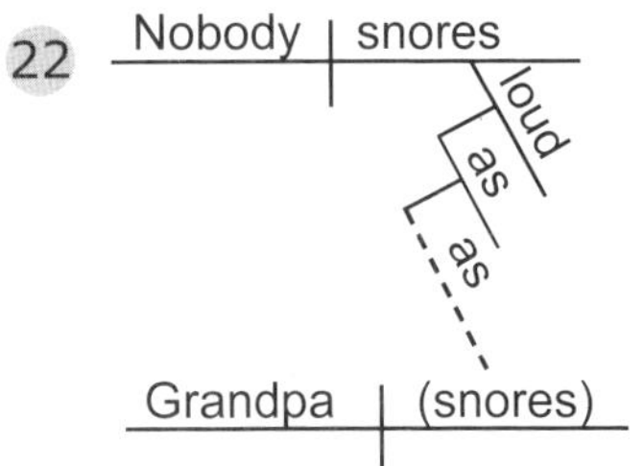

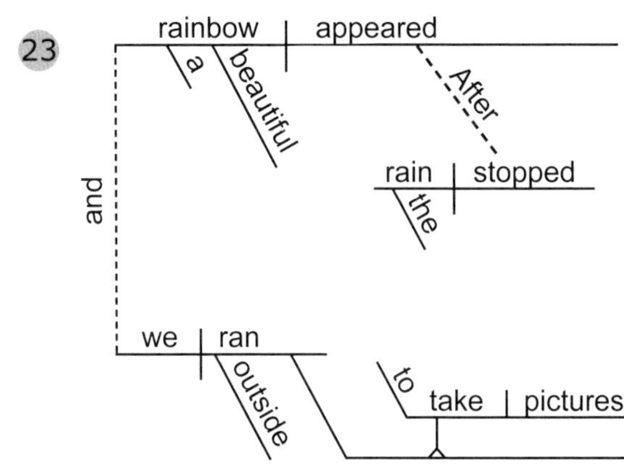

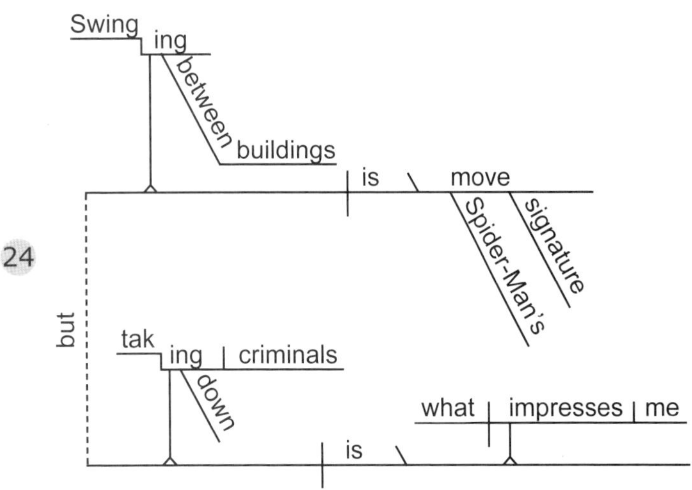

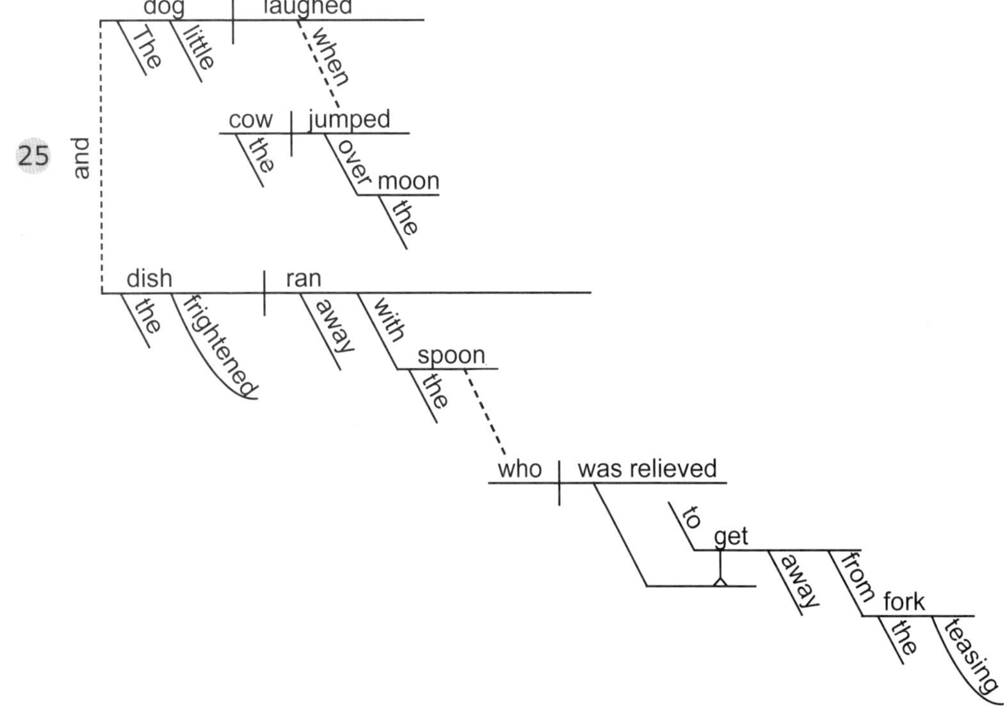